JERUSALEM
The Key to World Peace

Islamic Council of Europe  المجلس الإسلامي الأوروبي

ISLAMIC COUNCIL OF EUROPE
16 Grosvenor Crescent
London SW1X 7EP
Phone: 01-235 9832

First edition: 1980

ISBN 0 907163 30 0 Casebound
0 907163 35 1 Paperback

Set by Dessett Graphics Ltd, London.
Printed by Interlink Longraph Ltd, London.

JERUSALEM
The Key to World Peace

Contents

Introduction vii
Salem Azzam
Inaugural Address xiii
H.R.H. Prince Fahd bin Abdel Aziz
List of Contributors xvii

Part One JERUSALEM AND VARIOUS FAITHS

1 The Protestant Faith 3
Rev. Humphrey Walz
2 The Jewish Faith 21
Dr. Norton Mezvinsky
3 The Catholic Faith 39
Rev. Joseph L. Ryan
4 The Islamic Faith 77
Dr. Isma'il R. al-Faruqi

Part Two THE HISTORICAL PERSPECTIVE

5 Judaization of Jerusalem 109
Rouhi el-Khatib
6 From Ancient Times to the Beginning of Muslim Era . . 123
Dr. Demetri Baramki
7 Jerusalem under Islamic Rule 141
Dr. A.L. Tibawi
8 From British Mandate to the Present Day 155
Peter Mansfield
9 The Conflict on Jerusalem: Causes and Contradictions . 173
Dr. Afzal Iqbal

Part Three JERUSALEM TODAY AND TOMORROW

10 Jerusalem and International Organisations 189
John Reddaway

11 Jerusalem and Palestine in International Law 211
Dr. Henry Cattan

12 The Future of Jerusalem 259
Khalid al-Hassan

Appendices

I Welcome Address by H.E. Mr. Salem Azzam, Secretary General, Islamic Council of Europe 277

II Message from His Majesty Hassan II, King of Morroco 280

III Address by H.E. Mr. Habib Chatti, Secretary General, Organisation of the Islamic Conference, Jeddah 284

IV Address by H.E. Mr. Chazli Klibi Secretary General, League of Arab States 292

V Address by Mr. Khalid al-Hassan, Chairman, Foreign Relations Committee, PLO 296

VI Paper by Mr. Khalid al-Hassan, Chairman, Foreign Relations Committee, PLO 303

VII Remarks by Session Chairmen: 320

(i) H.E. Mr. Kamel Al-Sharif (First Session)
(ii) Mr. Christopher Mayhew (Second Session)
(iii) Dr. Musa Mazzawi (Third Session)
(iv) Lord Caradon (Fourth Session)

VIII Text of the Communique 329

Introduction

Few other questions of our time have so deeply moved the world conscience and so gravely threatened world peace as the Zionist usurpation and continued occupation of Jerusalem and Palestine. It has perpetrated untold human misery and unleashed a seemingly unending reign of terror in a land held sacred by Muslims, Christians and Jews alike. As a result, more than a million men, women and children have been hounded out of their homes and forced to become refugees, while merciless Zionist persecution goes on throughout the length and breadth of their homeland.

Unfortunately, the treacherous and massive misrepresentation of facts by international Zionism has tended to mislead public opinion in many parts of the world, particularly in the West. It was precisely to identify, analyse and bring out the true facts, in a correct historical, academic and multi-religious perspective, that an International Seminar on Jerusalem was held in London from December 3-5, 1979, sponsored by the Ministry of Information, Saudi Arabia, and organised by the Islamic Council of Europe. The participants at the Seminar included distinguished Christian, Jewish and Muslim scholars and jurists from all over the world, as well as eminent lawyers, statesmen and public figures, who examined objectively and in depth various aspects of the problem of Israel and Jerusalem.

The papers presented at this Seminar are reproduced in this volume, and serve to highlight the fact that the question of Jerusalem is at the heart of the Palestinian problem, and that the only real solution of this problem is the return of Jerusalem to Arab and Islamic sovereignty. As the respected Jewish scholar, Dr. Norton Mezvinsky, pointed out in his paper: "Peace must be based on justice. This means primarily justice for the Palestinians. Make no mistake: Justice for the Palestinians is impossible, a solution of the Arab-Israeli conflct will not be forthcoming, positive resolution of the fate of Jerusalem will not occur so long as Israel continues to be dominated by Zionist nationalism. The liberation of the state from its Zionist political philosophy in favour of non-discriminatory democracy is therefore a necessity."

Indeed, as Dr. Mezvinsky asserted, what he proposed "was solidly based in Jewish faith and, if accepted by a sufficient number of Jews, might help prevent further human tragedy in the troubled Middle East." And he unequivocally told the Seminar participants: "As a religiously committed Jew I say to you that the establishment of the Zionist state of Israel in 1948 was a tragic mistake; it caused a major blemish in Jewish history; it contradicted the essence of the land of Israel theme in the Jewish faith. The creation of this demographically Jewish exclusivist state, shrouded in false religious clothing, resulted in immediate oppression of Palestinian Arabs who constitute the non-Jewish indigenous population of this part of historic Palestine. Oppression of the Palestinians in the State of Israel has continued to such an extent since 1948 that it has become a central feature of that state's Zionist character."

Another participant, Rev. Humphrey Walz, former Chairman of the Middle East Studies Department of the United Presbyterian Synod, in his paper on "The Protestant Faith and the Problem of Israel and Jerusalem", exposed a number of views "skilfully publicised, often with Zionist financing and co-operation, as standard Biblical doctrine." Among them he mentioned the following: that the promises made 25 centuries ago to Judahite exiles in Babylon and, more than a millenium earlier, to Abraham, are fulfilled today by giving all Jews and only Jews unconditional rights to Palestine; that the Christian guilt for the Nazi holocaust must be atoned for by turning Palestinian property over to Jewish possession and control; and that the creation of the "State of Israel" and the in-gathering of the Jews thither is a necessary step towards the conversion of the Jews and the second coming of Christ. He said the Protestant Church rejects these, and that "examined in the total Biblical context, they are found to be at odds with Biblical ethics and theology, and untenable by all Protestant denominations and ecumenical bodies."

In his paper on "The Catholic Faith and the Problem of Israel and Jerusalem", the Rev. Joseph L. Ryan, a Jesuit priest and Rector of his community, who was on assignment in the Lebanon for many years, traced the essential problem to the launching of the Zionist movement by Herzl in 1897, which was a "political movement by European Jews aimed precisely at establishing a Jewish state - a state that would be essentially and predominantly Jewish - in Palestine, and in a Palestine where at the turn of the century the population and land ownership were nearly 100 per cent Arab and were, moreover, as the Zionist Movement became known, overwhelmingly opposed to it." He therefore argued that Zionism at that time intrinsically constituted a deliberate, basic and massive violation of the rights of the Arabs then in Palestine, especially their right of self-determination." And he added: "If the argument of equal rights is adduced, namely, that Jews had a right to a state too, one must ask: by what argument can one rationally justify European Jews setting up a state that instrinsically aims to force the Arab natives to leave or, in remaining, to become inferior? If one argues that European Jews had some right, some tie to the land, the right of Palestinian Arabs was vastly stronger, the two sets of rights were by no means equal. If one argues that the pressure of anti-Semitism in Europe forced the Jews into the Zionist Movement, one argues that it forced them to violate the rights of Palestinians . . . By one of the bitter ironies of history, at the end of World War I the West was extolling the principle of the self-determination of people, while in practice, by blessing the Zionist Movement, it was hypocritically denying that principle to the Palestinians."

Analysing the problem of Israel and Jerusalem from the Isalmic viewpoint, the well-known Muslim scholar, Dr. Ismail al-Faruqi, emphasised that Islam does not oppose the Jew because he is a Jew, and that Islam's opposition is to Zionism, which is "a plan to dispossess Palestine of its legitimate owners, to set up a racist state and community in their stead, and to exercise a policy of subjugation and exploitation of non-Jews." As he explained, for Islam Jerusalem, or the precinct of Al Aqsa, is blessed by God. It is the third *Haram* or sanctuary after Mecca and Madinah. It is hallowed by Muslims because of its associations with the Prophet Mohammad's (Peace be upon him) Isra' and Miraj, with the Prophet 'Isa ibn Maryam and all the Prophets of Judaism (on whom be peace). "In the past 14 centuries, neither the Jewish nor the Christian shrines would have survived were it not for this very attitude of Islam towards Judaism and Christianity. Only an Islamic government, therefore, would be permanently and absolutely committed to honour and safeguard the places holy to the three faiths."

Apart from the religious factors, dealt with by the Jewish, Christian, and Muslim scholars, the Seminar also served to out the many other positive and incontrovertible historical, legal and political facts which were marshalled by experts and specialists in their respective fields. As Dr. Henry Cattan, former Member of the Palestine Bar and Tutor at the Jerusalem Law School, argued: "The Zionist claim to Jerusalem and

Palestine is spurious both in the light of historical facts and international law." Tracing the history of Palestine since it was founded four thousand years ago by the Canaanites, the ancestors of Palestinian Arabs, Dr. Cattan said that: "In sharp contrast to the uninterrupted presence of the Arabs in Palestine and Jerusalem, the Jewish presence there was merely transient during the Biblical times." Secondly, he asserted that there is absolutely no racial link between the Israelis of today and the Israelis of the Bibilical times, and added: "Both these facts conclusively refute the Israeli claim to their right of annexation of Jerusalem and Palestine on historical grounds."

But above all, as the Chairman of the Foreign Relations Committee of the Palestine Liberation Organisation, Mr. Khalid al-Hassan, argued in his paper presented to the Seminar, "The problem of Jerusalem is not an academic question to be dealt with by academic means; it is the essence of a political cause — that of the people of Palestine which the world recognises as being the central element of the conflict in the Middle East." And he made it plain that "All we are asking for, and are urging the Super Powers to do is to let the real future become a reality in as short a time as possible to avoid more victims, more hatred, more sacrifice, so that we can be the symbol of peace — not only in Palestine and the Middle East, but for the whole world."

It was in this context that Mr. John Reddaway, Director General of the Arab-British Centre in London, and former Deputy Commissioner General of the U.N. Relief and Works Agency (UNWRA), spoke in anguish about "the wretched failure of the international community over so many years' to do anything effective towards carrying out "the well-meaning, highly principled sentiments expressed in so many U.N. Resolutions on Jerusalem." He drew pointed attention to "the outrageous reality of what is happening in Jerusalem", and said that "in the end it is political action, not legal analysis, that must provide the solution." And, as Lord Caradon put it in his introductory remarks as Chairman of one of the Sessions of the Seminar, "the centre of the Middle East problem is the Palestine problem . . . the centre of the Palestine problem has been the problem of Jerusalem . . . and there will never be peace in Jerusalem if one part of the population is a subject people."

In offering, through this volume, these and the other papers presented at the International Seminar on Jerusalem, to a wider audience in all parts of the world, the Islamic Council of Europe hopes to clarify the real issues involved and to put these in their true perspective so that truth and justice shall prevail.

I should be failing in my duty if I do not put on record my thanks to all those whose advice, guidance and generous co-operation has been available to me at every stage of the Seminar, and in the preparation and production of this volume. Apart from the distinguished participants whose erudition and scholarship was matched only by their vision and integrity, I am grateful to the many individuals and organisations, including my own colleagues in the Islamic Council of Europe and others outside it, but for whose tremendous personal and institutional support a project of this dimension could not be undertaken. May Allah bless them all.

Salem Azzam
Secretary-General, Islamic Council of Europe

Inaugural Address

H.R.H. Prince Fahd bin Abdul Aziz

Following is the Inaugural Address of His Royal Highness Prince Fahd bin Adbul Aziz, Crown Prince and First Deputy Prime Minister, Kingdom of Saudi Arabia, delivered on his behalf at the Inaugural Session of the International Seminar on Jerusalem in London on 3rd December 1979.

Excellencies, Distinguished Guests,

It gives me great pleasure to deliver the inaugural address at this International Seminar on Jerusalem. This seminar is seized with one of the most important issues which have been of grave concern not only to the people of the Arab and Islamic world but to all those throughout the world who believe in love, peace and justice.

While the cause of Jerusalem is an inseparable part of the cause of Palestine, this holy city enjoys a unique status among the followers of the Divine Message, particularly so among Muslims. Jerusalem, it must be remembered, was their first Qibla before the blessed Ka'ba in the Holy Mecca.

It was the place of Isra and Mi'raj: the point to which Allah commanded the Prophet's night journey from the holy Mosque, Al-Masjid A-Haram, and from which the Prophetic ascension took place. There, Muhammad, may peace be upon him, led the other Prophets and messengers in prayers. This glorious event became an eternal symbol of the closest link between the holy mosque of Mecca and the Aqsa Mosque of Jerusalem, bearing evidence for the integration between religions and unity among Allah's Prophets in preaching His message, until Islam became the last of the prophetic missions, and our Prophet Muhammad, may peace be upon him, the seal of the Prophets.

It is to the sacred places in Jerusalem that millions of hearts of the faithful in the world are attached. Arabs were in Jerusalem more than 2000 years before the time of Moses, may peace be upon him. They remained there despite a series of invasions and occupations. They did not even abandon it when David, may peace be upon him, entered the city in 1007 B.C. and ruled for 70 years. Moreover, Jerusalem was under the sovereignty of the Islamic Caliphate for almost 14 centuries until it was put under British Mandate early this century. The fact that it remained Arab has not been affected by periods of invasion which lasted about 200 years, anymore than the current Israeli period of usurpation, annexation and settlement.

By stating these facts, I do not mean to embark on the content of any of the important topics which will be dealt with by a distinguished body of leading thinkers, politicians and specialists, together with the cream of honourable and devoted *Ulema* who have come from different parts of the world and who are devoted to the truth. They all have one thing in common: understanding of the deeply-rooted religious and historical bonds which link this with its past and future. This in itself is a great asset for the cause of Jerusalem that should not be relinquished.

The topics under discussion in this seminar vary from those dealing with religion to history, sociology and law. They may differ in their respective treatments and have even conflicting shades of opinion. This, however, springs from honesty of thought, objectivity in research, and sincerity to knowledge. Eventually truth and justice must emerge victorious. In the case of Jerusalem, the victory of truth is a matter of even greater importance, as a great part of the tragedy of Jerusalem stems from distortion of facts to such an extent that for a long time in the history of this cause, the facts have been absent. As a result unbiased and objective thinkers have not been able to give the matter the justice it deserves. Furthermore, victory of justice, in this particular cause, is of particular importance. Firstly, it means disarming aggression of its facade of legality which the aggressor comes to believe in through his *de facto* policy and use of power and coercion. Secondly, it means that the people are capable of using their legal rights in resisting imperialism, usurpation and occupation. Thirdly, it eventually means victory of justice against oppression and usurpation as well as the regaining of land and rights. In the cause of Jerusalem, victory of justice is after all an expression of the human conscience which has been shocked by the 20th century crime committed when the Palestinian people were expelled from their homes and made fugitives in refugee camps outside their homeland.

Members of the Seminar,

Undoubtedly the choice of London for this International Seminar on Jerusalem has pleased us in that it symbolises the role of civilisation which this country, with its eventful history, has played. This prominent location of London gives the widest possible opportunity to correct misinformation about the cause and to reveal the distortion and vagueness to which it has been subjected. From this seminar in London, facts will be communicated to the public opinion in the UK, Europe, and elsewhere in the world. This is the goal which the Government of the Kingdom of Saudi Arabia was keen to achieve when it welcomed the idea of convening this Seminar on a cause which it considers one of the most important cornerstones of the Kingdom's foreign policy.

We are very pleased to see that broad sections of the world public opinion together with thinkers in different countries have shown their readiness to understand the various dimensions of this cause. We hope that this Seminar will throw light on the true facts concerning this cause.

Finally, let me, on behalf of the King, the Government and the people of Saudi Arabia, and on my own behalf, express our thankfulness and appreciation for your attendance at, and contribution to this Seminar and our gratitude, in advance, for your valuable efforts towards explaining and interpreting the cause of Jerusalem. We appreciate the efforts of the Organisation of Islamic Conference, the Islamic Council of Europe, the Ministry of Information of the Kingdom of Saudi Arabia, and the Preparatory Committee, in planning this Seminar with which we wish you every success.

May peace be upon you.

List of Contributors

H.E. Mr. Salem Azzam
Secretary General, Islamic Council of Europe

Dr. Demetri Baramki
Noted scholar and archaologist

H.E. Mr. Mohammed Boucetta
Foreign Minister of Morocco

Dr. Henry Cattan
Author and International Lawyer

Lord Caradon
Well-known British politician, former Leader of the U.K. Delegation to the U.N.

H.E. Mr. Habib Chatti
Secretary General, the Organisation of the Islamic Conference

Dr. Ismail Al-Faruqi
Professor of Islamic Studies and History of Religion at Temple University, Philadelphia, U.S.A.

Dr. Khalid Al-Hassan
Chairman of the Foreign Affairs Committee of the Palestine National Council

Dr. Afzal Iqbal
Writer and Diplomat, former Ambassador of Pakistan to the Holy See

Mr. Rouhi Al-Khatib

Mayor of Jerusalem: he was forcibly removed from Jerusalem and sent into exile on 7th March 1968

H.E. Mr. Chazli Klibi

Secretary General of the League of Arab States

Mr. Peter Mansfield

Writer and broadcaster, member of the Executive Committee, Council for the Advancement of Arab-British Understanding.

Mr. Christopher Mayhew

Chairman of the ANAF Foundation and of 'Middle East International'; co-author, with Michael Adams, of 'Publish it Not'

Dr. Musa Mazzawi

Professor of International Law, London University

Dr. Norton Mezvinsky

Of Jewish origin and faith, he is Professor of History, Central Connecticut State College, U.S.A.

Mr. John Reddaway

Director General of the Arab-British Centre, and former Deputy Commissioner General of UNRWA (United Nations Relief and Works Agency in Palestine)

Rev. Fr. Joseph L. Ryan, S.J.

Jesuit priest and Rector of his community, he was on assignment in Lebanon for many years and has written and lectured widely

H.E. Mr. Kamel Al-Sharif

Minister of Awqaf and Islamic Affairs, Hashemite Kingdom of Jordan

Dr. Abdul Latif Tibawi

Educationist and scholar, Author of *Islamic Education: Its traditions and Modernisation under the Arab National Systems; Anglo-Arab Relations and the Question of Palestine*

Rev. L. Humphrey Walz

Protestant Minister, and former Chairman of Middle East Studies, Department of the United Presbyterian Synod of the Near East.

Mr. Alistair Duncan

Director of the World of Islam Festival Trust. Author of *The Noble Sanctuary*, he gave a lecture at the Seminar, illustrated with his own slides, on the religious significance of Jerusalem to Muslims and Christians, and the interrelationship between the two faiths.

PART ONE

Jerusalem and Various Faiths

1. The Protestant Faith and The Problem of Israel and Jerusalem

Rev. L. Humphrey Walz

The aspects of Protestant Christianity that cheer me most — in the Holy Land as elsewhere — are its works of mercy to the uprooted, the oppressed and the impoverished. My recent ten-day revisit to Jerusalem and environs, which ended only yesterday, put me in touch again with old friends and new trends in this type of service. I was, as of yore, heartened by their successes, hurt by their frustrations and impressed by their tenacity in the face of governmental dilatoriness, red tape and harassment.[1]

A Chinese proverb tells us: "Give a man a fish and you feed him for a day; teach him to fish and you feed him for life". Many Protestant programmes — providing food, clothing, shelter, medical care and legal aid — have ministered continuously since 1948 to short-term, immediate Palestinian needs. They are necessary but they are incomplete without follow-up programmes of self-help such as vocational training, student and small-business loans, seedling trees, pregnant livestock, water-conserving equipment and village development. And in all these undertakings, education — from pre-kindergarten to post-graduate — plays a crucial role.

It is on such projects and the people who guide them that I'd most like to dwell at this time, for it is they that stir me most deeply. But they are not peculiarly Protestant. Catholics,

Eastern Orthodox, Jews, Muslims and non-sectarian groups like UNRWA and ANERA have their own parallel and intertwining undertakings. So, since I have been asked to deal today with matters distinctively Protestant, I must shift my focus elsewhere — to the procedures and criteria with which we approach problem solving.

A central emphasis of Protestantism is on the democratic process under the authority of Holy Scripture. This is by no means an exclusively Protestant property. Nor do we Protestants always live up to it. Nonetheless, we do uphold this standard, and our failures and successes are to be judged in its light.

Pronouncement-Producing Procedures

Coming democratically to honorable, viable solutions for such complex problems as those underlying the Arab-Israeli conflict taxes the patience of all who feel the urgencies involved. Hearing out every expression of earnest concern is *so* time-consuming! Sifting out facts and opinions from all pertinent points of view and then struggling to formulate a sound, representative and intelligible recommendation has *so* many frustrating obstacles! And progress is additionally slowed down when one must, as Protestant consistency requires, attempt at the same time to include the full Biblical ethic: Loving thy neighbour, seeking peace and good will, judging friend and stranger by the same standards and doing justly and loving mercy while walking humbly with God.

Yes, the Protestant approach does have its hurdles! It also has its values. The Protestant statements which I shall summarize, having grown out of widespread participation, have accumulated substantial support along the way. They have also stimulated further study which will continue to reinforce the merits and correct the defects of past pronouncements.

Since 1947 I have collected well over 100 official Church

statements on the Arab-Israeli conflict. Let me limit my summary here, though, to the common points shared by American Protestant and ecumenical declarations reported in *Where We Stand,* the little 1977 book jointly published in New York by the Middle East Consultation Group and the Middle East Peace Project.

Like the pronouncements of the World Council of Churches, these statements are all characterized by a deep moral concern for all the people of the Middle East, for their well-being and full civil liberties. All declare that both Israelis and Palestinians have identical human rights, including the right of self-determination. (The Baptist statement assumes this. The others verbalize it explicitly). All grant that the double claim to the same land is at the heart of the struggle. All believe that a peace that benefits all is possible. They are convinced that breaking the continuing impasse will necessitate mutual recognition, mutual negotiations and reciprocal compromise. And they are unanimous in supporting the United Nations' insistence on "the inadmissibility of the acquisition of territory by war".

As US Ambassador Charles W. Yost testified to the UN on July 1, 1969, 'territory acquired by war' includes the walled city and the rest of East Jeruaslam. Hence the Churches may be seen currently as favouring the return of that area to Arab control. An alternative was put forward by the Executive Committee of the NCC (the US National Council of Churches) in the wake of war, on July 7, 1967. In the name of its Protestant and Orthodox constituency, it proposed "an international presence in Jerusalem which will preserve the peace and integrity of the city, foster the welfare of its inhabitants, and protect the holy shrines with full rights of access to all".

At the same time, it added, "We cannot approve Israel's unilateral annexation of the Jordanian portions of Jerusalem. This historic city is sacred not only to Judaism, but also to Christianity and Islam". In the furtherance of this spirit it encouraged the very practice you are sponsoring at this Seminar: "conversations with representatives of the Jewish, Christian and Muslim communities". And it went on to propose exploring "the possibilities for an Interfaith Centre in Jerusalem that would be a place for encounter, study and action among Jews, Christians and Muslims!"

That was over a dozen years ago — which leads me to point out that the democratic process does not allow Protestant pronouncements to remain static. For instance, while all mainline American denominations favour drawing Palestinians into negotiations on the future of the Holy Land, only the Presbyterians, Methodists and Brethren have gone as far as the Dutch Council of Churches in endorsing PLO participation in negotiations.[2] But now the forced resignation of Andrew Young — a United Church of Christ clergyman and former NCC staffer — from the US Mission to the UN is part of our common background. In its wake — on September 7, 1979 — the NCC Executive Committee supported his challenge to "the United States and Israel to desist from their no-talk policy" with the PLO. And it has assigned its Middle East panel responsibility for considering recommending that the US join the UN in recognizing the PLO as the "legitimate representative" of the Palestinians. The NCC is also taking seriously the Middle East Council of Churches' November, 1979, request for joint consultations before making pronouncements on the PLO, Jerusalem or other area matters.

Other 'input' is coming increasingly from peace-minded, rights-oriented and/or energy conservationist sources who are beginning to see the bearing of their special concerns on the Middle East. Such input, though not necessarily totally accepted officially, is always respected.

Interpreting the Bible

Speaking of non-acceptance, it may surprise you that certain views which are widely believed to be typically Protestant have, after careful scrutiny, been set aside as untenable by *all* Protestant denominations and ecumenical bodies which, in preparing their public policy statements, are committed to representative democratic processes under Biblical authority. These rejected views are as follows:

(1) "Promises made 25 centuries ago to Judahite exiles in Babylon[3] and, more than a millennium earlier, to Abraham[4] are fulfilled today by giving all Jews and only Jews unconditional rights to Palestine."

(2) "Christians must atone for the Nazi holocaust and previous mistreatment of Jews by turning Palestinian property over to Jewish possession and control."[5]

(3) "The creation of the State of Israel and the ingathering of Jews thither must be encouraged as a necessary step toward the conversion of the Jews and the Second Coming of Christ."[6]

Such views when examined in depth in the total literary and historical Biblical context reveal themselves to be at odds with Biblical ethics and theology. Still they do have lively acceptance in *some* Protestant circles, notably in Holland, South Africa and the US American Bible Belt. They have been skillfully publicised, often with Zionist financing and cooperation, as standard Biblical doctrine.[7] They have also been fostered by anti-Semites who see in such concepts a handy way to get their Jewish neighbours to go away![8]

With all this in mind, it becomes especially important in dealing with the terrestrial city of Jerusalem to recognise the place it holds in *mainline* Protestant preaching. There it is presented as the historic home city of several great prophets and as a key place in Jesus' ministry. What those prophets and Jesus said about *their* city is what *we* must say to and about our own communities. Let me cite how a few samples from almost 900 Biblical references to Jerusalem fit into this approach.

The prophet Jeremiah (cf. 5 and 7:17-20), seeing injustice, dishonesty, disobedience, idolatry and insensitivity to poverty flourishing on every level of Jerusalem's life, threatened divine punishment, even obliteration, unless its people — young and old, male and female — changed their ways. Another prophet, Micah (cf. 1:5 and 3:9, 12), deploring private immorality and public corruption, delared: "Because of you, Zion shall be plowed as a field: Jerusalem shall become a heap of ruins".

Turning to the New Testament, we find Jesus saying: "'O Jerusalem, Jerusalem, killing the prophets and stoning those sent to you! How often would I have gathered you as a hen gathers her brood . . . , and you would not . . .' And when he drew near and saw the city he wept over it, saying, 'Would that even today you knew the things that make for peace! . . . For the days shall come upon you, when your enemies will . . . dash you to the ground'" (Luke 13:34 and 19:41-44).

Such threats were not vindictive but incentives to repentance and reform. Micah (4:1-4) and Isaiah (2:2-5) shared a glorious vision of a transformed Jerusalem. They dared dream that the very people they denounced would change, would turn in obedience and trust to their Lord. Their community life would then be of such quality that people from afar would be attracted to learn of them, to repudiate war and to beat their swords and spears into plowshares and pruning hooks for beneficent productivity.

Protestant hymnals and conscientious expository preaching carry that challenge to their own churches and communities — seen as *their* Jerusalems. Like William Blake, the British poet who, distressed by the Industrial Revolution's "dark Satanic mills," longed to "build Jerusalem in England's green and pleasant land," they strive to make their home cities holy cities in the spirit of the great prophets.

At the same time, we have a responsibility for exalting Micah's and Isaiah's ideals for other communities. How proper influences can, without presumptuous intrusiveness, be exerted in such directions by outsiders is always problematical. Let me, however, ventilate for your appraisal, refinement and possible implementation some of my own thoughts that reflect my Protestant conditioning on behalf of present-day Jerusalem.

Personal Proposals

I feel we should make more persistent and coordinated efforts to inform our fellow-citizens — particularly our Jewish fellow-citizens — of the perversions of historic Jewish ethics now being perpetrated in, and ordered from, Jerusalem in the name of "Judaization".[9] Since that city is now under nominally Jewish control, I feel we should base our remedial recommendations in greater measure on insights gained from high-minded Israeli and Diaspora Jews.[10] At the same time we should reinforce the hands of our fellow-countrymen in high office who are concerned for fair play in international affairs.[11] We should press them, for instance, to implement all pertinent U.N. resolutions the U.S. has voted for. This would include the forbidding of further Israeli architectural and demographic disruption of — and prompt withdrawal from — occupied East Jerusalem.[12]

The people legitimately belonging in the to-be-liberated areas should, as a first step, be given every support for normalising their city. Families who fled in 1948 and 1967 or have emigrated under pressure should have their return facilitated. Where their former homes are occupied by strangers,[13] the present residents should be considerately helped toward finding satisfactory lodging elsewhere. Where their rightful homes have been levelled but not replaced, the homecomers should be aided in rebuilding on the spot. Where their property has been built on — whether with residential, commercial, or industrial developments — they should be given their full share in the new facilities.

The great complexities of these and other adjustments will require a wise and popularly backed political regime. Out of respect, long friendship and a sense of fair play, I recommend that the democratically elected mayor of East Jerusalem, Rouhi al-Khatib, be brought back from exile to head a provisional government and lay foundations for a permanent one. If the maintenance of law and order requires international help, I would suggest a *temporary* U.N. presence in the whole of Jerusalem, East and West.

A strong campaign through the mass media and educational institutions to help Jews and Arabs appreciate each other's cultures, wounds and aspirations would be important for creating an atmosphere for conciliation and cooperation.

For bringing harmonious and productive relations out of circumstances of controversy I have found the new techniques of MBO (Management by Objectives) useful: ideas for criteria and programming are brainstormed, evaluated for feasibility and effectiveness, tested and then put fully to work. The more the people directly involved in the problem can be brought into the solution the greater the acceptance and practicality of any plan. I'd recommend that such techniques be used in Jerusalem.

These specifics I submit very tentatively. Now let me conclude quite dogmatically: All of us, as believing Muslims, Jews and Christians, acknowledge the power of prayer. If we expect a right outcome, then we must join the Hebrew Psalmist (122:6) in *praying* for the peace of Jerusalem — a peace of justice and mercy, restitution and reconciliation. We must further pray that all people who honour Jerusalem as the Holy City, al-Quds, may be drawn together increasingly under God to bring that to pass.[14]

Jeru-Shalem originally got its name from the pagan, tribal

god, Shalem. We must wean it from its paganism and tribalism. We must help it become — in present reality as in historic symbolism — Jeru-Salaam, Jeru-Shalom, the City of Peace, indeed.

Footnotes

1. For reasons of their own, the Israeli ministries and military government delay visa renewals for foreign helpers, put off authorizations for specific undertakings, try to come between the voluntary agency and the people aided, impose taxes and import charges wherever possible, and set up non-legal requirements and complex procedures that hamper efficiency and effectiveness.

These handicaps exist on the welfare and social services level, chiefly with petty bureaucratic interference and delays, but the real problems are in connection with economic and community development programmes which help strengthen such basic Palestinian institutions as cooperatives and municipalities. These enterprises the Israeli government apparently resists as creating part of the infrastructure for a Palestinian state.

For over a year ANERA (American Near East Refugee Aid), to cite just one group, has been seeking government approval to build a wholesale fruit and vegetable market in Halhul on the road between Bethlehem and Hebron. The official excuse for the delay is that the proposed site is too near a school. However, the *Boston Globe* (July 5, 1979) reports a senior Israeli official as admitting that the real reason is that it might enhance the standing of Halhul's tough-minded, outspoken Mayor Milhem.

Another long-blocked ANERA project is a feasibility study for improving the irrigation system serving four Palestinian villages in the Jordan Valley. Replacing the present open conduits with buried pipes could reduce evaporation and otherwise make for increased efficiency and conservation. Not only has permission been withheld but a misleading mass-media campaign has been conducted against it under the general theme, "Americans help Arabs take control of West Bank waters!"

ANERA is not strictly a Protestant undertaking as it has non-Protestants on its board and most of its funds come from US AID. Quakers, however, *are* in the Protestant tradition and their work is entirely supported by private donations. One of their projects that the Israeli government has sharply curtailed is its East Jerusalem Legal Aid programme. It has provided lawyers to help West Bank Arabs who have, among other things, been arrested on security charges or want to fight land expropriation orders. The Israeli government asserts that Quaker work is licensed for exclusively humanitarian services, and that security and land cases, being 'political', are out!

2. The Dutch — who suffered heavily with their Jewish neighbours under the Nazi heel and who have a special awareness of the Hebrew roots of their Christianity — have until recently tended toward a strong pro-Israeli bias. What has led them to increase in sympathy for the Palestinians has been news — through the mass media and letters home — from their peacekeeping personnel in UNIFIL (the UN International Forces in Lebanon). These young Dutch men and women have observed at first hand — and reported — the death and devastation wrought by Israeli shooting, shelling and bombing (with US-made equipment) of Palestinian and Lebanese homes, farms, shops, warehouses, schools, churches, and mosques. They have acquired — and are giving the folks back home — a broadened view of the Arab-Israeli struggle.

3. In preparing the tribes of Israel to settle in the Promised land, Moses gave them warning that their continuation there would depend on their character and behaviour. "It shall come to pass," he insisted (Deuteronomy 28:15 ff.), "if thou wilt not hearken unto the voice of the Lord thy God to observe to do all his commandments . . . , the Lord shall scatter you among the peoples, from the one end of the earth to the other."

Largely because of indifference to spiritual, ethical and moral standards, the Kingdom of Israel split in two about 930 B.C. The major portion, including ten of the twelve tribes, continued as a separate Kingdom which rejected the authority of Jerusalem. Weakened by internal selfishness and strife, it fell in 722 B.C. before the Assyrians. Its citizenry was "scattered among the peoples," was assimilated by its neighbours and lost its identity.

The remaining two tribes, Judah and Benjamin, continued their oft-rebellious ways until 597 B.C. when, as again in 586 B.C., the Babylonians subdued Jerusalem and led the cream of the community into captivity. To them, as they gained new spiritual insights from their hardship and widened their understanding of God's universality through life in an alien land, their prophets promised that, contrite and cleansed by their experience, they would ultimately be allowed to return to Jerusalem and its environs to set up an exemplary community. This opportunity came about under King Cyrus in 538 B.C. Many did return to rebuild Jerusalem under Ezra and Nehemiah. But a sizable number remained to make the Babylonian Jewish community for centuries an outstanding one intellectually and spiritually.

It is thus wrong to suppose those promises weren't fulfilled until the Zionist movement started its modern-day ingathering. It is sacrilegious for Zionists to demand ancient territorial rights while rejecting the accompanying ethical-social requirements.

4. God's gift of "the Land" (variously and vaguely bounded) to Abraham and his "descendants for ever" was, as Prof. Alfred Guillaume long ago pointed out (in *Zionists and The Bible*), neither perpetual nor unconditional. "For ever" is an inadequate translation of the Hebrew *l'olam* which simply means "for an indefinitely long time", as when the Psalmist declared, "I will sing for ever". And the retaining of the land was to depend upon the quality of life of its inhabitants (cf. Deuteronomy 8:18-20; Jeremiah 7:13-15; Amos 3:10-15).

The present-day applicability of the territorial gift to Abraham has been confused by the assumption embodied in a Nineteenth-Century conundrum: "What's the difference between Abraham and opium?" To which the answer was: "Opium is the juice of the poppy; Abraham was the poppy of the Jews!" This assumption — that all Jews, and Jews only, are the descendants of Abraham — is less humorously and more politically played upon by Zionist nationalists. The Biblical account, however, includes Abraham's innumerable other descendants — "a multitude of nations" (Genesis 17:4), uncountable "as the dust of the earth" and the unnumbered states (13:16; 15:5). Through his three wives — Sarah, Hagar and Keturah (16:1-3; 25:1) — and his concubines (25:6), Abraham sired a prolific progeny that spread and intermarried all over the Middle East. A pocket calculator will reveal that if Abraham had had only *two* children and if each of his descendants had had a family limited to two, his physical heirs would now, some hundred generations later, far outnumber the earth's population. Intra-tribal marriages, war and pestilence have prevented this geometric progression from being fully carried out! Nonetheless, it would be harder for me to prove that I am *not* among the children of Abraham than to believe that I am.

In any case, the responsibility of Abraham's offspring is, wherever they are, to make their land a source of blessing to "all the families of the earth" (12:3). And whatever real estate they may claim for "family" sentiment they are expected, like Father Abraham, to negotiate and pay for (23:7-16).

5. There are honest differences of opinion over guilt for the mistreatment of Jews throughout the centuries and for the climax of anti-Semitism under Hitler's "Final Solution of the Jewish Problem". Jewish popular historian Max Dimont credits the Christian Church with the *survival* of European Jewry through the Middle Ages! He also indicates that there were *many* more Christians than Jews exterminated by the Nazis. And Hitler's minions were finally defeated by a war in which countless Christian soldiers were among

those who sacrificed life or limb.

A more widely publicized view sees Christians, by their attitudes, actions and inactions, as having been guilty of prolonged Jewish persecution, culminating in the Hitlerian programme of genocide. This interpretation is often accompanied by insistence that, to atone for their alleged record of inhumanity to Jews through the ages, present-day Christians owe them the security of a country where Jews, by being in control, may guide their own destiny. Such a country, Israel, was finally established in 1948 in Palestine. In the process, the overwhelmingly non-Jewish majority were displaced in large numbers to make room for Jewish newcomers.

The underlying problem here — of corporate guilt and what to do about it — bears fuller scrutiny than this space allows. A few comments are in order, however. In an overwhelming experience of the divine presence, the prophet Isaiah felt deeply the sin not only of his own "unclean lips" but of being an inseparable part of "a people of unclean lips" (Is. 6:5). And that corporate guilt, which involves corporate penalties (Exodus 20:5), can also include the sins of omission which Jesus took so seriously (Matt. 25:45; Luke 10:30). But wholesale application of this concept has its problems, too, as in blaming the Jews and/or Romans to this day for Jewish and Roman participation in the Crucifixion of Jesus Christ.

The element in Holocaust-related propaganda that is Biblically most unacceptable is the idea that our sins — individual or corporate — against others can be atoned for without our own personal sacrifice. Nathan's Parable of the Ewe lamb (2 Saul 12:1-7) sheds some light here. A traveller, it tells us, came to stay with a rich man who wanted to give him a great feast. The host had many flocks from which he could have prepared his hospitality. Instead, he slaughtered for the purpose the only lamb, a pet ewe, belonging to a poor neighbour.

He was right to give the hungry, weary traveller a sumptuous repast. But he was wrong in making another, less able, pay the price. Similarly, whether it is guilt feelings or hospitable motivation that leads Western Christians to be generous to threatened Jews by giving them not their own but the Palestinians' land, such action falls far short of Biblical standards and ethics.

Carolyn Toll, a freelance writer from New York and Chicago, is one of an increasing number of Jews who are feeling uneasy about the politicizing of the Hitler Holocaust for Zionist and Israeli purposes. She published a searching eight-page article on "American Jews and the Middle East Dilemma" in the August, 1979, *Progressive*. Her introductory paragraph quotes a character of Sol Yurick's as saying, back in 1968, "I am tired of you Jews throwing that six million up at us and hiding behind them corpses to do whatever you want to . . . ". Sadly but acceptantly she acknowledges the validity of that complaint.

6. The bearing of Biblical promises on the establishment of the modern state of Israel is variously interpreted by Dispensationalists and other types of millennarians, but one variety is this: Christ's Second Coming must involve the conversion of the world's Jews. This will be facilitated by having them all in the Holy Land at once. Therefore, the Zionist nationalist purpose to "liquidate the Diaspora and ingather the exiles" must be recognized as a forerunner of mass Jewish evangelization.

Such conclusions are based largely on interpretations of the Biblical books of Daniel and Revelation. These are part of the 'apocalyptic' literature which was written to bring to defeated and persecuted believers the assurance that their conquerors would pass away and their God would, in mercy and righteousness, triumph. Circulating promises of the overthrow of tyranny is hardly a safe pastime, so the apocalyptic authors wrote with imagery and symbolism which would be clear to their comrades and incomprehensible to their oppressors. Taking this ancient symbolism and searching the news media for possible applications, millennialists through the generations have not been deterred from their game by the fact that predictions similarly devised by their earlier counterparts have failed of fulfillment.

Morally and theologically they make the serious error of assuming that the passages they quote were irrelevant to their original audiences and to people in the centuries since. Quite self-centredly, for instance, they interpret Revelation's opening and closing words, "soon" and "the time is near" (1:1,3; 22:6,10,20) as inapplicable until nineteen centuries after they were written!

7. See Hertzel Fishman, *American Protestantism and the Jewish State,* Wayne University Press, Detroit, 1973, pp 93-5.

8. In the USA some of the strongest non-Jewish backing for Zionism comes from the areas where the Ku Klux Klan — anti-Catholic, anti-black and anti-Jewish — also flourishes. The interrelationship (*and* interdependence) of Zionism and anti-Semitism is a complex subject which needs fuller study. Suffice it here to make a few condensed observations:

British Prime Minister A. J. Balfour, who was a leading exponent of settling Jews in Palestine, was also a proponent of legislation to keep them out of Britain. In support of the discriminatory Aliens Bill, 1905, he specifically referred to the immigration of Jews as "not to the advantage . . . of the country" since those already in Britain, "by their own action, remained a people apart, and not merely held a religion differing from the vast majority of their fellow countrymen, but only intermarried among themselves." (See Oskar K. Rabinowitz, *Winston Churchill on Jewish Problems,* Yoseloff, London, 1916, especially pp. 164-7). Later (June 24, 1919) he derogatorily observed, "Jews now are not only participating in revolutionary movements but are actually, to a large degree, leaders in such movements" (*Documents on British Foreign Policy, 1919-1939,* Series 1, Vol. IV, London, Her Majesty's Stationery Office, 1952).

More than a century earlier, philosopher J. G. Fichte's racist rationale for dealing with Jews by ghetoizing them into Palestine was even blunter: "For our self-protection I see no other way than to conquer their destined land and to send them all to live there" (J. B. Agus, *The Meaning of Jewish History,* New York, Abelard-Schuman, 1963, p. 334). This may account in part for the fact that Theodor Herzl, the founder of Zionist nationalism, opposed Jewish emancipation in Europe and proclaimed that "The anti-Semites will be our most dependable friends, the anti-Semitic countries our allies" (Agus, pp. 334, 423).

Against this background one can better understand Jewish theologian R. L. Rubenstein's summation of present-day Zionism: "One of the supreme ironies of contemporary religious history is that the people who gave the world the prophetic vision of universal brotherhood and peace must effectively renounce its own heritage if it is to survive" (in *The Religious Situations, 1968,* Boston, Beacon, p. 50).

9. If one departs from the usual tourist, diplomatic, archaeological, academic or business routines and circulates freely among the Jewish and non-Jewish populations, one cannot avoid becoming aware of at least some of these perversions in Jerusalem and environs. On my most recent visit there, I observed Palestinian fruit trees dead or withering from diversion of their water to the fields and swimming pools of illegal Jewish settlements nearby. I checked out reports of private property, including church property, summarily expropriated by Israeli authorities. I talked with people who had to be pumped to describe their tortures in Israeli prisons, with academicians whose Palestinian students were being harassed and with relatives of prisoners arrested without charge. Rather than amplify this list, I should like to stress the more hopeful fact that many of my insights came from Israeli Jews who are working sacrificially to remedy the conditions they described.

10. Here are some examples of positive Jewish thinking from the Israeli League for Human and Civil Rights: As first steps toward future 'normalizing' of Jerusalem, a strong and wide effort should be made to ease the *present* life of its non-Jewish population by emphasizing certain personal rights. Important

items to insist on are: West Bankers living beyond the Jerusalem city limits should be allowed to settle at least in East Jerusalem. Palestinians who left before 1967 should be allowed to return to their East and West Jerusalem homes. Since Jerusalem is a holy city to Muslims, Christians and Jews, rights to settle there should be made equal for all three faiths.

There is considerable new subsidised housing in Jerusalem, most of it facilitated by money from the USA. 50,000 of these flats are for Jews, 350 for non-Jews. Equal-opportunity housing should be called for to remedy this discrimination.

A contemplated project to "clean the Muslim Quarter" within the walled city should be forestalled by publicity. It purportedly aims to destroy half the houses there and to remove the Muslim residents beyond the city limits into Azariah on the Eastern West Bank. Insistence should be made on enabling any persons so displaced to have new or equivalent housing, equitably priced, *within* the city.

11. The following instances came to my attention in October, 1979, as I was preparing this paper: On October 11, US Senator Mark Hatfield introduced a motion to cut Israel's share of Foreign Military Sales monies by $100 million. Although it was tabled, the subject had been brought out into the open for debate and seven Senators were willing to support it.

In connection with 1980 military assistance to Israel, the US House Appropriations Committee accompanied its October 4, 1979, report with this statement: "The Committee is deeply troubled by Israel's actions in Lebanon, by the continued establishment of settlements in the occupied territories, and by the administrative restrictions placed on the programmes of US Private and Voluntary Organizations in the West Bank and Gaza. Our concerns are amplified by the belief that those actions are harmful to the cause of peace and do not enhance Israel's security. Unless Israel modifies these policies, we fear that United States assistance in the struggle to achieve comprehensive peace will be to no avail".

On October 5, former Undersecretary of State George Ball clearly told the Middle East Institute: "Today Israel is able to continue on its present course only because of continued vast subsidies from the United States".

Much better known is Presidential Candidate John B. Connally's October 11 speech outlining his nine-point programme for peace and stability in the Middle East. While stressing that "the Arabs must be prepared to deal realistically with Israel's security concerns," he also insisted that "Israel must be prepared to deal realistically with the Arab requirements for a return to the 1967 borders and Palestinian self-determination". Other excerpts from his speech follow: "As long as the central issues in the Arab-Israeli dispute — namely, the disposition of the West Bank, Golan, Gaza and East Jerusalem, and the Palestinian questions go unresolved, peace will elude us . . . The time has come for American political leaders, from both parties, to face the Arab-Israeli problem squarely . . . A clear distinction must be drawn by the United States between support for Israel's security — which is a moral imperative — and support for Israel's broader territorial acquisitions . . .".

All these statements are in complete harmony with declared US Mideast policy. Few Americans would take exception to them. Polls on related issues suggest that most American Jews would go along with them. However, they are contrary to the positions of the well-organized, well-financed, vocal 'Zionist Establishment' which is equipped to undermine any individual or group that steps out of its prescribed line.

It is important, therefore, that when such people as I have quoted dare speak out boldly in truth for fair play, they hear supportively from those of us who claim to care.

12. Especially pertinent are such so-far disregarded elements of the UN Partition Plan as may still be viable, the Palestinian refugee right to return or be compensated as provided in UN Resolution 196 (paragraph 11) of 1948, and Resolution 267 castigating Israel for its persistent demographic and structural changes in Jerusalem in violation of international law. John Reddaway's masterful December 4, 1979, lecture on 'Jerusalem and International Organisations' before the London Seminar carried the castigation still further. He deplored "the wretched failure of the international community over so many years" to do anything effective toward carrying out "the well-meaning, highly principled sentiments expressed in so many UN Resolutions on Jerusalem".

13. Who are these people I refer to as 'strangers'? They are described in other terms in the 'tender' forms of various government-owned Israeli housing monopolies. Here is some of the wording from the form you will get if you reply to advertisements by The Company for The Rehabilitation and The Development of the Jewish Quarter in The Old City of Jerusalem, Ltd., announcing 'Offer of Apartments to the Public':

"(1.) Only one of the following alone may be permitted to participate in the offer:

(a) An Israeli citizen who is a resident of Israel, and served in the Israeli army, or served in one of the Hebrew organisations before 14 May, 1948.

(b) A new immigrant who is a resident in Israel."

This is the equivalent of 'Only Jews Admitted'. The 'Jewish Quarter' referred to is 30% larger than the historic section bearing that name, which was never 100% Jewish and was mostly Arab-owned. Thousands of non-Jews were evacuated from it, starting in 1967, and the above conditions were strictly applied to their replacements.

There were, of course, Jews who were evacuated from East Jerusalem in 1948 and are entitled to return, not as strangers, to their former homes — if, at the same time, a reciprocal arrangement is agreed to for Arabs evacuated from West Jerusalem in 1948.

14. One significant object of the joint prayers of Muslims and Christians is the momentum generated by the conference on 'The Reconstruction and Redevelopment of South Lebanon'. Though held at the World Council of Churches Centre at Bossey, Switzerland, the WCC served only as host and facilitator. The key convenors and coordinators — Gabriel Habib, General Secretary of the Middle East Council of Churches, and Professor Hassan Saab, the Muslim head of the Communications Department of the Lebanese University — invited some hundred leaders, with Muslims and Christians, Arabs and non-Arabs, in approximately equal numbers. They faced the challenge of finding ways and means for re-establishing good relations between the various competitive communities. Their goal: to plan how various concepts, projects and funding can best be applied to reconstructing a self-supporting and soundly governed Southern region of Lebanon. Something of this sort would be well to consider for Jerusalem.

2. The Jewish Faith and The Problem of Israel and Jerusalem

Dr. Norton Mezvinsky

The concept of Israel in the Jewish faith is multi-dimensional and complex. A major aspect of that concept is the modern land of Israel theme. Highlighting Jerusalem as a spiritually Judaic and historically Jewish city, Zionist theoreticians greatly adjusted and reshaped this theme. My proposition is that this Zionist-adjusted theme is invalid and dangerous. My advocacy is that it be discarded and positively replaced by those who have been its exponents.

What I propose may be regarded as heresy by some theologians and/or other religious commentators. What I propose will definitely be regarded as heresy by committed Zionists. What I propose, nevertheless, is solidly based within the Jewish faith, and, if accepted by a sufficient number of Jews, might help prevent further human tragedy in the troubled Middle East.

Before focusing upon Zionist formulations, it might be instructive to consider briefly the historical development of the concept of Israel and of the land of Israel theme contained in the *Old Testament* biblical text. Analyzing that development will reveal complexities in but may also illustrate certain major emphases in the Jewish faith.

The concept of Israel first appeared in God's promise to Abram, described in the *Old Testament Book of Genesis* and firmed in the divine Covenant. God gave the promise after delivering Abram by a special act of providence in the nineteenth century B.C. from the land of Ur of the Chaldees. God promised Abram would become the founder of a new nation, chosen not for domination but rather for universal service. God's promise, and thereby the Covenant, thus seemed to have both a national and a universal significance. God also promised that He would give to Abram and Abram's descendants a certain land (*Genesis* 15:7). The Covenant, ratifying this promise, was accompanied by, sealed, and according to the biblical text, enforced by the rite of circumcision. At the time of circumcision Abram's name was changed to Abraham. Literally meaning "the father of a multitude [of nations]", this new name signified that the promise, encompassed in the Covenant, went far beyond those who were Abraham's physical descendants and actually embraced all the families of the earth who were to be blessed in him and in his seed.

The textual explanation of the Covenant between God and Abraham, together with the promise contained therein, lacked adequate definition of certain key terms. Being aware of this, numerous students of *Old Testament* study, some of whom have claimed to be acting under Divine direction, have presented their interpretations of meaning. These interpretations have varied considerably. As matters of textual fact neither 'nation' nor 'land' nor possibly derivative terms were satisfactorily defined in the *Book of Genesis* account of the Covenant.

After the time of Abraham, according to the *Old Testament* text, God reiterated and renewed the Covenant and His promises to Isaac, Abraham's son, and to Jacob, Isaac's son. After a mysterious wrestling match with an angel, Jacob was renamed Israel. The term 'Israel', as used here, seemed to mean 'champion of God' and ultimately replaced the term 'Hebrews', by which the descendants of the family of Abraham had previously been known. A precise meaning of the concept of Israel, especially in the religious sense, was still lacking in the text.

Jacob had twelve sons from whom evolved the twelve tribes, constituting the people of Israel. Joseph, one of Jacob's younger sons, was most crucial for the historical development of the Abrahamic family. The full historical account need not be reiterated here. It is sufficient to state that through a series of unfortunate events the fortunes of the Israelites changed around 1580 B.C. They became terribly oppressed for over one hundred and thirty years.

At the critical moment, according to the *Old Testament,* God provided the great national liberator for the people of Israel. Moses, called by God to play this role, led his people out of Egypt into the Sinai in 1447 B.C.[1] (this is the date determined from biblical chronology). In 1448 B.C. God called Moses and named Himself as the "God of the Fathers, the God of Abraham, Isaac, and Jacob". Insofar as God was concerned, that appelation was sufficient and again indicated that the Israelites enjoyed a special relationship with Him. Moses, however, was not quite satisfied; he asked God to communicate a better name. God answered Moses, "EHYEH ASHER EHYEH [I am that I am]" (*Exodus* 3:14). The name for God in the *Old Testament* text thereafter became YHWH [He is that He is]. This name conveyed to Moses the important, if somewhat mystical, message that God was ever present with His people, Israel, with the children as with the fathers, through all the unfolding of their history — past, present, and future.

Moses brought the message of God, as he understood it, to His people who were in bondage in Egypt. He convinced them that he was to lead them out of Egypt and towards the place or land designated and promised by God. In traditional Jewish faith this part of the historical account is significant. The concept of Israel had here been re-emphasized; the land of

Israel theme could here be deduced; yet, the meanings of both the general concept and the specific theme remained on balance imprecise.

In the third month of the departure from Egypt, the Israelites arrived at Sinai, where another Covenant happening occurred. Some *Old Testament* scholars have maintained that a new Covenant was forged here which had its roots in God's Covenant with Abraham which in turn had its antecedents in a divine Covenant with Noah. Other scholars have maintained that the Covenant happening at Sinai was merely a reiteration of the one Covenant, entered into by God with the people of Israel. Through the perspective of either interpretation the Sinai happening became and remained centrally important for the Jewish faith. The Sinaitic Covenant defined the concept of Israel somewhat more clearly while at the same time tending to downplay the land of Israel theme.

The Sinaitic Covenant designated YHWH the God of Israel and Israel the people of YHWH. Still, the universal aspects of the Covenant that presumably applied to all human beings and not only to the Israelites emerged as the most important emphasis. This universalism was central in God's Covenant with Noah, according to the *Old Testament* text, and was therefore in effect for all human beings even before the time of the Hebrews. According to the universal character of the Covenant, human beings, created in the image of God, were required to conform to the character of God. God had been creative; human beings also had to be creative in maintaining and developing the work God had committed to their care. Creative cooperation was thereby stressed.

The basis of this creative cooperation was obedience to God, the creator. This was to be expressed in obedience to the moral law. The moral law was divided into two categories: (1) justice concerned with the recognition of human rights and (2) righteousness in which acceptance of duties was stressed.

From the vantage point of the Sinaitic Covenant God had entered into a Covenant with Abraham claiming him and his descendants as instruments for making known to human beings "the way of the Lord to do righteousness and Justice" (*Genesis* 18, 19) and in this sense performing the universal service for which he and his seed had been chosen. God's Covenant with Israel at Sinai ratified in all its implications the Covenant made with Abraham. The divine exhortation "And you shall be unto me a kingdom of priests and a holy nation" (*Exodus* 19:6) thus made clear the national selection of Israel to perform a universal service for God. As a 'kingdom of priests' Israel was to render a universal service. As a 'holy nation' Israelites were to follow a particular way of life, a life of holiness, which would set them off as a distinct and different people among the nations of the world. According to *Old Testament* scripture, and therefore according to traditional Jewish faith, Israel was by Covenant with God to be different from other nations.

The scope and substance of Israel's universal priestly mission was indicated and outlined to some extent in the Ten Commandments. The Decalogue is actually introduced by the statement: "I am YHWH your God who brought you out of the land of Egypt . . . " (*Exodus* 20:2). The clear indication is that God brought Israel out of Egypt to serve as the priestly nation for the deliverance of God's word. The specific duties and obligations involved in God's word for the holy nation were, according to the text, developed in a series of revelations by God to Moses that were then transmitted to the people. The revelations, including the Decalogue, finally became the Torah.

The Torah, denoting teaching and including doctrine and practice, religion, and morals, had, as a direct consequence of the Sinaitic Covenant, universal and national implications. The national implications, however, were actually encompassed with the universal, i.e. Israel was to exist as a holy nation with the priestly mission of delivering God's universal message. The concept of Israel within Jewish faith was then valid only from and through this perspective. The subsequent history of the Israelites affirmed the above. Journeying onward to the southern borders of Canaan, they sought to and did establish nation-states of their own in parts of historic Palestine. National feeling and the land of Israel theme at times appeared more secular than religiously oriented. Although God had promised "the land" to the Israelites, He made the promise conditional: the Israelites had to abide by the conditions of the Sinaitic Covenant and had to perform their priestly mission or "the land" would "spew them out". God's promise, moreover, did not necessarily posit the existence of a secular nation-state for the Israelites.

Obviously not following God's dictates, the Israelites strayed after strange gods and did not live up to the Covenant. Thus, according to the text, the northern Kingdom of Israel disappeared in 722 B.C.E. and the southern Kingdom of Judah, which lasted longer, was destroyed in 580 B.C.E. Still, Judah, including the small tribe of Benjamin, alone survived; the other tribes vanished by merging with their conquerors. In exile Judah emerged into a new people: the Jews. Spread throughout the world, Jews carried the dynamic message of the religion Judaism.

The Prophets who followed thereafter attempted to turn the nationalism of Judaism into an even more overriding universalism. Religion became more a matter of righteous living than mere ritual practice. The Prophets emphasized the unity of morality and religion. Jeremiah and Isaiah especially stressed Israel's world-wide mission. Isaiah discussed Messianism and declared that the restoration of land to Israel would occur when the Messiah had arrived.

Universalism, as opposed to nationalism, abounded in the later writings from *Psalms* through the wisdom literature of *Proverbs*, *Job*, and *Ecclesiastes*. This Universalism reached its highest point in the *Book of Ruth*. Primarily historical and concerned with tracing the ancestry of David, the *Book of Ruth* sought to teach that true religion was not confined to the boundaries of one people but was supra-national and that the principle of divine reward for good deeds was not dependent upon race but was equally valued for all people.

Many Jews, nevertheless, considered themselves in exile and still harboured national feelings. Influenced by new Prophets, scribes, and teachers they sought to settle again in what they considered to be their promised land. National feeling among Jews grew during the Babylonian captivity, which came to an end in 538 B.C.E. Some Jews made certain attempts to move back to their ancestral land, but difficulties abounded. Jews remained under the control of other people. Finally, in 143 B.C.E. the Jews expelled Syrians from Jerusalem and established a new Jewish state. This Second Hebrew Commonwealth lasted until 70 B.C.E. Soon thereafter, the Jews in Palestine began to rebuild religiously and socially. Their results, however, were decimated during the reign of the Emperor Hadrian from 117 to 138. Most Jews who had not been slaughtered or sold as slaves or forcibly deported by Hadrian fled the country, particularly to Babylon; organized Jewish life in Palestine fast approached extinction. The dispersion of Jews had clearly occurred. Following the death of Hadrian the situation changed. Improved conditions allowed active Jewish life to return to Palestine, especially in the Galilee region, which had been spared many of the ravages of the Hadrianic wars and persecution. Significantly, new Jewish schools of learning and an academic Sanhedrin, wherein distinguished rabbis decided matters of Jewish law, arose. All the while, the development of Jewish life and of Judaism continued and at times thrived in places other than Palestine. Babylonia, for example, became the major centre of Jewish learning and remained so for some time. The Babylonian Talmud became the leading compendium of

Jewish law and moral and ethical dictates, as derived by rabbinic interpretation from the *Old Testament*.

From the seventh century onward the spread of Islam affected Jews in many parts of what is now commonly called the Middle East. On balance, the spread of Islam was positive for Jews. After a few beginning difficult contacts with the Prophet Muhamad, Jews fared well, enjoying freedom, rights, and privileges in areas dominated by Islam.

In succeeding generations and centuries through the medieval period into the modern age, Jewish life in various other parts of the world so far exceeded the importance of Jewish life in Palestine that the two were hardly comparable. Jews became citizens of numerous nation-states. As was the case with some other people, Jews experienced difficulties and were persecuted at certain times in certain places. They, on the other hand, also thrived spiritually, intellectually, economically, socially and politically in many places much of the time. The major expressions of the Jewish faith emanated from places other than Palestine.

The concept of Israel and the specific land of Israel theme survived as important concerns in Jewish thought, feeling, and religious expression. But the meaning of both became increasingly symbolic and mystical rather than nationalistic. Jewish philosophy, literature, biblical commentary, and liturgy revealed this. The number of Jews who actually lived in or even visited Palestine at first diminished and then remained small.

In the mid-nineteenth century some Jewish thinkers were distressed with what they considered to be the disintegration of Jewish life. One of these was Moses Hess (1812-1875). Hess concluded that the only salvation for Judaism was Jewish nationalism. In his book, *Rome and Jerusalem*, published in 1862, he declared: "It is only with a national rebirth that the religious genius of the Jews, like the giant of the legend touching mother earth, will be endowed with new strength and again be inspired with prophetic spirit. No aspirant for Enlightenment, not even a Mendelssohn, has so far succeeded in crushing the hard shell within which Rubbinism has entrusted Judaism, without at the same time destroying the national ideal in its innermost essence . . . What we have to do at present for the regeneration of the Jewish nation is first to keep alive the hope of the political rebirth of our people and next to re-awaken the hope where it slumbers."[2]

Hess understood that he faced a problem of reconciling the idea of Jewish citizenship in a non-Jewish national state with loyalty to the Jewish nation. He argued that a good, patriotic, national Jew could participate in the culture and political life of the country of residence and actually have two fatherlands . . . For Hess only the return of Jews to their ancestral homeland in the land of Israel, i.e. Palestine, would provide them with the possibility of performing the high mission, given to them by God, of spreading principles of social justice and human cooperation and bringing permanent peace and unity to a troubled humanity. Hess did not specify what type of nation-state, if that, he thought best for the Jews in Palestine. He, for example, did not postulate either an exclusivist state nor a state in which others than Jews enjoyed the same secular rights and privileges.

During the time that Hess was advocating his brand of Jewish nationalism, some other Jews in Poland and Russia were advocating other ideas of Jewish nationalism in which redemption of Palestine, and especially Jerusalem, were stressed. One of these Eastern Europeans was Peretz Smolenski (1842-1885). Besides emphasizing the restoration of the Hebrew language, Smolenski posited the nationalistic idea that Jews were indeed a destined people and should act accordingly. At the same time, however, he insisted that Jews must consider themselves citizens of their respective countries. Their unity as a nation would thus be one of spirit only. Smolenski's Jewish nationalism interestingly was a nationalism without Palestine. For him the concept of Israel meant a spiritual nationalism in the diaspora.

Shortly after Alexander III acceeded to the throne in 1881, Jews as Jews were persecuted in Russia in a variety of ways. This persecution nurtured more numerous and even firmer expressions of Jewish nationalism. Relatively small, but nevertheless increasing numbers of Jews then began to express the idea that Jews should 'return' to Palestine, their promised land. By 1883, a few pioneers, financed by Baron Edmund de Rothschild of Paris, established struggling settlements in Palestine. This brand of Jewish nationalism was secularist based; it stemmed from persecution of Jews in this world. In order to acquire acceptance and backing from religious Jews, advocates attempted to cloak this brand of Jewish nationalism within the previously discussed land of Israel theme. This was substantially impossible since no adherence to the *Old Testament* Covenant conditions was stressed. Modern adjustment and reshaping of a major theme within the Jewish faith had begun.

Further theme adjustment and reshaping occurred in Western Europe in the 1890's. Under the leadership of Theodore Herzl (1860-1904) Jewish nationalism was transformed into an organized world movement with secular, political aspirations. The outbreak of virulent anti-Jewish anti-semitism, in the form of the Dreyfus case, in France, considered by some to have been the most civilized nation in the world at that time, convinced Herzl that Jews would be persecuted as Jews by non-Jews in all nation-states wherein they were in a minority and that the only solution of this Jewish problem lay in the establishment of a Jewish state. Herzl developed his ideas in his book, *Judenstaat* (*The Jewish State*), published in 1895. This book became the classic of the movement he inaugurated, a movement which assumed the name *Zionism*, which had been coined in 1892 by Nathan Birnbaum (1864-1937). In his early life Herzl neither associated with Jews nor with Judaism. His Zionism was unquestionably secular-based, he paid only lip service at certain times to his notion of the Messianic tradition for Jews. Herzl did argue that the Jewish state he envisioned would serve as a blessing not only for the Jewish people but for all the nations of the world. He, however, never made clear his meaning. Herzl organized the first Zionist congress in 1897 at which the programme of political Zionism was formulated in the words: "Zionism aims to establish a publicly and legally assured home for the Jewish people in Palestine".

Herzl did consider places other than Palestine for the establishment of a Jewish state. Herzl realized that the inhabitants of Palestine were mostly non-Jews. He was also impressed when certain members of the British Parliament early in the history of the Zionist movement suggested that an uninhabited part of Africa under British control should be given the Jews for their state thus avoiding settlement problems with non-Jews. Here Herzl again demonstrated the secular orientation of his advocacy of Jewish nationalism, i.e. Zionism, and his lack of concern for the *Old Testament* land of Israel theme. He acquiesed for internal political reasons within the Zionist movement to those who advocated Palestine as being the only place to establish the Jewish state.

Serious differences arose among those Jews who were committed Zionists. In their expressions of so-called 'spiritual' or 'cultural' Zionism, for example, Asher Ginsburg (1886-1927), commonly known by his pseudonym Ahad Haam, Martin Buber (1878-1969), and others stood in opposition to political Zionism. Expressing far more concern about the 'Arab inhabitants' of Palestine who were not Jews and being more interested in a Jewish cultural rather than religious rennaissance, many of these people opted at times to advocate something other than a Jewish nation-state in Palestine; they rather favoured a spiritual-cultural centre in Palestine for Jews. But such advocacy was torn asunder within the Zionist movement.

Jewish opposition to Zionism also existed outside the movement. This opposition stemmed from the most Orthodox to the most Reformist in religion and from one extreme of secular expression to the other. Although the Zionist movement gained strength and adherents within Jewry and although Zionism became the dominant new expression of Jewish nationalism before the 1930's, it was still the Holocaust, the killing of about six million Jews (one-third of the entire Jewish population of the world) in Europe by Hitler and the Nazis, that allowed Zionism to acquire the support from Jews and non-Jews that was necessary to bring about the establishment in 1948 of the Zionist state of Israel in historic Palestine.

As a religiously committed Jew I say to you that the establishment of the Zionist state of Israel in 1948 was a tragic mistake; it caused a major blemish in Jewish history; it contradicted the essence of the land of Israel theme in the Jewish faith. The creation of this demographically Jewish exclusivist state, shrouded in false religious clothing, resulted in immediate oppression of Palestinian Arabs, who constitute the non-Jewish indigenous population of this part of historic Palestine. Oppression of Palestinians in the state of Israel has continued to such an extent since 1948 that it has become a central feature of that state's Zionist character.

I could hardly begin to relate in one paper the record of oppression of Palestinians in the 'Jewish' state. Most of you in attendance at this conference know that record; some of you have personally experienced oppression, which has ranged from murder and torturing to economic exploitation and psychological assault of the personality structure.

I hope you will excuse a personal recollection at this point in my presentation. I recall a few years ago how appalled I became when studying Israeli official records and other documents pertaining to human and civil rights for use in a book manuscript I was preparing with an Israeli Jewish friend, Uri Davis, who is known to many of you for his courageous stands and anti-Zionist activities. I had expected to find some of what I found in my research and study. Yet, the magnitude of the evidence of oppression and persecution by Israeli Jews far exceeded my expectations. The evidence convinced me that the state of Israel, since inception, has been a racist entity wherein people have been discriminated against because of their origin. Palestinians have been denied basic human and civil rights by public policy simply because they were non-Jews. Please allow me to cite but one example from recently compiled evidence:

Most of the land in Israel belongs to or is administered by the Jewish National Fund (JNF), an institution within the over-all Zionist structure. The JNF forbids non-Jews to dwell on its land, to open businesses thereon, or sometimes even to work thereon. All the instruments of Israeli rule support this. Because of this policy many towns were created in Israel that were, as the colloquial phrase indicates, "clean of Arabs". In other towns, such as Upper Nazareth, only one special quarter was designated for Arabs. The opposition to an Arab's buying or renting an apartment or a house from a Jew has been both open and protected by all branches of the Ministry of Housing.

The 'salvation of the land' idea is still taught throughout the Israeli school system. According to the Israeli Ministry of Education a 'saved' piece of land is one that has been transformed to Jewish ownership. A land which has not yet been 'saved' still is in the possession of non-Jews. During the total period of the state of Israel's existence government officials have actively been involved in 'saving land', sometimes by employing force.

The Israeli Ministry of Housing has a special unit called the department for the housing of minorities. This department has dealt only with non-Jews. In Jerusalem, for example, while the Ministry of Housing has built apartments for Jews within the city, the department for the housing of minorities has attempted 'to thin out' Arabs by transferring them out of the city. Far more extensive confiscation by Jews of former Palestinian owned and occupied land occurred in other places.

In the opinion of this commentator no attempted analysis of the state of Israel's exclusivist, discriminatory character would be complete without mention of the Law of Return. The Law of Return was one of the first laws to be passed by the Israeli Parliament (1950), legally institutionalizing the political reality of an exclusivist Jewish state, granting privileged access and almost exclusive citizenship rights to members of Jewish communities throughout the world.

The Law of Return grants automatic citizenship to any member of the Jewish communities throughout the world on entry to the country. It follows necessarily from the elementary terms of the Zionist endeavour that a Jewish state, precisely to the extent it is Jewish, cannot be democratic nor offer equality of civil and political rights to all — least of all to the native Palestinian-Arab population. Against the reality of Palestinian refugees, clustered for years in camps around the borders, the law's focal point remains clear: any Jew throughout the world has prior access to Israeli citizenship as against the Palestinian Arabs, the native people of the country.

The Law of Return was cast within the classical Zionist land of Israel theme, put by Joseph Weitz (1890-1973), former Deputy Chairman of the Jewish National Fund and leading Zionist official for over forty years in the twentieth century, in his own diary in 1940 and quoted again by him in an article in 1967:

"Among ourselves, it must be clear that there is no place in the country for both peoples together . . . With the Arabs we shall not achieve our aim of being an independent people in this country. The only solution is Eretz-Israel, at least the west part of Eretz-Israel, without Arabs . . . And there is no other way but to transfer the Arabs from here to the neighbouring countries. Transfer all of them, not one village or tribe should remain . . ."[3]

Zionist theoreticians had already achieved a modicum of success by 1948. After the establishment of the modern state of Israel, however, apologists had even greater success. The fact that so outstanding a Jewish theologian as Abraham Joshua Heschel could write the following in his book, *Israel*, published in 1967, is proof positive of this success: "Intimate attachment to the land, waiting for the renewal of Jewish life in the land of Israel, is part of our integrity, an existential fact. Unique, *sui generis*, it lives in our hopes, it abides in our hearts. It is a commitment we must not betray. Three thousand years of faithfulness cannot be wiped off. To abandon the land would make a mockery of all our longings, prayers, and commitments. To abandon the land would be to repudiate the Bible . . . [Zionism] was a genuinely idealistic measure, and it was inspired far more by the Ancient Jewish relationship to the meaning of land than by modern single-tax or socialist theories . . . To the religious consciousness of the Jews, the people being in exile meant also God's being in exile and the return of the people to the land is also experienced in God's return to the land . . . The central theme of the story of the Covenant is the promise of the land to Abraham."[4]

Heschel stressed what he considered the central importance of Jerusalem in the Jewish faith and land of Israel theme: "Jerusalem is called the mother of Israel, and she is also used as a synonym for Israel . . . Jerusalem is not divine, her life depends on our presence. Alone she is desolate and silent, with Israel she is a witness, a proclamation. Alone she is a widow, with Israel she is a bride . . . For more than three thousand years we have been in love with Jerusalem. She occupied our hearts, filled our prayers, pervaded our dreams . . . The two most solemn occasions of the year, the Seder on Passover, and the Day of Atonement, found their climax in the proclamation: "Next year in Jerusalem."[5]

Almost unbelievably, Heschel and many other usually profound thinkers have accepted and advocated Zionist revisionism, for which the state of Israel is the living embodiment. They have failed to understand that Zionism is incompatible with the traditional, Judaic land of Israel theme. They have failed to observe correctly and/or to analyze carefully the obvious character and nature of this anti-Judaic, 'Jewish' state.

The command within Judaism to love one's fellow human beings with all its implications is all embracing, extending to all men, of whatever race or creed. Unmistakable in this connection is the biblical injunction "to love the stranger as yourself" (*Leviticus* 19:24). The great moral principle of human equality is enunciated in the words 'as yourself'; the non-Jewish stranger is 'as yourself'. Any distinction which Judaism makes between the Jew and the non-Jew is only of religious significance. Politically and socially no distinction is recognized between the two. "One law and one ordinance shall be for you and for the stranger that sojourneth with you" (*Numbers* 15:16). The law is one and the same for all. "Judge righteously between a man and his brother, and the stranger that is with him" (*Deuteronomy* 1:16). The stranger requires no patron to take legal action. "For the judgment is God's" (*Deuteronomy* 1:17). It is God who gives the stranger his share and full rights in the law of the land.

This equality is stretched even in regard to the land. "And it shall come to pass that you shall divide it (the land) by lot for an inheritance unto you and to the strangers that sojourn among you, which shall beget children among you; and they shall be unto you as homeborn among the children of Israel; they . . ."

The Talmud underlines the biblical attitude to the non-Israelite. Characteristic of such Talmudic teaching is the saying of Hillel: "Be you of the disciples of Aaron, one that loves peace and pursues peace, that loves human beings and brings them near to the Torah" (*Ethics of the Fathers* 1:12).

I suggest in conclusion that adopting the saying of Hillel is a good way for Jews and non-Jews to approach the future and to attempt to reconcile the great problems that exist in a part of the world that has such a holy tradition.

Yet peace must be based upon justice. This means primarily justice for the Palestinians. Make no mistake: justice for the Palestinians is impossible, solution of the Arab-Israel conflict will not be forthcoming, positive resolution of the fate of Jerusalem will not occur so long as Israel continues to be dominated by Zionist nationalism. The liberation of that state from its Zionist political philosophy in favour of non-discriminatory democracy is therefore a necessity.

Footnotes

1. Certain scholars have assigned other dates for the exodus from Egypt. These dates have varied from 1584 B.C.E. to 1144 B.C.E. Most acknowledged scholars, however, have accepted the Biblical date of 1447 B.C.E. A sufficient range of evidence has convinced this writer that 1447 B.C.E. is the best date to cite.
2. Hess, Moses, *Rome and Jerusalem* (English translation by M. Waxman, New York, 1943), p. 77, 146.
3. Joseph Weitz, quoting his own diary entry in 1940, in 'A Solution to the Refugee Problem: An Israeli State with a small Arab minority', *Davar,* September 29, 1978, p. 20.
4. Heschel, Abraham Joshua, *Israel* (New York, 1967, 1969), p. 44, 105, 25-26, 46.
5. *Op. cit.*, 14, 15, 26.

3. The Catholic Faith and The Problem of Israel and Jerusalem

Rev. Joseph L. Ryan

The word 'Israel', as often used in Scripture, both in the old and new Testaments as well as in Catholic writings, refers to the people of God in salvation history. We are not using that meaning here.

We are primarily interested, I believe, in contemporary questions: Israel as a Jewish state, today particularly and also for the immediate future; Jerusalem as a political problem involving questions of sovereignty, religious and cultural identity, human rights, etc.

'Catholic Faith' usually refers to the faith of Catholics in the sense of their act of believing (one says of a person, his faith is strong) or of the essential truths in which they believe (such as the articles of the Creed and other dogmatic statements). In matters which are not directly connected with the essentials of the Catholic faith but are of some interest or concern to Catholics, one may ask what members of the Catholic faith think of such matters, what stands they take.

Hence, here we might ask: How does a person or persons professing the Catholic faith look at these issues of Jerusalem and Israel? To try to answer that complicated question would be extremely difficult. A superficial view might cite opinion polls which show in the US that Catholics, like other American citizens, have been supportive of Israel.

Rather, we would do better to begin looking at attitudes expressed and actions officially taken in recent years by the Church, especially by the Church in Rome, and in the light of our finding we might more profitably and with less confusion examine other Catholic views. Those other views may be of other Catholic churches, e.g. in the Middle East or the US, or of significant Catholic groups and individuals.

1. Inter-faith affairs vs. political affairs

At the outset I would like to stress the distinction which the Catholic Church in Rome makes between inter-faith activity, on the one hand, and political activity, on the other, between dialogue by Catholics with Jews, and the foreign policy of the Vatican regarding Israel and Jerusalem.

A recent striking example of this distinction was given by Pope John Paul II in his visits to the US. At the UN the Pope spoke succinctly about the Arab-Israeli conflict and stressed the centrality of the Palestine problem. He then went on briefly to repeat the Vatican's view of Jerusalem. It is true that he referred in the UN speech to the camps of destruction in Europe during World War II and especially of Auschwitz, but he had nothing to say expressly about Israel, nor, for that matter, about the other Arab states. On the other hand, at Battery Park he warmly greeted Jews in New York, but that was clearly outside the context of Vatical foreign affairs.

This separating of interreligious affairs from foreign affairs is hardly new but its context here (regarding the Middle East) is. The Vatican Secretariat of State is quite distinct from the other Vatican offices, and far older than most of those which deal with interreligious affairs, such as the Secretariat for Christian Unity in which activities involving relations with Jews take place.

What is the scope of the secretariat for Catholic-Jewish relations?

In a report given at the secretariat's plenary session in Rome,

February 8-16, 1972, Father Jerome Hamer, OP, secretary of the Secretariat for Promoting Christian Unity, cited the document Regimini Ecclesaie, Article 94, to the effect that the secretariat "has competence also in questions concerning the Jews under their religious aspects". Then he added: "The article defines both the scope of this task ('questions concerning the Jews') and its proper character ('under their religious aspect')".

Father Hamer continued: "Are we the only ones in Rome who deal with Jewish questions? No. There is the Council of Public Affairs for the Church to which it belongs 'to deal with everything concerning relations with civil governments' (Article 28). Thus relations with the State of Israel are the business of this council, whose president is the Secretary of State, Cardinal Villot."

"This shows", Father Hamer went on, "the importance and interest of the specifications 'under their religious aspects' when the competence of our secretariat is in question. The specification does not restrict the field of our duties but it throws a certain light on it and it traces out a method. Whatever the problem we have to study it together, it is under its religious aspect that we are asked to tackle it." (Father Hamer's report appeared in the Christian Unity Secretariat's information service, No. 17, April 1972/11).

A striking instance of the separation of interreligious affairs and foreign affairs was given when on March 9, 1976, the Vatican denied a statement by one of its own officials that the Holy See had changed its views on the political status of Jerusalem. (*Christian Science Monitor,* March 10). Rev. Pierre de Contenson, secretary of the Vatican's Commission on Religious Relations with the Jews, said in an interview with Israel Radio the week before that the Holy See no longer demanded that the city be administered by an international regime as proposed by a UN resolution in 1947. He said that the

Pope now wanted only international guarantees for preserving the status of the city's holy sites. But the Vatican press spokesman said that Father de Contenson was not competent to discuss political matters and added that there had been absolutely no change in the Holy See's policies.

Another example of the difference between inter-faith and foreign policy affairs is seen in the Vatican's disavowal of two paragraphs of the resolutions issued by the Seminar on Islamic-Christian Dialogue in Tripoli, Libya, February 1-5, 1976. (The decrees were published in *The Christian Science Monitor*, March 9, 1976. The disavowal by the Vatican was announced in *L'Osservatore Romano*, February 11, 1976).

For an explanation of the subordinate role of ecumenical relations in policy statements about the Middle East, see the 'Background: the Structure of the Question' by Rev. J. Bryan Hehir, Director, US Catholic Conference Division of Justice and Peace. Fr. Hehir's explanation accompanied the US Bishops' statement 'Towards Peace in the Middle East', November 1973.

2. Jewish-Catholic relations

Having stressed the difference between Catholic inter-faith activity and Vatican political activity, let me take up that inter-faith activity between Catholics and Jews.

At the beginning of Vatican II, Arabs — not only Muslims but also oriental Christians — did not understand why the Catholic Church at the Council spent so much time discussing what to do about the centuries-old charge that Jews after Jesus were responsible for the death of Jesus. By the time Vatican II was over, however, I think Arabs had a far better understanding of Catholic motives even if they still feared that the Vatican decree would be used (against the Vatican's intention) for Israel's political advantage. Arabs came to learn, I believe, that especially after the anti-Semitism in Europe and the Holocaust during World War II, Catholics particularly in the West felt bound in conscience to remove anything in Catholic teaching which might appear to be a basis of hatred of Jews and discrimination against them. And that in fact was done through the process which produced one part (part 4) of one of the decrees, *Nostra Aetate*, namely the Declaration on the Relationship of the Church to non-Christian Religions.

But it is interesting to note, especially for Muslims, that during the long and sometimes painful discussion on the charge of Jewish responsibility for the death of Jesus, the original decree, which had only been concerned with Jews, was marvellously widened to encompass all other believers (including Muslims) who are not Christians. The Catholic Church is wonderfully enriched by this widening, and the developments in relations between Catholics and Muslims since then are deeply indebted to the enlargement of the scope of the decree.

Let me offer a few brief comments on the decree.

Personally I feel that the Church's stand on anti-Semitism was necessary and timely, if not, sadly, long overdue. The decree explained that "what happened in His (Jesus') passion cannot be charged against all the Jews, without distinction, then alive nor against the Jews of today . . . the Church . . . decries hatred, persecutions, displays of anti-Semitism, directed against Jews at any time and by any one".

Further I believe that the Holocaust, the systematic destruction of many peoples during World War II, in as much as it included Jews, deserves very serious attention, especially by Christians of the West because of the anti-Semitism in our culture; and in as much as it included, with these Jews, millions of other persons of various ethnic and national groupings, deserves the most earnest consideration of the whole world. This attention and consideration were expressed by Pope John Paul II in his recent speech before the UN.

A secondary but practically important consideration regarding anti-Semitism is that it is used at times as a political weapon held by some over the heads of others who disagree with them regarding Israel. This abuse of the campaign against anti-Semitism must be firmly checked, especially by Christian leaders in inter-faith activities.

The Vatican II Declaration on the Relationship of the Church to non-Christian Relations, *Nostra Aetate,* marks an altogether extraordinary development in the Roman Catholic church's view of other religions, a turning point in our history and an incentive for us to look at other religions in a new, positive and understanding way.

3. Other declarations

Nostra Aetate was issued in October 1965. Ten years later in January 1975 Rome issued a document entitled 'Guidelines and Suggestions for Implementing the Conciliar Declaration *Nostra Aetate* (n.4)'. This document came from the Vatican Commission for Religious Relations with the Jews, a commission which had been set up by Pope Paul VI in October 1974. (These documents are given in Helga Croner, compiler, *Stepping Stones to Further Jewish-Christian Relations,* London, New York: Stimulus Books 1977, pp. 11-16).

The 1975 document stated that "such relations as there have been between Jew and Christian have scarcely ever risen above the level of monologue. From now on, real dialogue must be established" (p. 12).

The document also said that Christians "must strive to learn by what essential traits the Jews define themselves in the light of their own religious experience", but it did not go into any details (p. 11).

The absence of details is significant. What the 1975 'Guidelines' do not say, or avoid saying, may be suggested by an earlier working document, submitted to Rome but never accepted by Rome as its own. In December 1969 at a meeting at Loyola College, Baltimore, Cardinal Shehan of Baltimore, who had returned from a meeting in Rome of the Secretariat for Christian Unity, released a document which was described, incorrectly, as having been approved by Rome. The document stated:

> "Fidelity to the covenant was linked to the gift of a land, which in the Jewish soul has endured as the object of an inspiration that Christians should strive to understand. In the wake of long generations of painful exile, all too often aggravated by persecutions and moral pressures, for which Christians ask pardon of their Jewish brothers, Jews have indicated in a thousand ways their attachment to the land promised to their ancestors from the days of Abraham's calling. It could seem that Christians, whatever the difficulties they may experience, must attempt to understand and respect the religious significance of this link between the people and the land. The existence of the State of Israel should not be separated from this perspective; which does not in itself imply any judgement on historical occurrences or on decisions of a purely political order". (Croner, p. 7).

In the uproar which ensued after the meeting at Loyola College, it became clear that the document had not been approved in Rome but had simply been submitted as a working paper. The Cardinal expressed regret over the circumstances of its disclosure.

Allow me now to mention some other statements on Jewish-Catholic dialogue issued not by Rome but by other national Catholic offices. For example the US Catholic Bishops published one such statement in March 1976, (Croner, pp. 16-20) and another in November 1975 (Croner, pp. 29-34). A common statement was made in 1969 by the Archdiocese of New York and the adjacent dioceses of Rockville Center and Brooklyn (Croner, pp. 20-27). Other statements were issued by the diocese of Albany, NY (Croner, p. 28), the Archdiocese of Cincinnati, Ohio (Croner, pp. 28-29) and the Archdiocese of Detroit (*Origins* January 4, 1979, Vol. 8, No. 29, pp. 461-3). In April 1973 a committee of the French Bishops for relations with Jews (not the entire assembly of French bishops) made public a statement which provoked much controversy (Croner, pp. 60-65).

4. The link between Jews and 'the land'

What I am concerned with here is the reference in some of these statements to Israel and/or to a Jewish tie to the land.

No such reference is contained in the Vatican II declaration nor in the Vatican's 'Guidelines' of January 1975, nor in any of the US statements except the 1975 US Bishops' statement and the statements of the Archdiocese of Cincinnati and of Detroit.

The 1975 US Bishops' statement said:

> "In dialogue with Christians, Jews have explained that they do not consider themselves as a church, a sect, or a denomination, as is the case among Christian communities, but rather as a peoplehood that is not solely racial, ethnic or religious, but in a sense a composite of all these. It is for such reasons that an overwhelming majority of Jews see this tie to the land as essential to their Jewishness. Whatever difficulties Christians may experience in sharing this view they should strive to understand this link between land and people which Jews have expressed in their writings and worship throughout two millenia as a longing for the homeland, holy Zion. Appreciation of this link is not to give assent to any particular religious interpretation of this bond. Nor is this affirmation meant to deny the legitimate rights of other parties in the region, or to adopt any political stance in the controversies over the Middle East, which lie beyond the purview of this statement".

I have already discussed — and criticized — the above

paragraph. ('A Sensitive Middle East Topic: Jewish-Catholic Dialogue', *The Priest*, May 1976, pp. 23-29).

I said (in part):

" . . . Will Catholics recognise a tie to the land of all Jews (e.g., Jews in New York or Manchester) and, in a highly controversial setting, be silent about the right to that same land of Palestinians who were born there and who have undergone traumatic suffering precisely because their right to the land happened to be an obstacle to the claim of Jews coming in from abroad? Whether Catholics admit it or not, silence on Palestinian right to the land in this context would be saying something. Do Catholics wish this? In the light of the tremendous emphasis which Catholics in the last decades have placed on justice and peace, one would think not. And that, in my opinion, is why the Holy See has refused, despite all the pressures, even to appear to slight the rights of a suffering and much maligned people.

. . . It is hard to avoid the conclusion that by their silence in this context on Palestinian rights to the land the bishops have, in fact, taken sides." (*The Priest*, p. 24).

The 1971 Cincinnati statement in two places mentions the state of Israel:

" . . . We must remember that before a real bond of understanding can exist between Roman Catholics and Jews, the task of examining our shared history is mandatory. The Nazi holocaust and the establishment of the State of Israel force us to look with compassion and candor on the magnitude of these two events.

. . . Roman Catholics should strive to understand the concern of the Jewish community for the State of Israel and should seek to support efforts that will ensure a just and lasting peace in the Holy Land for all concerned." (Croner, pp. 28-9)

The Detroit archdiocesan statement treats the return of Jews to the land in a curiously ambiguous way:

"e. The dispersion of the Jewish people and the present ingathering into the land of Israel should be understood in the light of Jewish history and Jewish perspectives.

f. It is difficult to make clear theological judgement on the return of the Jewish people to its ancient land. Scripture witnesses most strongly to the promise of this land to this people. (Gn. 12:7, 26:3-4, Is. 43:5-7, Jer. 16:15, Zeph. 3:20, *et al*). Therefore, Christians as well as Jews are faced with the question: Will the ingathering of the Jews effected under the constraint of persecution and the interplay of vast forces be one of the channels of God's justice for the Jewish people and at the same time for the Arab populations of the area and indeed, for all the peoples of the earth, or will it not? Together Christians, Jews and Moslems must face this great challenge as together they are the 'people of the book'.

Catholics should be sensitive to the deeply held feelings which American Jews hold for the state of Israel". (*Origins*, Jan. 4, 1979, Vol. 8, No. 29, pp. 462-3).

In April 1973 a committee of French bishops for Relations with Jews issued a statement which provoked much controversy, especially in France and in the Middle East. One controversial part concerned the land and the state of Israel . . .

"Today more than ever, it is difficult to pronounce a well-considered theological opinion on the return of the Jewish people to 'its' land. In this context, we Christians must first of all not forget the gift once made by God to the people of Israel, of a land where it was called to be reunited (cf Gn. 12:7, 26:3-4, 28:13; Is. 43:5-7; Jer. 15:16; Soph. 3:20).

Throughout history, Jewish existence has always been divided between life among the nations and the wish for national existence on that land. This aspiration poses numerous problems even to Jews. To understand it, as well as all dimensions of the resulting discussion, Christians must take into account the interpretation given by Jews to their ingathering around Jerusalem which, according to their faith, is considered a blessing. Justice is put to the test by this return and its repercussions. On the political level, it has caused confrontations between various claims for justice. Beyond the legitimate divergence of political options, the conscience of the world community cannot refuse the Jewish people, who had to submit to so many vicissitudes in the course of its history, the right and means for a political existence among the nations. At the same time, this right and the opportunities for existence cannot be refused to those who, in the course of local conflicts resulting from this return, are now victims of grave injustice.

Let us, then, turn our eyes toward this land visited by God and let us actively hope that it may become a place where one day all its inhabitants, Jews and non-Jews, can live together in peace. It is an essential question, faced by Christians as well as Jews, whether or not the ingathering of the dispersed Jewish people — which took place under pressure of persecution and by the play of political forces — will despite so many tragic events prove to be one of the final ways of God's justice for the Jewish people and at the same time for all the nations of the earth. How could Christians remain indifferent to what is now being decided in that land?" (Croner, pp. 63-4).

As a result of the clamour raised against the document throughout the French-speaking Catholic Church (in France, the Middle East and North Africa), Cardinal Marty, the Archbishop of Paris, in a clarifying statement explained that the document was published by an episcopal committee and not by the French episcopacy. Among the protests was a formal and public rejection of the document by forty-two Jesuits in Lebanon. They objected to the document's treatment of who

Jews are today and to the relation between the Old and New Testaments; they also challenged the statement's treatment of the state of Israel. (*Catholic Mind*, September 1973, pp. 58-60).

5. Growth in the dialogue

A generic word or two about the development of the Jewish-Catholic dialogue in the US (where it is most highly developed) might be helpful. The dialogue, which was promising before the June War of 1967, ran into a severe testing as a result of that conflict. American Christians did not respond in the way American Jews expected them to. For a while some Jews wondered if the dialogue could resume. It did.

It resumed, but it changed, perhaps as a result of the 1967 War, perhaps because of the essential clarification brought about (in the Jewish-Catholic dialogue) by the Vatican II decree *Nostra Aetate*, partly due to the sheer amount of time involved in the lengthening dialogue between Christians and Jews, and partly due to the 1973 War and all it meant to the West, the dialogue changed.

On March 24, 1974, the Apostolic Delegate to the US, Most Rev. Jean Jadot, speaking to the Synagogue Council of America, discusssed the question whether, as was widely conceded, the ecumenical movement and the Jewish-Catholic dialogue had slowed down. Focusing his talk on the Jewish-Catholic dialogue, he concluded that it had not.

On October 17 of the same year, speaking to Jewish leaders in New York, the Delegate spoke of the controversial problems and the resulting tension between Jews and Christians.

He said: "To put the matter quite bluntly, some Catholics feel that on the issues of Israel and Soviet Jewry, Jews have been successful and we have helped them; whereas, in regard to abortion and state aid to private schools, we have not been successful and Jews have opposed us".

While he challenged the factuality of the objection, he

acknowledged the intercommunity difficulties. He said: "The chief obstacle on this path is not hostility . . . Today, it is perhaps a fear of one another. It is also apathy".

As a result of the 1973 War, Christians and Jews in the US had their eyes opened to the Palestinian problem as never before. Because Christians were better informed, they put aside some of their hesitancy in speaking their mind to Jews and expressing their dissent. The new expertise in political analysis of the US Catholic Bishops' Office of International Peace and Justice contributed to a clearer understanding of the essentially differing points of view, namely, the point of view of interreligious affairs and the point of view of political foreign affairs. Further, more and more Americans began to reflect on their own interests, as the Andrew Young affair, the visit to the Middle East by Jesse Jackson and other blacks and the speech of former Texas governor John Connally on the Middle East showed.

6. Multiple contacts of the Holy See

I have stressed the great difference for Catholics between inter-faith affairs and political matters. Having discussed inter-faith activities between Catholics and Jews, let me pass now to political matters.

I would like to make some general observations about the Holy See and about Popes Paul VI and John Paul II. Then I will take up some practical questions.

To begin with, the Holy See, because of a great variety of contacts, is very well informed about the Middle East, and in particular about Palestine.

First of all there are Catholics in Palestine and other Arab countries, Catholics of both the Latin and various Oriental rites with a Latin Patriarch, bishops, churches, schools, hospitals, etc. Although there is a small number of Catholics of Jewish origin in Israel, most of the Catholic people and many of the priests and prelates in Palestine are Palestinian Arabs; there is in Palestine also a significant number of Latin-rite priests and sisters. As a result of the presence of these Catholics, the Holy See understands in very great detail what has gone on in Palestine for decades, what has happened to Palestinians, etc. I believe that for Westerners, especially in the US, it is impossible to overestimate this knowledge on the part of the Holy See. It is in such striking contrast to the great ignorance and/or indifference in the US generally, at least up to the 1973 War.

And this is not all. The Holy See has multiple other contacts, e.g. with the Orthodox both in Palestine and the other Arab countries who are very sensitive to the threat of Zionism to the future of their communities.

The Holy See also has contacts with many Arab countries, either through direct or indirect diplomatic representation and through the apostolic delegates.

It also has relations with other non-Arab Muslim countries.

Each of these sources provides the Holy See not only with abundant evidence about conditions but also with significant — and differing — points of view.

7. The Holy See's wider perspective

Further, in addressing itself to the Arab-Israeli conflict and the problem of Palestine, the Holy See brings to that conflict a very wide perspective.

One element in that perspective is time. The Holy See is not hurried. It sees situations in the long term. Being the oldest governmental institution with continuous existence in Europe, it has an extraordinary historical experience to fall back on to help itself assess conditions and take action on them.

Because of its long-term perspective and its special religious character, the Holy See generally uses quiet diplomacy. It tends to speak privately rather than publicly. It prefers to take milder steps rather than strong ones. A striking instance of quiet papal protest regarding Palestine was provided at the first visit of an Israeli prime minister to the Vatican when Mrs. Golda Meir went to see Pope Paul VI. Some of the significance of the meeting can be inferred from the statements issued afterwards.

The Vatican spokesman Frederico Allesandrini, countering Israeli government claims that Mrs. Meir had come to Rome at Pope Paul's invitation, stated that the audience had been requested by her. Alessandrini pointed out that the meeting "does not signify nor imply the least change in the attitude of the Holy See concerning the problems of the Holy Land."

The tenor of the Pope's remarks to Mrs. Meir would not have been publicly known had she herself not revealed them, as she did in an interview with the Israeli newspaper *Ma'ariv*. Pope Paul apparently started off the meeting by speaking to Mrs. Meir about Israeli mistreatment of Palestinians. Mrs. Meir, according to *Ma'ariv*, said: "I didn't like the opening at all. The Pope said to me at the outset that he found it hard to understand why the Jewish people, who are supposed to act mercifully, respond so fiercely in their own country". How strongly the Pope spoke we may infer from the vigour of her reaction. "I can't stand it when we are talked to like that," she said. "I won't give in to anyone who begins a conversation in this way." (For a discussion of the visit, see Alfred M. Lilienthal, *The Zionist Connection*, NY, Dodd, Mead & Co., 1978, pp. 505-7.)

If one perspective of the Holy See is time, another is the universality of the Church. It encompasses the whole world and it brings to any local conflict that world view. This perspective of universality may be suggested by some of the themes of talks by Popes Paul VI and John Paul II. Generic as some of these themes are, they indicate some of the background of papal thinking, some of which has an application to conditions in the Middle East.

8. Themes of Pope Paul

Let me illustrate these elements of time and universality by citing some passages. The first passage is from Pope Paul VI's Message on the World Day of Peace. It was addressed to Catholics everywhere. May I suggest that you listen to it, if possible, as both a world citizen and then as a Palestinian.

What is real peace?

Reaffirming his message of the previous year, namely, that "peace is possible", Pope Paul continued: "it is more than possible — it is a duty, a moral necessity, a supreme ethical objective." He scorned the politics of fear and of balance of power, saying that such politics operates on "the unspoken and sceptical conviction that, in practice, peace is impossible".

The Pope argued against "the confusion of peace with weakness (not just physical but also moral), with the renunciation of genuine right and an equitable justice, with the evasion of risk and sacrifice, with cowardly and supine submission to other's arrogance, and hence with acquiescence to enslavement."

He said: "This is not real peace. Repression is not peace. Cowardice is not peace. A settlement which is purely external and imposed by fear is not peace. The recent celebration of the 25th anniversary of the Declaration of Human Rights reminds us that true peace must be based on a sense of the untouchable dignity of the human person, from which arises inviolable rights and corresponding duties".

Prospects of War

A year later, January 11, 1975, delivering a 2,500 word address to the diplomatic corps accredited to the Holy See, Pope Paul warned of dangerous world conditions. He then went on to discuss Vatican diplomacy and expressed some of its limitations and strengths.

First, his warning. He referred to his "growing preoccupation" with the current situation in the world, a

situation that "appears to be gradually deteriorating, to the extent that it causes some to speak of a transition, already begun, from a 'post-war' to a 'pre-war' phase". The prospect, he said, has a "terrifying import" for all concerned. He asked:
concerned. He asked:

> "Has there not perhaps been till now a sort of convergence of judgements — and of fears — concerning what could be the meaning for the world of the outbreak of a conflict that — should it prove impossible to keep it in proportion, always very painful for the victims, but at least territorially limited — would almost inevitably become atomic, because of its seriousness and extension?"
>
> The 'terror' of such a war, the Pope continued, "is currently considered to be the main if not perhaps the only guarantee against events that would appear for that very reason too dangerous for the very people who would have felt sufficiently strong to be able to win by surviving the other contenders."

Some Vatican observers interpreted the Pope's words as a reaction, diplomatically phrased, to the declaration of US Secretary of State Henry Kissinger that the United States has not ruled out the possibility of military action if oil-producing countries should threaten to strangle the economies of the industrial nations.

However, Vatican officials were unwilling to take the Pope's words any further than he had himself. (Cf. NC News Report from Vatican City by James C. O'Neill, Boston *Pilot,* January 17, 1975),

He rejected the formula of 'the balance of terror' as a means of safeguarding peace and gave four reasons. It is too detached from the moral basis of peace. It involves extravagant waste of energies which are diverted from the well-being and progress of all peoples. It is destructive of harmony and mutual understanding. And fourthly, it is too fragile.

Having rejected the 'balance of terror', the Pope went on: to "the voice of force" it is necessary to "oppose the strong and serene voice of reason". The world today needs "perhaps more than in past years, the courageous and persevering action of wise diplomacy oriented towards the safeguarding of peace, in all its dimension, in its causes and in the conditions that render it possible and secure".

Diplomacy of the Holy See

In the second part of his address, Pope Paul discussed the diplomatic activities of the Holy See.

He began by saying:

> "This diplomacy is not inspired by a desire for self-affirmation and human prestige, or by a wish to interfere in matters which are alien to the nature of the Catholic Church. On the contrary, the first and fundamental purpose of this diplomacy is precisely to render faithful service to the Church, to her potentialities for life and action, in all places and in all historical, political or social situations, and to her legitimate freedom, even if this service is not easy and not always adequately appreciated."

The Pope said that in defending the legitimate interests of freedom of religion, the Church also makes a significant contribution to civil society itself and to the defense particularly of human rights. Summing up his argument, Pope Paul declared:

> "On a vast stage of today's (world) the Holy See's diplomacy intends to operate with fidelity to its own principles but with loyalty, cooperation and friendship towards the other members of the community of peoples, even when, on some crucial problems, the respective positions may not be fully concordant . . .
>
> In other words, the Holy See intends to act with strength in order that operative principles of solidarity and brotherhood may replace those which are ever present as a continuing

threat to the peaceful coexistence of peoples, namely egoism whether national, group-oriented, racial or cultural".

9. Themes of Pope John Paul II

From Pope Paul VI, let us turn to his successor. Although Pope John Paul II has been in the Vatican only a year, he has made several statements which, while general, have a very interesting application to the Middle East.

Warfare against humanity

Towards the end of his address to the United Nations the Pope spoke of how serious is any threat to human rights. He said: "Any violation of them, even in a peace situation, is a form of warfare against humanity". He then went on to two main threats in the modern world, both of them concerning human rights in the field of international relations and human rights within individual states or societies.

His remarks have a general applicability. But anyone familiar with the condition of Palestinians since the rise of Zionism cannot fail to be struck by the Pope's words and apply them to this conflict.

The first of these systematic threats against human rights, Pope John Paul said, is linked in an overall sense with the distribution of material goods.

> "Various forms of inequality in the possession of material goods, and in the enjoyment of them, can often be explained by different historical and cultural causes and circumstances. But, while these circumstances can diminish the moral responsibility of people today, they do not prevent the situations of inequality from being marked by injustice and social injury".

The second systematic threat to man in his inalienable rights in the modern world involves the various forms of injustice in the field of the spirit.

> "Man can indeed be wounded in his inner relationship

with truth, in his conscience, in his most personal belief, in his view of the world, in his religious faith, and in the spheres of what are known as civil liberties. Decisive for these last is equality of rights without discrimination on grounds of origin, race, sex, nationality, religion, political convictions and the like. Equality of rights means the exclusion of the various forms of privilege for some and discrimination against others, whether they are people born in the same country or people from different backgrounds of history, nationality, race and ideology."

The Pope spoke of recurring threat and violations, often with no possibility of appealing to a higher authority or of obtaining an effective remedy. Structures of social life often exist in which the practical exercise of these freedoms condemns man, in fact if not formally, to become a second-class or third-class citizen.

Torture and oppression for 'security' reasons

Earlier in the speech the Pope spoke of the lesson that Auschwitz and other such camps teach. He said that such experiences must disappear. He condemned especially "the various kinds of torture and oppression, either physical or moral, carried out under any system, in any land". He added — and the addition is poignant for Palestinians: — "This phenomenon (torture and oppression) is all the more distressing if it occurs under the pretext of internal 'security' or the need to preserve an apparent peace."

Right of self-determination

Pope John Paul II, speaking in Poland at Jasna Gora on June 5, 1979, addressed himself to unity and reconciliation. For any one concerned about the problem of Palestine, the Pope's words have a special meaning.

"As inward unity within each society or community, whether a nation or a family, depends on respect for the rights of each of its members, so international reconciliation depends on recognition of and respect for the rights of each nation. Chief of these are the rights to existence and self-determination, to its own culture and the many forms of developing it. We know from our own country's history what has been the cost to us of the infraction, the violation and the denial of those inalienable rights." (*Origins*, June 21, 1979, Vol. 9, No. 5, p. 71)

Right to the land

Another theme of Pope John Paul II which would find resonance among Palestinians concerns the right to work and the right to the land. In his pilgrimage through Poland, he visited Nowy Targ, in the southern mountain region of Poland. Nowy Targ is beautiful land but difficult — rocky, mountainous, less fertile than some other parts.

" . . . may I be permitted precisely from this land . . . to refer to what has always been so dear to the heart of the Poles: love for the land and the work of the fields . . .

This is the great and fundamental right of man: the right to work and the right to land . . . the right to land does not cease to constitute the basis of a sound economy and sociology.

. . . I wish with all my heart that . . . the personal link with the land, may not cease to be so even in our industrialised generation." (*Origins*, June 21, 1979, Vol. 9, No. 5, pp. 74-75)

10. Pope Paul VI on Palestine

Having spoken about the generic approach to political questions by the Holy See and about the possible applications to the Palestine problem of several papal statements of principle by Pope Paul VI and John Paul II, I would like to take up some specific Vatican statements concerning Palestine.

Jerusalem and Palestine

In his Christmas message on December 22, 1967, Pope Paul VI took up both the Jerusalem question and Palestine. He said:

"The question . . . offers . . . two essential and indispensable aspects.

The first regards the Holy Places properly so called . . . and intends to safeguard the freedom of worship, the respect, the preservation and the approach to the Holy Places themselves protected by a special immunity by means of a special status of its own, the guarantee for the observance of which should be made by an institution of international character . . .

The second aspect . . . has reference to the free enjoyment of religious and civic rights, which legitimately regard the persons, the homes and the activities of all of the communities present in the territory of Palestine."

Four years later in his 1971 Christmas message Pope Paul, commenting on the peace initiatives, said they should "take into account the legitimate interests of all parties" and added: "and one must include . . . (among these parties), in their proper place, the populations which the vicissitudes of the last decades have constrained to abandon their lands."

Pope Paul VI repeated his concern for people and places on other occasions, e.g. on March 14, 1971, April 9, 1971 and June 24, 1971. For instance, on January 19, 1978, addressing Israeli Foreign Minister Moshe Dayan on his visit to the Vatican, Pope Paul VI again spoke of Jerusalem and the holy places and said: "We fervently hope for a solution that will not only satisfy the legitimate aspirations of those concerned, but also take into account the pre-eminently religious character of the Holy City".

On April 29, 1978, on the occasion of the visit of King Hussein to the Vatican, Pope Paul VI said:

"In particular we once again express our hope that a just end may be put to the sad situation of the Palestinians, and that Jerusalem, the Holy City for the three great monotheistic religions . . . may really become the 'high place' of peace and encounter for peoples from every part of the world . . . " (*L'Osseratore Romano*, May 11, 1978).

Mutual recognition

In his December 22, 1975, Christmas message, Pope Paul called on Jews — and by clear implication Israeli Jews — to recognize the rights of the Palestinians. He said:

> "Even if we are well aware of the tragedies not so long ago which have compelled the Jewish people to seek a secure and protected garrison in a sovereign and independent state of their own, and because we are properly aware of this, we would like to invite the children of this people to recognize the rights and legitimate aspirations of another people which also have suffered for a long time, the people of Palestine."

Vatican recognition of Israel

The question of Vatican recognition is often raised. Some pro-Zionist Jews and Christians have critized the Vatican for not recognizing Israel.

Dr. Eugene Fisher, executive secretary of the US Catholic Bishops' Secretariat for Catholic-Jewish Relations and a person very sympathetic to Israel, explained:

" . . . while there has been no official diplomatic recognition of Israel, there has also been none granted to the state of Jordan either, since the Vatican traditionally waits for the resolution of outstanding border conflicts in such cases." (*Origins*, Aug. 16, 1979, Vol. 9, No. 10, p. 158)

Pope Paul has received in audience an Israeli Prime Minister, Mrs. Meir, and Foreign Minister Moshe Dayan. It is interesting to note that during the very month when Yasir Arafat spoke before the United Nations, Pope Paul received for a forty-five minute audience Mr. Gibrail Shukri Deeb, the PLO delegate to the UN Food Conference, who was in Rome at the time. They discussed Jerusalem. (*Houston Post*, Nov. 17, 1974)

Christians in Palestine

In an apostolic constitution (March 25, 1974) Pope Paul

discussed the increased needs of the Church in the Holy Land. Precisely because that document focused on the religious and charitable aspects of the situation, it suggests some elements of a Christian view of the Holy Land: the continuous link for two thousand years between the 'geography of salvation' and Christians who have been living there: and the concern and responsibility of Christians everywhere; the intimate bond between the land and the Christians everywhere, and particularly of the Pope, for working towards an improvement of the situation.

The Pope said:

"The Church in Jerusalem . . . has a privileged place among the cares of the Holy See and the whole Christian world . . .

. . . the continuation of the state of tension in the Middle East . . . constitutes a serious and constant danger . . . In addition, the continuing existence of situations lacking a clear juridical basis internationally recognised and guaranteed, far from constituting a fair and acceptable solution which takes account of everyone's rights, can only make such an achievement more difficult. We are thinking especially of Jerusalem . . . towards which there turn more intensely in these days the thoughts of Christ's followers, and of which, on a par with the Jews and the Moslems, they ought to feel fully 'citizens'.

. . . Were the presence (in Jerusalem of the community of believers in Christ) to cease, the Shrines would be without the warmth of the living witness and the Christian Holy Places of Jerusalem and the Holy Land would become like museums. We have already had occasion to express openly our anxiety at the decreasing numbers of Christians in the ancient regions that were the cradle of our faith . . .

If this Christian community which originated in Palestine two thousand years ago and is still there today is to ensure its continued survival . . . then the Christians of the whole world must be generous and help the Church in Jerusalem with the charity of their prayers, the warmth of their understanding and the tangible expression of their solidarity."

Father Tucci, the head of the Vatican Radio, explained at the press conference on April 5 at which the apostolic exhortation was made public, that in the document, which calls for financial support of church activities, "the accent is placed more on the Christian community living in the Holy land rather than on the mere maintenance of the shrines themselves".

Father Tucci was asked why, in the following sentence, the word 'citizens' was put in quotation marks:

"We are thinking especially of Jerusalem . . . towards which there turn more intensely in these days the thoughts of Christ's followers, and of which, on a par with the Jews and the Muslims, they ought to feel fully 'citizens'."

Father Tucci answered that he presumed that the Pope meant to say that people living in the Holy land "should be fully endowed morally and juridically with the rights of liberty and the full exercise of rights without hindrance". (Boston *Pilot*, April 12, 1974, p. 15; for the full text, see *The Link*, May/June, 1974, p. 1-3).

Pontifical Mission for Palestine

On July 16, 1974, Pope Paul VI in a letter to Msgr. Nolan, on the 25th anniversary of the Pontifical Mission for Palestine, expressed his "heartfelt sharing" in the sufferings of the Palestinians "and our support for their legitimate aspirations". In the light of activity towards peace, Pope Paul hoped that Palestinians would "look to the future with a constructive, likeminded and responsible attitude". As for the work of the Pontifical Mission, it will have to expect, the Pope said, "in the situation that is now evolving, to contribute to projects of aid, of rehabilitation and of development for the population of Palestine."

While urging Christians to be generous witnesses on behalf of their Palestinian brethren of the Holy Land, the Pope made a very significant statement: "We . . . exhort you and your collaborators to become the voice of those who are suffering."

A word should be said about the Pontifical Mission for Palestine. Founded in 1949 by Pope Pius XII as the Vatican agency for relief to the refugees, the Mission concentrates on self help through education, vocational training and medical aid. In its first twenty-five years, it dispensed over $100 million in money, goods and services for educational, cultural and humanitarian assistance. Because the Mission uses the fund-raising facilities of the Catholic Near East Welfare Association, its central office is in New York City and Monsignor John G. Nolan, National Secretary of the CNEWA, is its president. But it is an international organization with regional offices in Rome, Beirut, Jerusalem and Amman. The Mission owns neither land nor buildings, but works through existing structures in close cooperation with the United Nations, and the governments and hierarchies of the host nations.

Catholic Bishops, Roman Periodicals

In addition to the papal statements which have just been cited, there was a remarkable chorus of other declarations in the 1970's from Catholic bishops and from the Catholic press in Rome about Palestinians and places in Palestine under Israeli control. It would be difficult to argue that these statements were issued without some kind of papal approval or support.

Thus on March 1, 1971, three bishops of Jordan, one Orthodox and two Catholic, sent an appeal to Pope Paul about conditions in Jerusalem. On May 10, 1971, nine Christian leaders in Damascus issued an appeal to the conscience of the world about Jerusalem. The Melchite (Greek Catholic) convention in Washington, DC, June 24-27, 1971, passed a resolution about the dangers threatening Jerusalem.

During the October 1971 Synod of Catholic Bishops in

Rome, the Catholic bishops of Egypt wrote a letter to the bishops of the US asking for understanding and support. The Egyptian bishops asked that the Palestinians be considered not as refugees who ask for charity, but as a people who ask for justice and their rights. The letter also protested that the process of Judaizing Jerusalem was against the fundamental rights of its Arab inhabitants.

On July 9, 1974, the Catholic hierarchy of Lebanon, in a letter to the Catholic bishops of the world, spoke incisively on several issues touching the Arab-Israeli conflict, Palestinian rights and Jerusalem.

The conditions about which these episcopal statements spoke were detailed in two prominent Catholic publications in Rome.

L'Ossaveratore Romano dedicated its March 22-23, 1971, editorial to a sharp protest against Israeli steps to Judaize Jerusalem. The paper spoke of conditions which were forcing Muslim and Christian Palestinians to leave their homeland because of an Israeli government policy "which seems to aim at slow suffocation".

This editorial was followed by three very long articles in the Romas Jesuit periodical *Civilta Cattolica* in June and July 1971. The series exposed in detail the ways in which Palestinians were being oppressed: the Defence Emergency Regulations, the pressures in Israel which prompted the exodus of Arabs, the Judaization of territory in Israel and in Jerusalem, and the aims and plans for Jewish housing in Jerusalem.

Catholic Bishops of Palestine

Mention should also be made of the letter of December 15, 1971, sent by all the Catholic Bishops of the Holy Land to the Catholic Bishops of the US. This brief, modest document is extremely significant, because in a quiet manner these Catholic leaders of the area make several important points:

(1) That there is need of a solution that "will safeguard the rights and legitimate aspirations — and consequently the

human dignity — of all those involved in the conflict . . . In particular the rights of Palestinian refugees to return to their homes or receive a just compensation;"

(2) That "an effective solution cannot be reached by a unilateral conception which would necessarily lead to domination by one ethnic group;" and

(3) That Jerusalem "be granted a special status, guaranteed internationally, in accordance with the Resolutions of the United Nations and in fulfillment of the statements of Pope Paul VI," and that "there should be no imposed settlement of people and town-planning schemes as at present".

(The text of the letter is in *Some Thoughts in Jerusalem*, Archbishop Joseph Ryan, pp. 24-26).

Archbishop Joseph T. Ryan

Archbishop Joseph T. Ryan, at the time Archbishop of Anchorage, Alaska, wrote a letter to the US bishops entitled 'Some Thought on Palestine'. The former head of the Catholic Near East Welfare Association and the Pontifical Mission for Palestine, he returned early in 1972 to the Middle East to study the situation at first hand. In his letter he reflected on conditions in an astonishingly frank and extensive analysis. One may assume that this letter would not have been written nor have received the reception it did if it were against the wishes of the Holy See. (The text is in *The Link*, Vol. 5, No. 4, Sept./Oct. 1972, pp. 1-7.)

Archbishop Ryan spoke of the "essential fact" concerning the Middle East today: "that the foundation and expansion of the State of Israel has constituted, for more than a million innocent Arabs, as grave a violation of human rights as any in the annals of history! It is a violation that we the Bishops of the United States must now begin to take into account lest the Church in future time be accused of condoning injustice to the peoples of Islam as She has been and is even today accused of being silent in the face of the horrible holocaust of Jews in the 30's and 40's".

Archbishop Ryan concluded his letter by this appeal to the American bishops:

"Speak up and speak up now. Make the world know that Christianity and Islam are in Jerusalem by right, not by sufferance. Make the world know that Christianity does not — cannot — accept the ethnic domination of, or the political sovereignty of, one religion over another."

Egyptian-Israeli Accords

A word must be said about the attitude of Pope Paul VI towards the Egyptian-Israeli rapprochement. He clearly encouraged steps that might lead to peace in the Middle East. Receiving President Sadat at the Vatican on April 8, 1976, the Pope said:

"With deep concern for this generation and for generations to come, we extend our sincere encouragement to continue to seek the peaceful and just solution to the Arab-Israeli crisis. This must include an equitable solution also to the problem of the Palestinian people, for whose dignity and rights we have repeatedly expressed humanitarian and friendly interest. And the question of Jerusalem and the Holy Places must be resolved with due regard for the millions of followers of the three great monotheistic religions, for whom these represent such exalted values." (*L'Osservatore Romano*, April 15, 1976).

In his annual Christmas message, given on Dec. 22, 1977, Pope Paul dwelt at length on the Middle East. He said:

"We must add some words on the Middle East. We are following the developments of the situation with very special attention and interest. We do not wish to take sides amidst the different and at times opposing opinions . . . but we cannot hide our hopefulness . . . that the initiatives now in progress, undertaken with a courage so daring as to appear rash, will succeed in setting in motion a process from which

> . . . solutions that correspond to the criteria of justice, equity and political farsightedness, as well as to human sensitivity, may at last take shape . . .
>
> The Holy See has not failed, also on this occasion, to express its thought discreetly but confidently, especially on the points most closely touching its mission of charity and its responsibility with regard to the legitimate interests of Christians." (*Origins*, Jan. 5, 1978, Vol. 7, No. 29, p. 457.)

11. Pope John Paul II and the Middle East

Pope John Paul II in his address to the UN spoke of the Middle East conflict and in particular Lebanon, Jerusalem and the Palestine question. On Jerusalem he said:

> "It is my fervent hope that a solution also to the Middle East crisis may draw nearer. While being prepared to recognize the value of any concrete step or attempt made to settle the conflict, I want to recall that it would have no value if it did not truly represent the 'first stone' of a general overall peace in the area, a peace that, being necessarily based on equitable recognition of the rights of all, cannot fail to include the consideration and just settlement of the Palestinian question."

He next took up Lebanon.

> "Connected with this question is that of the tranquility, independence and territorial integrity of Lebanon within the formula that has made it an example of peaceful and mutually fruitful coexistence between distinct communities, a formula that I hope will, in the common interest, be maintained, with the adjustments required by the developments of the situation."

On Jerusalem he said:

> "I also hope for a special statute that, under international guarantees — as my predecessor Paul VI indicated — would respect the particular nature of Jerusalem, a heritage sacred

to the veneration of millions of believers of the three great monotheistic religions, Judaism, Christianity and Islam."

When Pope Paul II, meeting Jewish leaders on March 12, 1979, spoke of "effective guarantees" for Jerusalem he omitted mention both of a "special statute" and of the international character of the guarantees. (*Origins,* April 12, 1979, Vol. 8, No. 43, pp. 690-1). Did the new Pope's words suggest a change of policy? The Jerusalem correspondent of the London Catholic newspaper, *The Tablet,* raised this question and wrote:

> "A senior ecclesiastic, when questioned as to the possible meaning of the change in the formula employed by the Holy Father, responded with an impatient dismissal of all speculation. He commented wryly that only international guarantees can be effective, that the legislation of a single state that can be unilaterally and arbitrarily changed cannot possibly be regarded as such. Like other ecclesiastics and diplomats he pointed to the fact that Israel did not even have a constitution on the basis of which legislation could be challenged by the Judiciary." (*Tablet*, July 28, 1979.)

12. Conclusion

I have shown how the Catholic Church in Rome, in its approach to the problems involving Palestinians and, in particular, the city of Jerusalem, distinguishes between inter-faith activities and foreign policy activities.

In this first category, I have shown, in the development of Roman Catholic initiatives since Vatican II, how some Catholics, but not the Church in Rome, have issued statements favourable to the link, in the present political context, between Jews and the land of Palestine.

In the second category, I have shown the variety of ways, in a style generally restrained and diplomatic, in which the Church in Rome has expressed its concern about events in Palestine, especially since the 1967 war, and how that same concern has also been voiced in other official Catholic circles.

One may conclude from these expressions of concern a deep understanding on the part of the Holy See of the conditions in Palestine and Jerusalem and, at the same time, a limited ability to affect directly major political decisions.

However, because of the Holy See's involvement in the Middle East and its moral influence on the world scene, one would rightly conclude that in the struggle for the rights of Palestinians, the Holy See ought to be encouraged to continue to play a significant role.

13. A Personal View

So far I have discussed what might be called the official Catholic view of some aspects of the current situation affecting Israelis, Palestinians, and the land of Palestine.

Let me conclude by stating my own view about some of the essentials of the Israeli Jewish-Palestinian Arab conflict.

To understand the essential problem we must, for clarity's sake, not consider the state of Israel today nor even its coming into existence in 1948; rather we must go back to 1897 and begin with the launching of the Zionist Movement by Herzl. It was a political movement by European Jews aimed precisely at establishing a Jewish state — a state that would be essentially and predominantly Jewish — in Palestine, and in a Palestine where, at the turn of the century the population and land ownership were nearly 100 per cent Arab and where, moreover, as the Zionist Movement became known, overwhelmingly opposed to it.

Herzl himself did not originally insist on the Jewish state being set up in Palestine — that insistence came a little later — but it was essential to the proposal that the state involve a population whose majority would be Jews. Hence, if the Jewish state was to be estabished in Palestine, where the predominantly Arab population vigorously opposed such a state, then somehow or other the Arab population had to be rendered a minority.

Hence the Zionist Movement at that time intrinsicially constituted a deliberate, basic and massive violation of the rights of the Arabs then in Palestine, especially their right of self-determination.

If the argument of equal rights is adduced, namely, that Jews had a right to a state too, one must ask: By what argument can one rationally justify European Jews setting up a state that intrinsically aims to force the Arab natives to leave or, in remaining, to become inferior? If one argues that European Jews had some right, some tie, to the land, the right of Palestinian Arabs was vastly stronger. The two sets of rights were by no means equal. If one argues that the pressure of anti-Semitism in Europe forced Jews into the Zionist Movement, one argues that it forced them to violate the rights of the Palestinians.

In the age of colonialism, that esential violation of Palestinian rights intrinsic to the Zionist Movement could be ignored practically, but it cannot be defended intellectually, especially today. Of course, even shortly after the Zionist Movement was launched, this violation could not have been defended intellectually. By one of the bitter ironies of history, at the end of World War I the West was extolling the principle of the self-determination of peoples — while in practice, by blessing the Zionist Movement, it was hypocritically denying that principle to the Palestinians.

And Zionist leaders, at least some of them, knew very well what the implications of the Zionist Movement were for the Arabs in Palestine. Not all Zionists, of course, desired to 'steal' the land from the Arabs, but even these Zionists supported a movement in which the denial of Palestinian rights was, in fact, implicitly contained as the Movement developed historically. Even today the necessity of an early confrontation between the

Arabs in Palestine and the Zionist Movement, as it began to develop, is explicitly recognized, I am told, in a quasi-authoritative source: the introduction to the *Book of the Haganah,* a special edition of which was used for the Israeli Defence Forces (see *Voice of Zionism,* No. 1).

I have stressed that we should consider the Zionist Movement first at the turn of the century — rather than after the Holocaust (when the plight of European Jewry became a powerful emotional justification for the West's acceptance of the Zionist Movement) or 1947, as Britain was about to withdraw from Palestine (when the number of Jews in Palestine had increased significantly and some practical decision had to be made) — because the essential violation of Palestinian rights was clearer at the turn of the century than at any later date. But the basic concept of the Zionist Movement — of an essentially Jewish state to the neglect of Palestinian rights — thrives within Israel today, both in the government and public Jewish attitudes.

Further, unless that basic injustice, inherent in Zionism, is recognized, Israeli Jews (and anyone else) do not begin to face the fundamental Arab problem regarding Israel or the Arab view of Israel, nor attempt to undo past injustices, inasmuch as they can be redressed today.

The basic injustice to Palestinians inherent in Zionism is expressed today in several very serious ways. Let me briefly describe four.

(1) The law of 'return' of the state of Israel. By this law any Jew from anywhere in the world may 'return' to Israel and be given automatic citizenship. But the law has another side. If it gives this right to Jews anywhere, it does not give it to those people, the Palestinian Arabs, who were born on the land and who wish to return to it.

Take the case of a Palestinian who was born in Nazareth, and whose family lived there for generations, and who, in 1948, to avoid the fighting, crossed the border into southern Lebanon. Since then, he has not been able to return. Even if he did come back, he still would not enjoy the same automatic rights of citizenshp which a Jew from New York or San Francisco enjoys. And the reason is precisely because he is *not* Jewish. This discrimination is heightened in our day because the Universal Declaration of Human Rights has recognised the right of every person to return to his land.

(2) The Jewish National Fund. Early in the 1900s, people in the Zionist movement decided to set up a fund to acquire land in Palestine and to establish settlements in it. But the fund had another side. Regulations were written which provide that once the land was bought, it could be developed by the fund or leased to others, but only to Jews.

Then in 1961, as a result of a covenant with the government of Israel, these restrictions of the Jewish National Fund — forbidding land to be sold or leased to non-Jews — were applied to all state lands. How much land is involved? About 90 per cent of all the territory of Israel. Thus, today, some 500,000 Arab citizens of Israel are legally prevented from owning or leasing or working on these lands precisely because they are not Jews.

Are these restrictive regulations in force today? They are. For example, in 1975 an Israeli newspaper reported that the government had recently begun an energetic campaign to eliminate the 'plague' of leasing lands and orchards to Arab peasants of western Galilee. Circulars sent to all Jewish settlements pointed out that the leasing of national land or its cultivation by Arab lessees, or the rental of the orchards to be picked and marketed by Arabs, is against the law.

(3) Defense laws. When Israel became a state, it took over some security laws which had been introduced in 1945 by the British Mandate government. In 1946 Jews in Palestine

severely criticized these laws as oppressive to Jews and inhumane, and called for their repeal. After the establishment of Israel, however, these laws were not repealed, but maintained and expanded — and used, not against Jews, but against the Arabs of Palestine.

Sabri Jiryis, a Christian lawyer from Haifa, has documented the oppressive use of these defense laws, especially in his book *Arabs in Israel.* Greek Catholic Archbishop Joseph Raya, formerly of Haifa and Galilee, vividly described in his 1970 Christmas message some of the deprivations suffered by Palestinians (Christians and Muslims) in his area because of Israeli government discrimination.

One particular use of the defence laws was in expropriating Arab land.

How much land was taken? About one-twentieth of the entire territory of Israel after 1948; and this takes account only of the land taken from those Arabs who remained within Israel. Additional land was taken from Palestinians who left their homes (which are now in Israel) and have not been permitted to return.

(4) The occupied territories. A varity of studies has documented the widespread and serious list of injustices being done to Palestinians in the West Bank and Gaza since 1967. These injustices include deprivation of property to torture of individuals.

This, in brief, is the view of 'this Catholic'. It could, of course, be the view of a Jew or Protestant or Muslim, and hence it is not a specifically 'religious' view.

What is important is that those, of whatever religion or no religion, who share this view should help others to understand it and to work together to correct the injustices involved.

Note:

(This personal view reproduces material previously published by the author: "More in the 'Anti-Zionism = Anti-Semitism' Debate", *World view*, September 1976, p. 47; and "Opinion: 'Zionism-as-racism'", *National Catholic Reporter*, March 5, 1976, p. 9).

4. The Islamic Faith and The Problem of Israel and Jerusalem

Dr. Isma'il R. al Faruqi

1. Not Judaism but Zionism

Islam is not opposed to Judaism but regards it as the religion of God. It acknowledges the God of Judaism, i.e., of Ibrahim, Isma'il, Ishaq and Ya'qub ('alayhim assalam), as the God. it recognizes Musa ('alayi assalam) as prophet and the Torah as revelation from God. Islam questions not Judaism but the Jews, first as to their faithfulness to the Torahic laws and second, as to the total integrity of the Torahic text. In doing so, Islam is at one with most Jews in history as regards the first point, and with those Jews (Reform, Conservative and Reconstructionist) who have accepted Biblical criticism as regards the second. Rather, Islam is opposed to Zionism, to Zionist politics and conduct.

Zionism is a movement launched by Theodor Herzl following his disillusionment by the 'Dreyfus Affair'. It is designed to transform Palestine and its adjacent territories into a Jewish state, "as Jewish as England is English". Its pursuit of this objective is thoroughly Machiavellian. Its singleminded purpose is given absolute priority over all considerations, including the moral. Prior to 1948, it sought to fulfil its purpose first by bribing and then by threatening the Sultan of the Ottoman State of which Palestine was a part. When this failed, it began to work for the destruction of the Ottoman State and put all forces at the service of its enemies. Zionism deployed all its powers — financial through Baron de Rothschild, and strategic science through Chaim Weizman — to extract from the British Government the Balfour Declaration in which the latter pledged its support to the Zionist cause.

Having obtained the Balfour Declaration, Zionism played its power to the hilt to acquire land. It stopped at nothing in this effort, including the application of pressure, blackmail, bribery, speculation and forced eviction of Palestinian farmers from lands which they had inherited from their ancestors through the millennia. Zionism wanted the land at any price; but in 1948, it got about three per cent of Palestine through all means — moral and immoral. Equally, Zionism sought to extract the Jews of Europe and settle them in Palestine. To this end, it used indoctrination and bargained with Fascist and other governments. Its strategy was not to save all Jewish lives, but only those that could serve its purpose of military occupation and agricultural colonization of Palestine.

It was after 1948 that Zionism uncovered its nature and began to operate in the open. Its plan was to empty Palestine of its native inhabitants and to seize their lands, farms, homes and all movable properties. In so doing, Zionism was guilty of naked robbery by force of arms; of wanton, indiscriminate slaughter of men, women and children; of destruction of men's lives and properties. In order to obtain the human resources necessary to complete the plan, Zionism undermined the Jewish communities of the whole world. In the Arab World, where uprooting of Jewish communities would provide argument presenting the emptying of Palestine of its inhabitants as one half of a 'population exchange', Zionist action was brutal. Zionism terrorized Arab Jews by bombing their synagogues, destroying their businesses and assassinating their questioning or reluctant leaders. In its occupation of Palestine since 1948, Zionism has perpetrated immeasurable injustice against the Palestinians who survived its onslaught and remained in their homes. Internationally, the Zionist State has, since its establishment in 1948, terrorized the whole region, massacred the innocent by the thousands, destroyed innumerable villages, and drained the resources and energies of a whole generation of a hundred million awakening Arabs on futile wars which it imposed upon them.

2. Undoing the Injustice against Non-Jews

For this long list of crimes against the individual Palestinian men and women, against the corporate existence of the Palestinians, against the individual Arabs of the surrounding countries as well as the *ummah*, Islam condemns Zionism. Islam demands that every atom's weight of injustice perpetrated against the innocent be undone. Hence, it imposes upon all Muslims the world over to rise like one man to put an end to injustice and to reinstate its sufferers in their lands, homes and properties. The illegitimate use of every movable or immovable property by the Zionists since the British occupation of the land will have to be paid for and compensated. Therefore, the Islamic position leaves no chance for the Zionist State but to be dismantled and destroyed, and its wealth confiscated to pay off its liabilities. This obligation — to repel, stop and undo unjustice, is a corporate religious obligation (*fard kifayah*) on the *ummah*, and a personal religious obligation (*fard 'ayn*) on every able adult Muslim man or woman in the world until the *ummah* has officially assumed responsibility for its implementation. Defence of the *ummah*, i.e., of every province over which the banner of the Islamic State has once been raised, is *jihad*, or holy war, and it is a prime religious duty. Fulfilment of this duty is *falah* (felicity) in this world and the next, i.e., victory in this world, martyrdom and paradise in the other (Qur'an 3:169). Moreover, God commands the Muslims "to avail themselves of all means and instruments of force in order to overwhelm the enemy and bring the war to a quick end" (Qur'an 8:60).

However, dismantling the Zionist State does not necessarily mean the destruction of Jewish lives or of properties. Such destruction will, however, be regarded by Islam as necessary evil in case Zionist forces resist the dismantling and seizing process. It is a first Islamic principle that aggression and injustice be met with an identical proportion of same (Qur'an 2:194). Excess is absolutely forbidden. Moreover, hostilities must, according to Islam, be immediately stopped as soon as resistance stops. To continue them beyond acquiescence of the resistant is unpardonable injustice (Qur'an 8:61; 5:87). Islam commands the Muslims never to transgress, never to go beyond the termination of injustice, never to give vent to any resentment by increasing the suffering one atom's weight, but to deal to the enemy exactly what he had dealt them, measure for measure (Qur'an 5:45). Islam equally commands its adherents to spare no effort, no *materiel*, no wealth needed to bring the war to victorious conclusion. It lays no time limit on the declaration or conduct of the war; for a moral religious obligation is *ex hypothesi* timeless. Islam further recommends pardon, mercy and forgiveness (*Ibid.*). But these virtues cannot be forced; and they have moral value only if they are practiced from a position of strength and self-sufficiency. Moreover, they are strictly personal. They must be the object of a personal decision on the part of a free personal subject for them to be the moral value they purport themselves to be.

The injustice perpetrated by Zionism is so complex, so compounded and so grave that there is practically no means of stopping or undoing it without a violent war in which the Zionist army, state and all its public institutions would have to be destroyed. Even if the Western world forsook the Zionist State altogether, its Zionist leadership would still muster enough desperate courage to persist. For it is, by nature, an ideological state, necessarily prepared to save itself at all costs to human life and property. All the more reason, therefore, for the

Muslims of the world to take it more seriously, and to prepare realistic plans which they are unquestionably capable of executing.

3. De-Zionization

Once the Zionist State, its army and other public institutions are destroyed, the problem of what to do with its population would have to be faced. That Islam cannot and will not compromise on Zionism is a lesson which must be taught to every Jew living in the Muslim World. Hence, Islam will not tolerate the establishment of a Zionist alternative to the Zionist State. All Zionists who wish to live within the Muslim World would have to de-Zionize themselves, emigrate, or face prosecution for their Zionist activities. De-Zionization, it must be borne in mind, is the rejection of Zionism, the political programme to transform Palestine into a Jewish state on the European or Western model.

Islam's unequivocal condemnation of Zionism is not restricted to it as a political programme in which individuals were unjustly dispossessed of their personal properties. It goes beyond even the corporate Palestinian existence which the Zionist State has destroyed in its agression and which exacerbates its crime and responsiblity. The condemnation in fact extends to the realm of thought and emotion. For, even if the injustice against the Palestinians were to be terminated and the Palestinians were to be adequately compensated for their damages incurred since the Balfour Declaration, Islam still would condemn a Zionist programme whose object is not Palestine, but some non-Muslim corner of the world. Indeed, Islam will condemn a Zionist State even if it were set up on an isolated island or on the other side of the moon.

The cause of Islam is universal. The truth and value which God granted through Islam is meant for all mankind, not merely for the Arabs, the Semites, or the Asians. The moral and religious imperatives deriving from the Islamic revelation are valid — and hence, obligatory — for all men. The most basic of these, which are the other side of *tawhid*, or unization of God, and are hence inseparable from it, are the egalitarian creatureliness of all men before God, their universal obligation to do justice, and their innate, personal and inalienable right to hear the word of God. Whether or not they are convinced by it is their own individual decision which may not be made for them, ultimately, by any ruler or government. Any violation of these first principles is a defiance of God, an attack upon His unity, transcendence and ultimacy.

4. The Injustice of Zionism against Judaism

Firstly, Zionism interprets Judaism in accordance with a preconceived stand of European romanticism based on arbitrary feeling. It understands God's election of the Jews as racist superiority over all God's creatures, and His covenant as irrevocable promise to His children whom it ambivalently understands in biological and spiritual terms by referring to it as being 'in the flesh' and independent of moral conduct. This is discrimination among God's creatures in so far as they are His creatures. Such discrimination is a reflection of God's nature; for the first and essential definition of God is that He is the Creator of all. Zionism redefines God as the Creator of all men in one way, but the Creator of the Jews in another special way. This characterization reduces the Godliness of God, i.e., His unity and transcendence, because it distinguishes varying defining characteristics in His essence. Thus, Zionism is an attack upon divine transcendence. This error, this blind judgment which Zionism accepts absolutely and bases its whole life- and world-perspective on, leads its adherents to a life of moral casuistry and turpitude. The very same cause led Nazi Germany first to extend its domain so as to have an empire. For there is no sense to racist superiority if there are no other races over whom to exercise that superiority, just as expansionist Israel has been seeking to do during its thirty years of history.

Secondly, racist discrimination of Nazi Germany led it to commit untold injustice against those of its own citizens, as well as those citizens of other nations who fell under its sway, who did not fulfil the requirements of racist superiority as the standard bearers of Nazism defined it. The 'Holocaust' of Jews, Poles, Slavs, and numerous others followed with logical necessity once the premises of German racism were postulated. Likewise, the Zionist State has reduced its non-Jewish citizens to second status; confiscated their lands and properties; subjected them to martial rule; jailed, banished or executed them without process of law — all in the name of Jewish racist purity and Zionist political ideals. Regardless of whether these unhappy humans are Arabs or non-Arabs, Christian or Muslim, the discrimination is against them as *goyim*, i.e., as non-Jewish humans. Indeed, the children of mixed marriages where the mother is non-Jewish have been subject to the same discrimination in the Zionist State, recalling what a racist redactor had reported about an earlier occurrence of racist discrimination and disowning of legitimate wives and children (Ezra 10:10ff; Nehemiah 10:28-30). Being directed against humanity at large, racist discrimination is a sin, an injustice, of which Zionism is guilty on a large scale. Islam binds its adherents to rise against injustice wherever, whenever, by whomsoever and against whomsoever it is committed.

Thirdly, no racist regime can maintain itself without setting up an iron curtain around it. Its ideology cannot withstand alternatives, for it is arbitrary and dogmatic. Its adherents are necessarily single-minded and bent on intolerance for other views. It does not make its claim rationally — i.e., with evidence and in openness to further evidence — but doggedly on a 'take it or leave it', or 'if you are not with us you are against us' basis. That is why the Zionist State has been a police state in every sense of the term, placing those of its citizens who do not share its ideology in a category which amounts to a large concentration camp if they are *goyim*, and under special supervision if they are Jews. That is also why no man, Jew or *goy*, may settle in the Zionist State unless he adheres to Zionism's racist ideology. Differences of opinion with the ruling ideology may be tolerated to mislead the outside observer into thinking the state to be a free, democratic one. But such differences can only be those which refer either to strategy or incidentals, never to basics. The very thesis of Zionism cannot ever be put to question by those who dwell under its dominion. The policy of a Zionist state must therefore be isolationist, shutting its people off from the word of God which challenges its essential doctrine.

5. Undoing the Injustice against Judaism

Islam demands of its adherents and institutions to make the word of God known to all humankind. It recognizes no state authority which shuts off a people from hearing the word of God. True, Islam can only present the word of God and cannot force its acceptance. But when the presentation of the word of God is itself prohibited or proscribed, the Islamic state is obliged to confront the prohibiting authority and break it up. For, the shutting off of any ear other than one's personal own is a grave injustice, a sin committed not only against the person who is the object of it, but against humanity, and ultimately against God. Just as the conscience of humanity would be aroused to condemn a regime bent deliberately upon starving its citizens to death, the conscience of Islam is aroused to condemn, and demand action against, a regime bent upon starving the souls of its citizens, upon de-sensitizing them to rational evidence, to moral and religious obligation — in short, to deface and dehumanize them as creatures of God.

It is not therefore beyond the jurisdiction of the Islamic State to transcend its own frontiers and to wage *jihad* or holy war against such Zionist State wherever it may set up its house to imprison its adherents therein. This obligation derives from the very nature of the moral law. Holding the moral law to be universal, based upon a primary sense of value that is innate to all humans as well as upon reason, the accumulated wisdom of mankind, Islam regards any restriction of the universal validity of the moral law as contrary to the nature of morality. Certainly, some restrictions of some moral laws are valued and permissible if they are made in the interest of realizing higher moral laws. Such restriction is always rational, critical, open to contrary evidence, and supported by the cumulative moral wisdom of mankind. When the restriction is arbitrary, dogged, based upon 'feeling' or 'romantic experience' and running against the very grain of moral wisdom, it must not be valid. Charity and love of neighbour demand that what the moral subject has found to be the *summum bonum* be communicated by him to all other humans. If it is a sin deliberately not to inform one's neighbour in an apartment house of a fire in the building, it must be a sin *a fortiori*, deliberately not to communicate to him the *summum bonum*, the ultimate meaning of human life and man's destiny in eternal bliss or fire.

If, contrary to its nature, the Zionist State were to open its frontiers and permit its citizens to be exposed to the word of God, then the Islamic State can take no further action against it. The Islamic obligation to undo injustice cannot go beyond the penetration of the domain of injustice and the presentation to its sufferers and perpetrators with the alternative of morality and justice. This is the meaning of the Qur'anic verses: "No coercion in religion . . . The Prophet's duty is limited to communicating the message clearly; etc." (Qur'an 2:256; 5:102; 13:42; 16:82; etc.). It does not imply a toleration of isolationism, or mean any kind of axiological relativism. It simply means that should the sufferers and perpetrators of injustice persist in their injustice despite the presentation of the word of God to them, no more could be demanded of the Muslim than to continue to call them to the divine word and to warn humankind against following their example. The fact that that to which the Muslim calls is through and through moral, obliges him to present his case and have it heard, but not accepted. To accept it freely and deliberately is the moral value the Muslim is seeking. The facts of acceptance and all that follows upon them by way of moral conduct have from his perspective as moral inductor of them only utilitarian, not moral, value. Moral value is that which is involved in the free acceptance of value and acquiescence to its ought-to-do. It should be borne in mind that this restriction applies to the Zionist State which has set up its house on an isolated non-Muslim island. It does not apply to the Zionist State of Israel, which is guilty of injustice perpetrated against the Palestinians and all the Arabs. In her case, the Islamic requirement is *jihad*, to the end of stopping the ongoing injustice and undoing the injustice committed by it, or on its behalf by the British, since the Balfour Declaration.

6. Islam and the Jewish Problem: The Negative Aspect

What, it may be finally asked, does Islam have to say to the Jewish problem itself, to which Zionism had come as an attempted solution? If Zionism is a false doctrine, and the Zionist state is to be dismantled on account of its injustice, what is to be made of the problem for which Zionism and its state had provided solution?

(i) Failure of Zionism to Provide Security

The first fact to be faced is that Zionism has provided no solution at all to the problem it set itself to solve. The majority of the Jews have not accepted its call to uproot themselves and emigrate to Palestine. An overwhelming majority of them still live outside Israel and are most likely to continue to do so in the future. New York City alone has more Jews than the whole Zionist State. Although the number of Jewish residents in Europe has been largely reduced by World War II and its aftermath, their numbers are steadily growing again. Neither they, nor their co-religionists in the USSR or the Americas are immune from persecution. Indeed, the success of Zionism and the establishment of its state, Israel, have made such persecution nearer, not farther away.

Zionism has cast a frightful question mark on the national loyalty of any Jew around the world. By its insistence that Judaism is a religion, a polity, a race, and a land all in one, Zionism has made it impossible for a Jew to identify himself as a Jew without inviting suspicion from the guardians of the national state and national integrity. The bombastic claim of Zionism in the world press which it largely controls, its posing as the guardian of Jews everywhere, and its acrobatic arrogance in demanding the surrender, and actual commando-like lifting of anti-Jews or anti-Zionists to judge them in its state, are having a world-wide effect of resentment and disgust which may explode one day against the guilty as well as the innocent.

More particularly, in Palestine itself, Zionism has won the deepest enmity of the Palestinians and of all the Arabs and Mulsims around them. The latent enmity of the Muslim masses aginst Zionism and its current protector, the USA, has burst into fury in as far places as Jakarta, Manila and Kuala Lumpur. Despite its internal divisions and other weaknesses, the Arab World and beyond it, the Muslim World, stand bristling with antagonism, awaiting the proper opportunity to pay the Zionists with their own currency. And it is always a question when a change in the international situation will send world Jewry plummeting into another holocaust precisely because of the arrogant use of their power after World War II and the impertinent display of their resentment against humankind.

Zionism has not only contributed to this sad state of affairs. It is directly responsible for it. How, then, can it be said that it had succeeded in providing security for the Jew? Even in the very heartland of Zionism, in Israel, the Jew sits in the midst of an armoury, surrounding himself with barbed wire, minefields and all kinds of weaponry to prevent an onslaught which he knows for certain is coming, sooner or later. His very existence is a regimented spartanism, due in greatest measure to the bounty of international imperialism and colonialism. Thus, Israel, the so-called greatest achievement of Zionism, is really its greatest failure. For the very being of the Zionist state rests, in final analysis, on the passing whim of international politics. Zionism has built its 'fortress' on shifting sands.

(ii) **Failure of Zionism to Stop Assimilation**

Zionism is supposedly the solution to the problem of assimilation. Assimilation, it must be remembered, was a problem for the Jew living in Christian Europe. The Jews of the rest of Christendom sympathized and many adopted the Zionist view (without opting to emigrate to Palestine) because they felt the problem of the European Jew to be equally their own. To any religiously conscientious Jew, the university campuses of America where the majority of Jewish intelligentsia receive their training is a 'disaster area' as far as Judaism is concerned. These Jewish leaders of the future are as secularized as their Christian colleagues. They may be ethnocentrists; but in their minds and hearts there is no faith in God, in revelation, in the absoluteness of the moral law, in man's ultimate responsibility, or in the Day of Judgment. This secularism is so widespread and deep in the Zionist state, excluding the older generation of emigrants from the Muslim World, that the claim that this is the state where Judaism is the be-all and end-all is ridiculously false.

Certainly, it is Zionism which encouraged the spread of such secularism among Jews. It ridiculed the orthodox Jew's faith in a restoration that is eschatological, and hence completely divine in authorship. It repudiated the nature of restoration as being spiritual, and taught the restoration of a kingdom in real estate, rocks and gunpowder. It enlandized God by its insistence that the Jew can only be a Jew in Palestine, echoing the enlandizing Biblical redactor who, in praising David, asserted that God may be worshipped in and only in David's political capital, Jerusalem (Psalms 132:13-17; II Kings 5:8-19). Finally, it is Zionism which substituted 'ethnic feeling' for the faith in God as source of the ultimate good; and, by its unscrupulous defiant flouting of all moral laws in dealing with those who stood in its way whatever their faith may be, spread cynicism among the Jews of the world.

After the Arabs, the greatest contempt in Israel is reserved for Muslim World Jews who brought with them a remnant of faith in God. It is the clear objective of the Zionist state to Zionize the 'oriental Jews'; and this in practice means to 'Westernize' them, to cause their thinking to run in Western channels from which God has been banished. Indeed, Zionists are proud that the whole of Israel is a 'Western' unit, a 'Western' transplant, a 'Western' oasis in the Muslim 'desert'. Western culture, with its basic secularism, cynicism, materialism and nihilism, constitutes the '*forte*' of the Zionist state.

(iii) **Failure of Zionism to enable Judaism to Blossom Forth**

Has Zionism succeeded in enabling Judaism to recreate itself in thought — philosophy, theology, the sciences; in the arts — literature, the visual arts and music; in action — piety and righteousness? The sad truth is that Zionism has not inspired any such attempts. To this day, the world of scholarship knows of no Jewish social sciences, of no Jewish humanities. In the realm of thought, Zionist Jews are trailing the West in all fields. Indeed, Zionist theory itself has been formulated in Hegelian terms. Even in Biblical studies, Zionism has been led by Western scholarship. Nothing is more incongruous than the modern Jewish scholar who makes all sorts of claims for Judaism and Zionism, but does so under a Western Christian doctrine of revelation, a Western Christian understanding of the role of his ancestors in Heilsgeschichte, or a Hegelian or Marxist interpretation of history.

The same is true of the other domains of thought. The universities and colleges of Israel do not as yet know of a Jewish sociology, a Jewish anthropology, philosophy, political science or economics. All that is being taught and written by Jewish intellectuals stands squarely within the Western tradition.

In the arts, Jewish creativity has been thoroughly Western. Israel, the sovereign state where Jewish genius is to flourish, as yet knows of no music, no dancing, no sculpture, no painting, no architecture that is not Western. What the Jews have brought with them from the Arab countries, from East Europe, the Balkans, North and West Europe, and from America is syncretized and labelled 'Jewish'. The only non-Western element, if any exists at all, is what they have taken from the Arab countries and the Palestinians. But that, because of their hatred of and contempt for everything Arab, is extremely little. When the work of art has a Jewish objective content, like the works of Chagall in painting, or Ernest Bloch in music, it is as little Jewish in form (which after all, according to romanticism, is the definitive aesthetic category!) as Rimsky-Korsakov's Scheherezade and Mozart's Il Seraglio are Islamic. Mention needs not be made of the Zionists' circulation in the world of Arab *falafel*, *halawah* and bread as Israeli foods; of Arab peasant embroidery and couture as Israeli fashions; of Palestinian jewelry and the arts of decoration as Jewish and Israeli handicrafts.

Thus, in the realm of culture, Zionism has been as much a failure as in that of politics. In neither field has it fulfilled its objective. In either case, the reason is that Zionism is at contradiction with itself. In politics, it seeks to save the Jews from persecution by persecuting, from robbery by robbing, from suffering injustice by inflicting injustice. And in culture, it seeks to enable the Jew to be Jewish by Westernizing him, by making him a puppet and follower of the West in all fields of human endeavour, from the military to the musical. If the question is pressed further, why would Zionism suffer itself to be in contradiction with itself, the answer is that it itself is nothing but the romantic disease of the master (the European) passed to the servant-patient (the European Jew). It is of the nature of this European disease to hate that which is not European, especially the Semitic with which Europe has been at war — and unsuccessfully — ever since Alexander the Great.

In his Zionist stand, the Zionist is revulsed by all that has revulsed Europe, namely, by everything Semitic. In his subconscious mind, possessed by the disease of European romanticism, he hates himself, the Jew, the Semite, the non-European. In the person of the Palestinian, a being who, because of his descendence, traditions, association with the soil of Palestine and the lingering in him of so much of Semitic history, is in every drop the quintessence of Semiticism and Hebrew-ism, the Zionist sees himself as the European romanticist does — at his worst! Aggravating this psychic derangement has been the persistent Western Christian romantic identification of Jesus and the world he lived in as the Palestinian Arab, the Palestinian family, the Palestinian village and countryside, the Palestinian customs of today. As European, the Jew learned and believed this lesson of romantic Christian Europe. The Palestinian Arab was what he wanted as well as hated to be.

7. Islam and the Jewish problem: The Positive Aspect

If Zionism has proved itself to be such a poor solution to the problem of Jewish existence in Christian Europe, what is the alternative? The self-same law of Islam which requires of the Muslim to go to the end of the earth to put an end to injustice must equally apply to the *goyim* as to the Jewish sufferers of injustice. Can there be any doubt in the Muslim's mind that the Jew is a sufferer of injustice at the hands of the Christian West?

(i) The Question of Security

The answer is categorical. Certainly, the Jew has been victim of injustice in the West; and certainly, the Muslim is enjoined by God to come to his rescue, to relieve him from suffering and to help him achieve his freedom, security and peace. There can therefore be no doubt, Islamically speaking, that the World of Islam is religiously bound to champion the Jewish cause against Christendom; that it stands indicted as long as it fails to do so. Indeed, championing of the cause of the oppressed has been an essential component of the image of Islam in Makkah and Madinah, in the Muslim World and in Europe. That is why the Jews of Damascus, of Spain, as well as of Constantinople, the Balkans and Central Europe, have helped the Muslims in their conquest of these lands. The Jews themselves were convinced that Islam's and its adherents' championing of justice was genuine. What can Islam offer to the cessation of Jewish suffering in the modern world?

Following World War II and the defeat of Nazism and Fascism, the Jews of the West have made many gains in Europe and the Americas. Today there is no country in Europe and the Americas that does not grant its Jewish citizens the freedom to worship, to work, to elect and be elected to any public office. Equally, there is no country which does not give Israel, the Zionist state, respect far out of proportion to its size and real importance in the world. But since the aims of Zionism have coincided with those of Western imperialism and colonialism, the little state has become enormous by association with the

United States and Western Europe. This 'enormous' influence, however, is deceiving and, at any rate, temporary. The winds of politics shift suddenly and without reason. England, for instance, altered direction radically after 1973; and France, after De Gaulle terminated French colonialism in Algeria and composed France's quarrel with the Arab World. In fact, the great influence the Zionist State and Jews in general wielded since World War II hides behind it a growing resentment and impatience which may break out with the first economic or political crisis.

Moreover, ethnocentrism is still quite dominant in the West, and it is being nourished partly by the forces of romanticism internal to the Western soul, and partly by the success of Zionism, the *non-plus-ultra* cause of ethnic particularism. And yet, the Jews of the West, especially the Zionists, would certainly be the first victims, the first scapegoats and prey, should this ethnocentrism burst out. The other ethnic minorities of the West belong to the servant class and do not constitute a target. Not so the Jews. Masters of the professions, of trade and finance, of communications and the arts practically everywhere in the Western world, they stand at the forefront of the marked targets.

The Zionists are therefore right in their claim that Jewish security cannot be trusted to Westerners in the long run; that it is only an interval between one wave of anti-Semiticism and another in Western history. More important though is the other claim of Zionism regarding the future of Jewry in the West; and it is also the truer. That is the claim that wherever and whenever Jewish security is guaranteed in the West, it is certain to result in the dilution of Judaism, the dissipation of Jewish consciousness, and the assimilation of Jews in the Christian world through marriage or culture. It is this danger which is more intractable and insidious, and which prompted many Western Jews to adopt the Zionist cause. The solution of the Jewish problem cannot therefore rest with the guarantee of Western tolerance or the eradication of Western anti-Semiticism. More is certainly needed. It is this 'more' that caused Theodor Herzl to find the solution in a sovereign Jewish state. The solution was a tragic mistake though his assessment of the problem was true.

(ii) The Right to Immigrate to the Muslim World

Islam offers a perfect solution to the Jewish problem which has beset the Jews and the West for two millennia. This solution is for the Jews of the world to be given the right to dwell wherever they wish, as free citizens of the state of their choice. Those who feel themselves reasonably happy where they are and wish to continue to live there ought to be entitled by a world covenant to do so. As to those Jews who desire to emigrate from the West, they ought to be welcomed in the Muslim World. If, for reasons of religious attachment, they wish to live in those areas of the Muslim World associated with their history — Egypt to Mesopotamia — they ought to be entitled to do so by virtue of the respect Islam pays to the Prophets of God and the necessary extension of sympathy and love for those that honour the prophetic tradition and the spaces in which it conveyed its divine messages.

On this question of Jewish immigration Islam gives far more to world Jewry than Zionism. The latter wants only Palestine; Islam forces wide open the gates of the whole Muslim world, and *a fortiori*, of the Arab World; and still more, of the territory of the 'Fertile Crescent'. 'Immigration' however does not mean seizure of land, displacement or dispossession of others. Neither does it mean seizure of the state, or its transformation into a state for the Jews on the German or French model. *Ex hypothesi*, there must be an Islamic state comprehending these territories; an Islamic state whose constitution is the Qur'an, whose law is the *Sharī'ah*, and whose constituency is only partly non-Muslim. Such Islamic state, extending from the Atlantic to the Malay Basin, is certainly obliged to open its gates to any Jewish immigrant who travels thither. Such an Islamic state is the haven for world Jewry, as well as the protector and defender of prophecy and its peoples against all outside attack. Such a state is a world state, with infinite geo-political depth, infinite geographic and human resources. Endowed with the life- and world-affirming ideology that Islam is, and with a long history of confrontation with the world, and the richest culture and civilization, such an Islamic state can effectively contend on the world scene and has the capacity requisite therefor.

Contrasted with such an Islamic state, the state of Israel which Zionism presents is a miserable match. It consists of a few thousand square kilometres, a sliver of land, and three million people. True, it is at present armed to the teeth with the most uptodate and sophisticated weaponry. But it depends for its military muscle as well as the very food it consumes on Western Imperialism whose direction may change from moment to moment. Moreover, it is surrounded with a wall of resentment and hatred in the will of a hundred and thirty million Arabs and a billion Muslims, awaiting the shift in international relations which would give them occasion to pounce on it.

If world Jewry, or a substantial number of its members, or, if only the present Jewish citizens of Israel were to exist in an Islamic state, how may they live in accordance with Judaism? How may Jewish genius be given the chance to prosper and blossom forth?

(iii) **The Right to Peace**

The first requisite for any culture, civilization or religion to prosper — which is the same for any community to do so — is peace. The reassurance that one is safe as to life and property is absolutely necessary for the mind to operate in any long-term or constructive manner. Without it, no human can develop the taste or the will for truth, goodness or beauty. True, Nietzsche and von Treitschke have a point that war and danger do cultivate discipline as well as idealism. But no less true is the fact that they never sustain either value for any long time. Sparta, Imperialist Japan and Nazi Germany have not been able to do it despite the tremendously more favourable conditions they possessed by comparison with Zionist Israel. Such lasting peace cannot be assured to the Jews anywhere except by Islam and under its political dominion. The relation of Islam to Judaism being one of sympathy, nay of identity, Islam's religious honouring of the Hebrew prophets as God's prophets and of the Hebrew revelation as God's revelation furnishes the best guarantee. Here is a nation, an *ummah* of a billion souls on the march, maintaining this faith as an essential and constitutive element of its own religion, of its own consciousness of God, of itself and of the world. As with Muhammad (peace be upon him) and his companions, the *ummah* of Islam firmly believes that God is the Guardian of the Jews and other non-Muslims who opt for peace rather than war with the Islamic State. Indeed, in the faith and law of Islam, the guarantee is provided even against corrupt Muslim rulers who might be tempted to exploit or aggress upon the *dhimmis,* or covenanters who covenanted for peace under God's guaranteeship. Finally, there is the guarantee of tested history. Except for the briefest intervals in which Muslims have suffered even more than Jews or Christians at the hands of a corrupt ruler, the history of Islam's tolerance and coexistence with Judaism and Christianity is pure white. Throughout the fourteen centuries of its existence, its record is without blemish. Never has the *ummah* conceived of itself or of its mission, of its past or of its future, as involving a necessary decimation of the non-Muslims living in its midst.

The guarantee which Islam offers to the Jews is the best; for it is eternal as well as the most efficient. Whatever may be written in a constitution may be amended since the nation's will, a majority of 51 or 66 percent, have voted it as such and can as well vote its contrary. But when the law is God's writing and ordinance, it cannot ever be changed. Even national culture has modes and fashions and may change; not religion, which forms the very conscience of the overwhelming majority of the billion Muslims.

(iv) **The right to Self Determination by the Torah**

Before leaving the question of Jewish security under Islam, one more problem remains. Is it not necessary for the feeling of peace that the Jews enjoy national sovereignty like the European countries do? No! The feeling for national sovereignty is a very recent development, even in the West. It is an outgrowth of ethnocentrism and political nationalism and the offspring of European romanticism in the last two centuries. The European has existed and prospered for centuries without it. Loyalty to God, to the Church, to the universal community, to king and prince, does not require it. 'National sovereignty', as the third constitutive element of the state after 'people' and 'a piece of earth with defined borders', is itself a part of the disease of romanticism. 'Sovereignty' is a vague and woozy concept, supposed to weld 'people' and 'earth' into mystical unity precisely in order to exclude all other elements. When it was first called for in Europe, it was meant to exclude the jurisdiction of the church in affairs of the community. Later, as the church influence withered, it was meant to exclude Christian ethics and values from determining public affairs. It is neither needed nor called for by the nationalists when the matter is one of determining human lives in the conduct of concrete daily life. Its function is to nourish the *mystique* of nation as Fustel de Coulanges had conceived of it in the last century.

And yet, it is here, in the very domain of concrete daily living, that sovereignty is necessary. Islam grants it to the Jews as well as to other non-Muslims without reservations. Here, it means the authority of the Torah to guide concrete action, the Jew's freedom to observe the Law of God. The Western national state denies it to its Jewish citizens despite all assurances of the right to life, property and the pursuit of happiness the constitution may have granted equally to all citizens.

In the domain of concrete personal living, Islam unquestionably yields all authority to the non-Muslims to determine their lives as they alone see fit. It not only permits, but requires them to live in accordance with their own laws. To this purpose it regards them as an *ummah*, different and separate from the Muslims and all non-Jews, endowed with traditions and institutions. It requires the Jews to set up their own rabbinic courts, and puts its whole executive power at their disposal. The Shari'ah, the law of Islam, demands of all Jews to submit themselves to the precepts of Jewish law as interpreted by the rabbinic courts, and treats any defiance or contempt of the rabbinic court as rebellion against the Islamic state itself, on a par with like action on the part of any Muslim *vis-a-vis* the Islamic court.

Moreover, the whole ethic and culture of the state, the country and the population stress the value of religion, of piety and the ways of God, of righteousness and moral action, of the *ummah* — society and community — as the consensus of mind (vision), of heart (judgment) and of arm (action) in the service of God, as the universal brotherhood under the moral law. Such atmosphere is precisely what is required to promote the Jew's feeling for and commitment to Jewishness, to the revelation of Moses and the covenant of Abraham. The atmosphere provided by Islam is so favourable, and that provided by the secularist Christian West is so antagonistic to Judaism that the religion of Moses seems destined to flower under Islam's dominion, in cooperation and co-existence with the Muslims, or dissolve itself in secular Western culture.

Where a matter concerns a single Jew or more persons of Jewish faith, that matter is definitely to be disposed of by the Jewish rabbinic court alone, influenced by its own understanding of the Torah, of the Halakah and of the Jewish tradition. Whatever its judgment, the Muslims and the Islamic state are bound by law to acquiesce to it, and to attend to its execution as long as dominion and executive power is in their hands. Where a matter concerns two adherents, one of whom is a Jew and the other a non-Jew, Islam requires that each be treated according to his own law. Where the dispositions of the two laws are at variance with each other, Islam requires the state to interfere and compose the difference. Such composition by the state may not be arbitrary or capricious. It must be based on the principle of *maslahah* or benefit, of the parties concerned first, and the two *ummahs* behind them. This principle is so pervasive in Islamic jurisprudence that it can serve as legitimate base for composing the gravest differences. Even murder, under Islamic law, is compensable. The mediating judgment is always subject to appeal to the higher court. Above the highest court stands the law of God which is open to the inspection of and invocation by anybody against any authority, including that of the caliph himself. Moreover, in Islam, justice is free and available to anyone who seeks it.

(v) **Defence of the Islamic State**

The only area removed from the *dhimmi* community's jurisdiction is that of war and peace. This is the exclusive domain of the Islamic state whose *raison d'être* is the establishment of peace and the critical presentation of the word of God. This duty is that of defence of Dar al Islam — that is, the *ummah* of Muslims as well as that of the non-Muslims who have entered the *Pax Islamica*. Since the Islamic state is really a federation of community-states, it is only right and befitting that no community-state be held responsible for the conduct of foreign policy, of peace and war, and that the federal state be so. Two major differences exist between a federal state such as the Islamic state and one like the United States or Switzerland. The first is that in the latter the constituent is a mini-state based on territory, whereas in the former, it is based on humans in community, thus giving primacy to the humans rather than to real estate. The second is that the law of the Western federal state is positive in the sense that it is what the majority of the constituents (whatever its percentage) decide it to be at any time; whereas the law of the Islamic state is what God has ordained for it for all time.

8. The Islamic Solution and the *Status Quo* in the Arab World

Finally, it may be asked, how would the application of the Islamic solution affect the actual state of affairs in the Near East?

First, the Arab states of the Near East must undergo a transformation from being caricatures of the Western national states to becoming a single, united Islamic state. The Arab states are literally all creations of Western colonialism. They must all be dismantled and their populations reorganized into an *ummah* of Islam. Their laws which again for the most part they had inherited from Western colonialism ought to be discarded in favour of the Shari'ah, or law of Islam. The Islamic state emerging from their union should abolish all frontiers between them, all their individual defence establishments, and assume all responsibility for defence and foreign affairs. Only if this is achieved may the Arab Muslims of the Near East stand ready to implement the Islamic solution of the problem of Israel.

Second, Israel, the Zionist state, would be dismantled; by force, if necessary. The institution of the Zionist state is a positive evil, and so is all its defence establishment. This leaves the *ummah* of Jews as covenanter with the Islamic state for peace. The Jewish citizens of Israel would not be required to move. On the contrary, they would be invited to dwell in any city or village of the whole Islamic state, not only in some pieces of real estate on the West Bank of the Jordan and in the Gaza strip as Zionism is presently asking. But no Jew may dispossess a Muslim of his land, house or other property as Zionists have so far done. The transaction is personal; and both parties, buyer and seller, have to will the sale and be satisfied with it. As for the Palestinians, they would have to be rehabilitated in their own homes and lands, out of which they had been forcefully ejected first by British and then by Zionist arms. Moreover, they would have to be compensated, under Islamic law, for their damages.

This means that the Jews presently living in stolen homes and cultivating stolen lands, will have either to vacate or to compensate their owners. If the owners insist on evacuation, the capital necessary for compensation could be used to buy new land and homes elsewhere. If, as Jews claim, the Kingdom of David extended from the River of Egypt to the Euphrates, there is still plenty of land for them to purchase and occupy. According to Islam, as it has been already said, there is no restriction whatever on the number of Jewish immigrants, nor on the area or locality of land they may purchase to dwell in thoughout the Muslim World.

Thirdly, once the bouleversement this solution brings has settled down, there is no reason why the Jews, as *dhimmi* citizens of the Islamic state, may not keep all the public institutions they have so far developed in Palestine (Courts of law, learned societies of art and culture, public corporations, schools, colleges and universities) to continue in their operation, whether in any locality of Palestine or anywhere else where Jews might choose to dwell. Henceforth, their vision and their efforts would be directed toward upholding and promoting Judaism, not the Western ideologies of decadence and aberration. No one will make war against them. No one will persecute or molest them. Their task is to be as Jewish as they care to be.

Then, when the Jews of the emerging Islamic state have organized themselves and begun to breathe as Jews, free from any threat, the chief of the Islamic state might repeat the message which an earlier predecessor of his (Muhammad, 'the second', Conqueror of Constantinople) had sent to the chief of an earlier non-Muslim *ummah* in the Islamic state (Gennadius Scholarius, Patriarch of Constantinople): "Be the Patriarch of your *ummah* in peace. May Allah protect you. To you, our friendship is pledged in all circumstances and under all conditions, wherever it may benefit you. May you enjoy all the privileges hitherto enjoyed by your predecessors!" (G. Papadopoloulos, *Les privilèges du patriarchat oecumeniques (Communauté grecque-orthodoxe) dans l'empire ottoman*, Paris, 1924, p. 10).

9. The Problem of Jerusalem

The solution of the problem of Israel is at once the solution of the problem of Jerusalem. This city was Canaanite, i.e., Palestinian, for centuries before King David set foot in it. Indeed, he chose it in its non-Jewishness for capital in order to win the loyalty of non-Hebrews whom he sought to rally to his political cause. The Hebrew opposition was so strong that even David could not build his temple in Jerusalem. His son Solomon did, after Canaanization of the Hebrews had been accomplished. Solomon's success where David had failed, was due to the Hebrews' acculturation by the Palestinians. The Hebrews had by then learned Hebrew, the Canaanite language, abandoned their pastoral ways and settled down for agriculture, adopted the agricultural feasts and celebrations of the Palestinians, exchanged their calendar for that of Palestine, and began to feel the need, like the Palestinians, for permanent temples of worship and for a sacrificial system manned by a priesthood.

Jerusalem remained capital of the Hebrew state for only 39 years, 961-922, the dates of the accession and death of Solomon. At his death, the state split into Israel and Judah, and Jerusalem became capital of one half of the people, and lost much of its importance. It was invaded and sacked by Sennecharib in 701 and by-passed as unimportant by the Assyrians in their march toward Egypt. It was finished off in 587 when the Babylonians sacked it under Nebuchadnezzar and drove its inhabitants as slaves to the East. Thereafter, none of the attempts to rebuild it succeeded. The Greeks de-Judaized it almost completely, and finally the Romans ploughed it and renamed it Aelia Capitolina in 70 A.C. The Romans prescribed that no Jew shall enter it. This law remained in force until the Muslims eased its restriction. The Temple site was used as a garbage depot until 'Umar ibn al Khattab cleansed it with his own hands in 635.

Islam does not deny the sanctity of Jerusalem. This sanctity is proclaimed in the Qur'an; and for Muslims, it is an item of their very faith. On the contrary, Islam applauds and commends all those who, like the Muslims, regard Jerusalem as 'blessed' on account of its association with many of the Prophets of God, from Ibrahim to 'Isa ibn Maryam (peace be upon him). The problem of Jerusalem is that of finding for it a political and cultural regime which would not violate the relation of the city to any of the religions associated with it.

First, there is the association of the human inhabitants who regardless of their faiths (and they have changed their faiths through the centuries) continued to associate themselves with Jerusalem by inhabiting it. Like the rest of the Palestinians, these humans have the first right to continue with their habitation and to exercise political dominion over the city. To pull them out of their ancestral habitat by force as Zionism has done, is unpardonable crime and must be undone.

Second, there is the association on the level of religion and hope on the part of people who lived far away from Jerusalem. These are certainly entitled to visit the city, to worship in its shrines associated with their faiths. This category includes Jews, Christians and non-Palestinian Muslims around the world.

Sovereignty over the city may not be exercised in the name of Judaism because Judaism does not regard either Christianity or Islam, and hence their presence in Jerusalem, as *de jure*. It may not be exercised in the name of Christianity because Chritianity may regard the Jewish presence as religiously relevant to the drama of salvation, but it does not regard the presence of Islam as *de jure*. Finally, sovereignty over Jerusalem may not be exercised in the name of the United Nations, a secular institution in whose consideration all religions are, as it were, irrelevant by definition. A secular atmosphere is not one in which the religious concerns can exist with reassurance of safety and dignity, with confidence in the future.

There remains only one solution, *viz.*, an Islamic state exercising sovereignty in the name of Islam. Under it, Judaism and Christianity are religiously and publicly as legitimate and constitutional as Islam. In the past fourteen centuries, neither the Jewish nor the Christian shrines would have survived were it not for this very attitude of Islam toward Judaism and Christianity. Only an Islamic government, therefore, would be permanently and absolutely committed to honour and safeguard the shrines holy to the three faiths. Only an Islamic government would be an affirmation of the Palestinians and Jerusalemites' right to continue their physical association with (i.e., their habitation of) the city. What Jewish sovereignty may do to Jerusalem is already before your eyes, *viz.*, de-Islamization, de-Christianization, de-Palestinization. What Christian sovereignty may do to Jerusalem has been witnessed by history when the Crusades set up the Kingdom of Jerusalem and transformed al Aqsa into a stable. What Islamic sovereignty may do is equally witnessed by history. It began with 'Umar's covenant with Sophronius, followed by his refusal to pray in the Church of the Holy Sepulchre, and his cleansing of the Haram site with his own hands. It is corroborated by the honour in which the Muslims of the world have held Jerusalem throughout the fourteen centuries of history, namely, as the third Haram after Makkah and Madinah. May Jerusalem enjoy that honour for ever and ever.

PART TWO

The Historical Perspective

5. The Judaization of Jerusalem and its Demographic Transformation

Rouhi El Khatib

The tragic history of Jerusalem since the turn of the century has passed through the following four distinct phases:

The First Phase was characterised by the preparatory measures adopted by World Jewry to infiltrate into Palestine generally, and into Jerusalem particularly. These preparations were formally adopted as a Zionist policy program at the Basle Conference held in 1897 under the chairmanship of Theodor Hertzl, and they fitted in with the recommendations of an international committee composed of representatives of the European Colonial Powers which was set up at the initiative of the British Prime Minister, Mr. Campbell Bannerman, and which met in London in 1907. The task of this special committee was to recommend a long-term policy for the colonial powers whereby their imperialistic and colonial interests could best be secured and safeguarded. Its basic recommendation, which, for obvious reasons, has not been widely published, was the creation of an alien ethnic wedge on the eastern coast of the Mediterranean Sea which would separate the Arab peoples of Asia from the Arab peoples of North Africa, and which would serve as a staunch ally and a permanent base for the colonial powers from which they could protect and further their colonial interests in Asia and Africa.

Thus it came about that the Zionist programme to infiltrate into Palestine which had been adopted ten years earlier became the ready-made tool which the European colonial powers, with Great Britain at their head, were able to use in order to implement their grand colonial design. It is in this context, and against this sinister background of collusion that the British Balfour Declaration of 1917 must be viewed. Under that Declaration Great Britain undertook to establish a National Home for the Jews in Palestine, thus ignoring and reneging on its previous undertakings and assurances to its Arab War allies led by the late King Hussein Ben Ali during the First World War, to support their national aspirations for establishing a unified independent Arab state, comprising the territories of Hedjaz, Syria, Iraq, Palestine and Jordan.

The Second Phase extends over the thirty years from 1918 to 1948 when Palestine was placed under British Mandate by agreement among the Western Powers. During the whole of that period, Great Britain, through the Mandatory Government, spared no effort to implement its undertaking to World Jewry under the Balfour Declaration to establish a National Home in Palestine for the Jews. The program of massive Jewish immigration and settlement in Palestine was forcibly implemented by the British Government with the aid of British troops who were constantly called upon to quell Palestinian Arab protestations and uprisings throughout that period.

The program was given moral and material support by the so-called German Reparation Funds which were extorted by the Zionist Movement from a guilt-ridden German Government, and by the powerful Zionist Lobby in the USA with its disproportionate influence on the formulation of American foreign policy. As a result of this massive Jewish immigration into Palestine during the thirty year period of the British

Mandate, the Jewish population of Palestine increased from 56,000 in 1918 to about 650,000 in 1948, whereas the Arab Moslem and Christian population of Palestine increased during the same period from about 600,000 to about 1,400,000 only. Thus the proportion of Jews to Arabs in Palestine rose from 8.57% in 1918 to about 25% in 1948. In so far as the City of Jerusalem was concerned this rapid demographic transformation during that period was even more phenomenal, as the Jewish population of Jerusalem increased from about 10,000 or 25% of the City's population in 1918, to about 100,000 or about 50% of the City's population in 1948. This is no doubt due to the fact that the Judaization of Jerusalem has always been a basic feature of the over-all Zionist design. Representation of Jews on the Jerusalem Municipal Council was accordingly increased from four members in 1925 as compared with six Moslems and two Christian Arab members during that period, to 50% of the membership of the Jerusalem Municipal Council in 1948.

Land ownership by Jews during the period of the British Mandate increased from 2% in 1918 to 5.66% in 1948 for the whole of the country, and from 4% in Jerusalem to 14%. The disproportionate increase in Jewish land-ownership was in large measure due to legislation enacted by the British Mandatory Government in violation of terms of the Mandate and the Declaration of Human Rights.

The Third Phase (between 1948-1967) started with the establishment of the state of Israel, and its usurpation, with the connivance and assistance of the Western Powers and the USA, of most of the Arab Lands in Palestine, and the expulsion of over one million Moslem and Christian Arab Palestinians, whose lands, houses, and movables were appropriated by the state of Israel. These Palestinian Arabs, who became homeless refugees, were never allowed to return, despite numerous resolutions by the United Nations Organisation that they should be permitted to do so. Their lands, houses, and even their household furniture, were used to settle hundreds of thousands of Jewish immigrants who were lured into the newly established state of Israel from the four corners of the earth with promises of financial and material aid and support by the Jewish Agency and the Government of Israel. The magnitude of this flood of immigration resulted in a rapid increase of the Jewish population of Palestine from 650,000 at the end of the British Mandate in 1948 to 2,400,000 in 1967. It was during this phase that the state of Israel forcibly expanded its area to cover about 70% of the area of Palestine. In the course of the fighting which took place in 1948, the Hashemite Kingdom of Jordan rescued and retained the Eastern part of Jerusalem including the ancient walled City together with the Moslem and Christian Holy Places. Jerusalem thus became a divided city with Israeli forces occupying about 80% of its Municipal area. Sixty thousand Moslem and Christian Arab inhabitants of Jerusalem lost their lands, houses and possessions in the area occupied by the Israeli forces, became refugees and were never allowed to return. Their lands and houses were immediately assigned to Jewish settlers, thus increasing the Jewish population of Jerusalem from 100,000 in 1948 to 190,000 in 1967.

The total area of lands occupied by Jews rose from 14% prior to 1948 to about 73% after the 1967 War, most of it being land that belonged to the Arab inhabitants of Jerusalem who fled the city and became refugees, and are still awaiting the implementation of United Nations resolutions permitting them to return to their houses and homeland.

The Fourth Phase started with the occupation in 1967 of the remaining part of Palestine including the Gaza strip, the Western Bank Sector of the Jordan River and the Eastern Sector of Jerusalem, including the Old City within the Walls. It was in this fourth and final phase that the Israeli Authorities set about the systematic Judaization of the city in phases and by various military, terroristic, legislative and administrative measures which they implemented in flagrant violation of the Geneva Conventions, and the Universal Declaration of Human Rights and United Nations Resolutions. I would like to enumerate for your information, and to describe briefly the more outstanding of these measures in the sequence in which they were implemented, and as I personally witnessed them during the first nine months after the occupation of the Eastern Sector of Jerusalem and before my expulsion from the city to Amman on the 7th of March 1968, and subsequently on the basis of information gathered from documented accounts conveyed to me by responsible Arab bodies and citizens of Jerusalem, and on information published in newspapers and magazines within the occupied areas, and broadcast by Israeli radio and television. These criminal measures and violations are as follows:

1. The use of terror tactics to drive out the remaining Arab inhabitants.

This was the course adopted in 1948 by the Jewish terrorist organisation known as the 'Irgun Zvi Leomi', headed then by the arch terrorist Menahem Begin, who has since become the present Prime Minister of Israel, and which committed the massacre of Deir Yassin, a suburb of Jerusalem, when about 400 peaceful Arab villagers, most of whom were women and children, were systematically slaughtered at night and their bodies paraded by their killers in the streets of Jerusalem the next morning. In the wake of that massacre, tens of thousands of Arab inhabitants of Jerusalem and the rest of Palestine fled the country in terror, thus enabling the Jews to occupy the major part of the City and the country as a whole virtually devoid of its Arab inhabitants, whose houses, lands and chattels were immediately appropriated by Jewish settlers.

The same terror tactics were used in the 1967 War on the inhabitants of the Arab Sector of Jerusalem after the withdrawal of the Jordanian army from the City. Although the armed Arab resistance had ceased and the fighting had stopped, the occupation Israeli force continued to terrorise the civilian population by continuous fire from the air and on the ground, deliberately killing about 300 civilian Arab inhabitants, and causing the flight of about 5000 others from the city as part of their design to reduce the number of Arabs in the occupied areas to a minimum.

2. Demolition of buildings to compel the Arab occupants to leave the City.
Four days after the cessation of hostilities, and the withdrawal of the Jordan army, Israeli army units brought in their bulldozers and demolished all the buildings of the Maghrabi Quarter of the Old City of Jerusalem inside the walls, and rendered 135 Arab families numbering 650 persons homeless refugees. Another 24 buildings and a plastic factory adjacent to the Armenian Quarter were also demolished at the same time, depriving another 300 inhabitants and the workers of the factory of their homes and their livelihood.

3. The annexation of Jerusalem administratively and politically as from June 28th 1967 to the sovereignty of Israel, against the wishes of its Arab inhabitants and international opinion, and in violation and flagrant defiance of United Nations Resolutions. Subsequently Israel announced the unification of the Jewish and Arab sectors of the City and declared it as the capital of Israel, contrary to the Geneva Convention and the Universal Declaration of Human Rights.

4. Dissolution of the elected Arab Municipal Council of Jerusalem, and the confiscation of its records and its movable and immovable properties, and the amalgamation of the Arab Municipality as from June 29th, 1967, with the Municipality of Israeli occupied Jerusalem, and the subsequent expulsion on March 7th, 1968, of the Arab Mayor of Jerusalem (who is addressing you now) to Amman.

5. **Abrogation of Jordanian Laws** and the enforcement of Israeli Laws and legislation in the occupied Arab Sector of Jerusalem, and the closing of the Civil Courts, thus compelling the Arab inhabitants to refer to the Israeli Courts, contrary to the Geneva Conventions.

6. **Stay of execution of all judgments issued by the Sharia Islamic courts in occupied Jerusalem,** in order to compel the Moslem inhabitants of the City to refer to Jaffa Sharia Court which was ordered by the Israeli authorities to apply Israeli Laws in all matters of personal statute, contrary to the principles of Islam.

7. **The confiscation and expropriation of about 120,000 Dunoms of the remaining Arab Lands in Jeruslem and its suburbs (equal to 30,000 acres),** and depriving no less than 10,000 Arab owners and farmers of their right of ownership and earning their living in addition to the threat of becoming dependent on Israeli employment or forced to leave the area.

8. **Confiscation and appropriation of four Arab quarters inside the walls of the Old City of Jerusalem,** which contained 595 residential apartments, 437 shops and business premises, one girl's school in which 300 students were enrolled, and two mosques, in addition to the Arab buildings and lands which had previously been taken over and occupied by Jews in Jerusalem in the 1948 War, and which at that time constituted about 80% of Arab owned lands in the city as a whole in 1948.

9. Demolition of 640 buildings, including the girls' school and the two mosques, inside and around the walls of the Old City, and the expulsion of the occupants of these buildings, who numbered about 6,000 Moslems and Christians, in addition to the 60,000 Arabs who had fled the City in 1948 and were never allowed to return.

10. Carrying out of illegal excavations around the Western and Southern Walls of the Sanctified Area of the Aqsa Mosque and Dome of the Rock Mosque in violation of the Hague and Geneva Conventions. As a result of these excavations fourteen historic buildings either collapsed or were damaged causing cracks to appear in the walls and subsequently were bulldozed and demolished by the Israeli occupying authorities. Tens of other historic buildings in the area were also damaged. Additional excavations were also carried out which penetrated the southern wall of the Sanctified Area of the Aqsa Mosque and the Dome of the Rock Mosque. As a result of these excavations a total of about 300 buildings which include cultural and religious inhabitations, historical buildings and residential apartments are now exposed to the damages of collapse, and their 3000 Arab occupants face the threat of being deprived of their homes and their livelihood and becoming refugees in the neighbouring Arab Countries. The numerous resolutions adopted by the UNESCO condemning these excavations and calling upon Israel to discontinue them have been totally and flagrantly ignored.

11. The Burning of the Aqsa Mosque on August 21st, 1969, and the repeated attacks by Israeli political and religious leaders and their followers into the sanctified area of both Mosques, the Aqsa and the Dome of the Rock by forcible entry to hold Jewish religious services in the yards, and the issue of judgment by an Israeli magistrate recently condoning the holding of such

Jewish religious services in the Aqsa Mosque area. These constant and repeated violations of the sanctity of the most venerated of the Moslem Shrines has created an extremely tense atmosphere among the Moslems in Jerusalem and in all occupied Palestine, which threatens to explode into violence that would endanger the lives of the unarmed Arabs therein.

12. **Repeated and Continued attacks against Christian Churches in Jerusalem** including the Church of the Holy Sepulchure and the Coptic Convent, and the sustained pressure by the Israeli Authorities on Christian clergy to sell or to agree to long-term leases of lands owned by Christian Churches of various denominations. As a result, large areas of Church owned lands have passed into Israeli ownership or possession.

13. **Closing of Arab banks and confiscation** of their funds, thus compelling the Arab inhabitants of Jerusalem to deal with Israeli banks, and in general undermining the Arab economy in the occupied areas and rendering it totally dependent on the economy of Israel.

14. **Imposing Israeli education curricula in Arab schools** and placing them under strict Israeli supervision, and prohibiting the use of many standard Arab school textbooks in existing Arab schools. Terrorising dissenting Arab educators by imprisonment of the Director of Education and his Assistant for refusing to co-operate in implementing Israeli curricula and expelling many other teachers and educators, in addition to the demolition of a girls' school inside the old city which I have already mentioned, and damaging the building of a technical training school for Arab orphans which has become exposed to the danger of collapsing as a result.

15. Subjecting Arab businessmen, craftsmen and companies in the city to the provisions of Israeli tax and commercial laws and Israeli municipal laws and regulations contrary to the resolutions of the Security Council and the Geneva Conventions.

16. Preventing Arab Citizens of the City who were absent during the fighting in June 1967, whose number is estimated to be about 20,000, from returning to their homes and the confiscation of their properties. This same policy was adopted in the 1948 fighting.

17. Closing of all Government health centres and clinics in Jerusalem and transferring them to locations outside the city, to compel the Arab citizens of Jerusalem to seek medical care and treatment from Israeli medical institutions, in order to increase the dependence of the inhabitants of the Arab Sector of Jerusalem on the Israeli occupation authorities and to consolidate its annexation and absorption to the Israeli sector of the City, in violation of the resolutions of the United Nations General Assembly and Security Council.

18. Closing the Government Social Services Centre in Jerusalem and transferring it to a location outside the city, and subjecting all existing Arab charitable societies and institutions with their hospitals, clinics, various human services, to the control and supervision of the Israeli Social authorities, contrary to the United Nations resolutions.

19. Changing the Arabic or historical names of many of the main streets and public squares of the Arab sector of the city into Israeli names, and the obliteration of all outward landmarks and signs which connect these streets and public squares with their Arab and Islamic history.

20. The adoption of a new Town Planning Scheme for the City of Jerusalem, and its suburbs, the implementation of which calls for the gradual demolition and obliteration in stages of large parts of some existing Arab quarters in the City, and the transfer of their present Arab inhabitants to other parts of the country, and the subsequent obliteration of the features of the Arab quarters which connect them with their Arab and Moslem history and culture. Needless to say, this master plan requires as a pre-request for its implementation the prohibition of constructing any new buildings by Arabs in any of these areas which are destined for expropriation under the plan. The number of Arab residents whose properties and homes are affected by this town planning scheme is estimated at 10,000.

21. The transfer of title to the shares of the Arab Municipal Council which was dissolved in the Jerusalem Arab Electricity Co., to the name of the Israeli Municipal Council of Jerusalem, and applying various means of pressure including increased taxation, in order to compel the Board of Directors of the company to amalgamate with the Israeli Electricity Company. The continued resistance of the Arab Board of Directors of the company to this illegal duress has brought about veiled threats by the Israeli authorities to cancel the concession of the company and confiscate its assets. The purpose of these oppressive measures is obviously to render the Arab sector of Jerusalem and its remaining beleaguered Arab population completely and totally dependent on the Israeli authorities not only for its medical, social, educational, water, and other public services, but also for its electric power.

22. The adoption and public announcement of a Greater Jerusalem Plan, which would include an additional nine Arab townships and sixty Arab villages with a total Arab population of about 250,000 or about one third of the total population of the occupied West Bank area. Under this plan all the area would be annexed and become part of Greater Jerusalem, subject to the sovreignty of Israel. The implementation of this long-term plan has already started with confiscation of large areas of Arab lands for Jewish settlement in the suburbs around Jerusalem.

23. **The expulsion of numerous Arab citizens from the city to neighbouring Arab countries,** particularly prominent citizens including religious leaders, the Mayor of Jerusalem, physicians, lawyers, school teachers, farmers and students.

24. **Establishment of sixteen new Jewish quarters and areas of dense Jewish settlement on confiscated Arab lands inside and outside the walls of the old city,** in accordance with the master plan to encircle the Arab inhabited areas of Jerusalem and its suburbs. The fortified multi-storey buildings encircling areas of Arab settlement can be seen in the photograph, copies of which are printed in the booklet already distributed earlier. It is estimated that about 100,000 new Jewish settlers have been housed in these buildings which were constructed on Arab lands.

25. **Arrest, imprisonment and torture of Arab citizens without trial** is one of the ugliest and most brutal forms of terror which is being used as a means to induce the remaining Arab inhabitants to leave the city. At present, the number of Arab prisoners in occupied Palestine exceeds five thousand, many of whom have been brutally tortured and all of whom are subjected to inhuman treatment and prison conditions which have nothing in common with the basic standards of treatment of prisoners applied in civilized countries. By far the greatest number of these prisoners are held for months without trial and on unsubstantiated charges of resisting the Israeli occupation.

26. **The dismantling of the motors and water pumps of the water pumping stations of the Arab Municipality of Jerusalem,** and their removal to the Israeli sector of the City, and connecting the water pipe network of the occupied Arab sector to the Israeli Water Distribution network of Jerusalem, thus compelling Jerusalem Arabs to be dependent on Israeli water.

27. **Promotion of Jewish immigration and settlement in Jerusalem, and the prevention of the return of its Arab citizens,** and the prevention of the settlement of any other Arabs in the Greater Jerusalem area. As a result of this discriminatory policy, the number of Jewish residents in Jerusalem has been artificially increased to over 300,000 as compared with about 100,000 Arab inhabitants, namely a proportion of 75% Jews to 25% Arabs, a complete reversal of the proportion which prevailed at the beginning of the British Mandate in Palestine in 1918 when the Arab population of Jerusalem constituted 75% of the total, and the Jewish population about 25%.

28. **Permitting the Israeli owners of property in the Arab sector of Jerusalem to take back their properties after the Arab sector was occupied by the Israeli forces in 1967, and denying the same right to the Arab owners of property in the Israeli sector of Jerusalem.** These Arab properties are still confiscated and their Arab owners of the Israeli occupied territories are still considered as absentees. This is a flagrant example of racial discrimination sanctioned by Israeli legislation.

29. **Confiscation and expropriation of Arab lands for Jewish settlement has resulted in a reversal of the proportion of Arab and Jewish land ownership in Jerusalem.** In 1918 Arabs

owned 94% of the lands in the Jerusalem area, and Jews owned 4%, the remaining 2% was owned by foreigners. At the present time, Jewish ownership of lands in Jerusalem is about 84% of the Municipal area and Arab ownership is about 14%.

30. The reduction of the number of Christian residents, as a result of terroristic pressures. Large numbers of Christians fled and have taken refuge in neighbouring Arab countries, while others have emigrated to the United States of America, Canada and Australia as a result of continued Israeli repressive and oppressive measures. The number of Christian residents in Jerusalem has declined from about 30,000 before the Arab — Israeli War in 1948, to about 18,000 before the Arab — Israeli War in 1967, and it now stands at about 12,000 only.

These are briefly some chapters in the recent tragic history of Jerusalem under the Israeli occupation, and it is also the sad story of my country Palestine from which I have been expelled, and of the whole of the Middle East which has been the victim of Western veiled imperialistic designs, led first by Great Britain, and presently sponsored and financed by the United States of America.

6. From Ancient Times to the Beginning of the Muslim Era

Dr. Demetri Baramaki

The evidence derived from archaeological exploration demonstrates that Jerusalem was founded sometime in the first half of the Second Millennium, about 1800 B.C. However, pottery only, but no remains of architectural structures, has been found which is attributed to the Third Millennium.

The Middle Bronze Age city has been for the most part excavated by the late Kathleen Kenyon, who discovered parts of the city walls including a massive gate. The ancient city lay some 200m. south of the present city walls which form the enclosure wall of the Temple Area and stand 2,500 ft. above sea-level. It was enclosed between two valleys, the Kedron on the east (known at present as Wady ne Nar) and the Tyropaean Valley on the west, ending on the south side at the tips where the two valleys converge. Thus the city was long and narrow and roughly elliptical in plan. The gate stood at its north-east corner. The city received its water supply from the spring called Bihon in the Old Testament, but at present it is known as the Virgin's Fountain or Ain Umm ed Daraj (the spring with stairs). Excavations have proved disappointing as apart from a few sections of the city wall here and there, as well as the gate mentioned above, no substantial structures of any description were found as most of the ancient masonry was dismantled for use in later structures. Evidence for the date of this city was given by the Middle Bronze Age pottery found associated with some sections of the city wall.

The city was founded by the Canaanites or Amorites who called themselves Jebusites after the name of the city Jebus. The Amorites and Canaanites hailed from Arabia. A German historian influenced by the Biblical myth of the story of Noah called them Semites and their language Semites after Shem the son of the mythical Noah. As they hailed from Arabia, it is more appropriate and more scientific to call them Arabs.

Yet Jerusalem, in spite of its unpretentious size, as it covered an area of eleven acres only, lays claim to some importance because of its strategic position; for it commands the highway from the sea-coast to the hinterland and lies athwart the ridge road leading from the south to the north. Without Jerusalem it is impossible to unite the two parts of the country north and south.

The area of the city and its position remained unchanged during the second millennium B.C. Yet in spite of this, it was impregnable and withstood many assaults throughout the first eight centuries of its existence. Its historical importance and significance is apparent from the role it played during the Amarna Period, when messages were exchanged between Akhenaton, the dilettante pharaoh of Egypt, and Abd Khiba, the King of the city. Abd Khiba (note the Arabic construction of the name which means worshipper of the goddess Khibat), together with many other Near Eastern Kings like Ribudda, King of Byblos, Abimilki, King of Tyre and Ammunira, King of Beirut (modern Beirut), sent urgent messages to the Egyptian court asking for help against the marauding Apiru or Habiru nomads who were harassing the Eastern littoral of the Mediterranean, by their continuous excursions from the desert. However, in spite of frequent assaults, Jerusalem stood its ground and repelled the invaders who were presumably the Israelites. The city remained independent for over three and a half centuries after these assaults, until it was captured by David about 1000 B.C., at least 800 years after its foundation as a city by the Jebusites who had originally come from Arabia. Joab, David's general, captured the city by a ruse infiltrating some of his men through the shaft that led from the Virgin's fountain to the centre of the city. Joab was unable to capture the city by direct assault. The archaeological record shows that under David, the city remained essentially the same as he embarked on no additions or modifications.

When King Solomon ascended the throne about 960 B.C. he more than doubled the area of the city by adding a large section of the slope on the north side incorporating part of the present Haram enclosure. He built a temple and a palace nearby. The land on which the temple and palace were built had already been acquired by King David from Araunah the Jebuzite who had been using it as a threshing floor. Solomon engaged Phoenician masons, carpenters and other craftsmen sent to him by his ally Hiram, king of Tyre, as there were no craftsmen in Israel. The remains of this temple, if any, lie under the platform which was flattened a thousand years later by King Herod. However, remains of temples and palaces have been found at Tell Achana and Tell Ta'yinat in Turkey in the plain of the Amuq near Antioch. These conform to the description of the temple and palace given in the Biblical narrative. The temple at Tell Ta'yinat consists of a porch (called 'Olam in the Bible), the front of which was decorated with two columns. (In the Old Testament these are called Jachin and Boaz). But whereas the two columns at Tell Ta'yinat are functional in that they support the roof of the porch, the impression gained from the Biblical account is that the Jachin and Boaz stood freely and independently in front of the porch and were rather ornamental than functional. The porch led through a door to a large hall (called hekal in the Bible). This was reserved for the priests and Levis. A door led from the hekal to an inner sanctuary called debir or Holy of Holies in the Bible. Here there was an altar. The Ark of the Covenant was kept in the debir, to which only the High Priest had access. With regard to the decoration and furniture of the Temple, whereas until the excavations carried out since World War I these were a complete enigma to us, now since the excavations carried out in various sites of the near East especially at Megiddo and Byblos we are better informed, as a great deal of light has been shed on the Biblical narrative. We now know that the cherubim mentioned in the Bible as decorating the ceiling and various parts of the Temple are small sphinxes of which a few have been found in recent years, notably on the sacophagus of Ahiram at Byblos, and on an ivory magic wand at Megiddo. With regard to Temple furniture, a bronze brazier was discovered at Beisan, ancient Beth Shan, which may well have been similar to the brazier made for the Temple. We are also told in the Bible that a large altar decorated with a horn at each corner was set up in front of the temple. A few small stone altars ornamented with horns have been discovered at Megiddo and other sites. Similarly, Solomon's palace was probably built on the same plan as the palace at Tell Ta'yinat. Sargon II of Assyria tells us that the Amorites called this type of building Bit Hilani. The palace at Tell Ta'yinat consists of a flight of stairs leading up to an enclosed porch, the roof of which was supported by three columns. Three doors led from the porch to the throne room, consisting of a large hall. A door on the left led to the King's bed chambers, while another door at the back of the hall led to offices; on the right a door gave access to a large storage chamber.

Jerusalem remained the capital of the Kingdom of Israel for about seventy years. During the reign of Solomon the outlying districts occupied by David were lost. Even the Shephelah was lost, as we are told in the Bible that Pharaoh captured Gezer and gave it to Solomon as a dowry when Solomon married Pharaoh's daughter.

On the accession of Rehoboam, the Kingdom of Israel split into two and Jerusalem became the capital of the Kingdom of Judah only. It retained that position until 586 B.C. when Nebuchadnezzar captured it and razed it to the ground. At the time he took the bulk of the population of Judah into captivity. But Jerusalem was brought to great straits between 930 and 586 B.C. It was sacked by the Pharaoh Shishak or Sheshonk in 922 B.C. and again by the Philistines in 850 B.C. Furthermore, during the frequent wars between the two Kingdoms of Israel and Judah, Joash the King of Israel sacked it in 781 B.C. Sennacherib the King of Assyria besieged Jerusalem during the reign of Hezekiah. However plague struck the Assyrian Army and Sennacherib was content to receive tribute from Hezekiah and raised the siege and departed. Thus Jerusalem was free for only short intermittent periods of time and the Kingdom of Judah lasted from about 930 B.C. to 586, in other words 344 years only as against the 800 years it was held by the Jebusites of 'Semitic' or Arab origin. Yet in these 344 years Jerusalem, as capital of the Kingdom of Judah, was not wholly independent, but was tributary of Assyria.

There was a slight expansion of the site on the east side during the lifetime of the Kingdom of Judah. This was probably due to defensive purposes as after the division of the Kingdom of Israel and the creation of two kingdoms, independent of each other, the Kingdom of Judah was subjected to many attacks. Besides the three attacks which we have already mentioned when Jerusalem was sacked in turn by Shishak, the Philistines and Joash of Israel, the city was often attacked by the Ammonites and Moabites of Transjorden and by the Edomites from the south. Hezekiah, in order to insure the supply of water to the city, dug a tunnel in the rock from Gihon (the Virgin's Fountain) to the lower pool of Siloam.

After the fall of Nineveh in 612 B.C. at the hands of the Medes and Babylonians, Judah changed masters and became the vassal of Babylon. Necho II, the Pharaoh of Egypt, contested the claim of Babylon over Palestine, Phoenicia and Syria, and advanced with a large army through Palestine against Nebuchadnezzar, the Crown Prince of Babylon, but his passage was contested by Josiah, the King of Judah, who attempted to halt Necho's advance; but he was defeated and slain at the famous battle ground of Megiddo. Necho continued his advance north and met the army of Nebuchadnezzar at Carchemish on the Euphrates in 605 B.C. where he was utterly defeated, and fled helter-skelter to Egypt hotly pursued by Nebuchadnezzar as far as the Egyptian border.

Babylon was left in control of the eastern littoral of the Mediterranean for a few years; but Necho, still smarting under the defeat at Carchemish, proceeded to instigate the tributaries of Babylon to revolt. Jehoiachin, the King of Judah, listened to the Egyptian machinations and revolted. Nebuchadnezzar did not waste time but advanced at the head of a large army, captured Jerusalem in 596 B.C. without difficulty and carried away part of the population into captivity. It seems that a lesson was learnt from this unsuccessful venture and Egypt, absorbed with problems elsewhere, left Babylon in control of Palestine, Phoenicia and Syria. When the Pharaoh Uahabra (the Biblical Hophra and the Greek Apries) ascended the throne he instigated Judah and Phoenicia to revolt, the lesson of 596 B.C. having apparently been forgotten. Using Phoenicia as his base Uahabra gathered together a large force and made preparations for a campaign against Nebuchadnezzar in support of Phoenicia and Judah. Nebuchadnezzar moved with alacrity against the rebels with a large force. (The Bible says he had one thousand thousand men at his command but this is obviously an exaggeration.) The bulk of the Babylonian army was sent against Zedekiah, the King of Judah. Jerusalem was besieged and succumbed after a short siege in 586 B.C. Zedekiah was taken prisoner and his sons were slain before his eyes which were later put out. The bulk of the population of Judah was taken captive and deported to Babylon except the very poor. The remnants of the Jews who managed to escape sought refuge in Egypt and were settled at Tahpanhes. Thus came the end of the Kingdom of Judah after flourishing for 344 years. The Kingdom of Israel in the north had already been destroyed by Sargon II, King of Assyria, in 722 B.C.

Jerusalem lay derelict and in ruins for about 70 years. However, when the Achaemenid Persian Dynasty captured Babylon in 538 B.C. and inherited its vast empire, Palestine came under Persian rule, which was benign and tolerant compared to the two empires that went before it. Some Jews were allowed to return to Jerusalem and other points in Judah in several batches. The first contingent returned under Zerubbabel in 516 B.C., seventy years after their captivity or rather the captivity of their forebears. Zerubbabel rebuilt the temple on a modest scale, but like its predecessor, there are no visible remains of this as it must have been submerged by the Temple Platform built later by Herod. Nehemiah returned with another contingent of Jews in 445 B.C. and was allowed to build the city walls, which except for some slight variations followed the line of the Solomonic wall. Nehemiah extended the wall in the west over the edge of the Tyropaean Valley which had already silted up to a great extent. We hear of no persecution under the Persians and it seems that the Jews returning from exile enjoyed peace, prosperity and a small measure of autonomy.

In 333 B.C. Jerusalem was captured, apparently without resistance, by Alexander the Great and thus came under Macedonian rule. It has been suggested that the Jews gave Alexander a lot of information about the Persian Empire and Alexander reciprocated by allowing them to practise their religion freely and accorded them a measure of autonomy. For about 140 years Jerusalem led a precarious existence; it lost its importance as the centre of Jewish faith had already shifted to Egypt as we have seen. Under the foreign rule of the Ptolemies the city enjoyed a period of prosperity and peace, but after the Battle of Paneion in 198 B.C. Jerusalem came under the rule of the Seleucid Kings of Syria and a period of turbulence ensued because of the struggle for succession with which the Seleucid Kingdom was plagued. Furthermore, among the Jews there arose a party which favoured certain aspects of the Hellenistic culture introduced by the Seleucids which was however vehemently opposed by the conservative Orthodox Jews. The constant squabbles between the two opposing parties induced Antiochus IV Epiphanes to intervene on the side of the progressive element in the population. Under the plea of re-establishing law and order and in order to carry out his policy of creating a homogeneous state out of the heterogeneous elements in the population of his kingdom he captured Jerusalem, profaned the Temple by slaughtering a pig to the God Zeus Olympus. He furthermore built a fortress called Akra on the west hill, overlooking the ancient city. Akra was probably built on the site of the present citadel. The harsh measures adopted by Antiochus, and especially the desecration of the Temple infuriated the large Orthodox section of the Jewish community and led to an open revolt. In 167 B.C. Mattathias, the son of Hasmon and his son Judas Maccabeus, led the revolt and captured Jerusalem. They fought off the Seleucid armies sent against them successfully. When the Seleucid King Demetrius I ascended the throne in 162 B.C. he defeated the Jews and in the space of one year overcame their resistance leaving Judas Maccabeus dead on the battlefield. But the internecine wars among the various and numerous claimants to the throne emboldened Jonathan, the son of Judas Maccabeus, in 157 B.C. to resume the struggle for independence. He would pass as the ally of one of the claimants and when that claimant became strong, Jonathan would change sides and move over to help the other. Eventually his treachery led to his doom and he was executed by King Tryphon when he moved over to his side, after he had been helping Demetrius II. Jonathan's son, Simon Maccabeus, captured the Fortress of Akra in 142 B.C. and again re-established the independence of the Jews. His success is again due to the squabbles between the various claimants to the Seleucid throne. The Jews were left unmolested for eight years. However, in 138 B.C. Antiochus VII Sidetes succeeded to the Seleucid throne, and having put this house in order, he turned his attention to Jerusalem. He attacked the city in 134 B.C., captured it and destroyed its fortifications. At his death in Parthia in 129 B.C., and the turmoil which ensued in the Seleucid Kingdom, the Jews regained their independence which they maintained until the arrival of Pompey in 63 B.C. because of the patricidal war of the Seleucids.

Simon was succeeded by his son John Hyrcanus I who, fearing no reprisals from the Seleucids, annexed Galilee 'of the Gentiles' into the Jewish state and forcibly converted its inhabitants to the Jewish faith and circumsized them. The Seleucid Kings were too engrossed with their wars of succession to pay much attention to what was going on in Palestine. henceforth, the Maccabaeans or Hasmoneans became virtually independent and remained so for some 66 years.

Taking advantage of the disruption of the Seleucid Kingdom the Maccabaean Kings extended their dominion over their neighbours on both sides of the Jordan. However, the later Maccabaeans deviated from the lofty principles and ideals which inspired and guided the founders of the dynasty. Judas Aristobulus I (105-104 B.C.) murdered his own mother and forcibly circumcized the inhabitants of the Arab district of Idumea and converted them into the Jewish faith. Judas Aristobulus I was the first to assume royalty and proclaim himself King. His predecessors contented themselves with the title of high priest.

It is not known when Jerusalem was rebuilt after its partial destruction by Antiochus VII Sidetes. It was probably soon after his death. Josephus says that Judas Aristobulus I restored the worship in the Temple and evidence points to John Hyrcanus I for the restoration and expansion of the city. It was most probably during his reign that the city was expanded to the west to include Mt. Zion as well as the Citadel Hill. Thus the western boundary became the Valley of Hinnom. In the meantime the Tyropean Valley which had formerly formed the Western boundary had silted up. The Citadel had already been built as we have seen by the Seleucids.

Alexander Jannaeus (104-76 B.C.) succeeded his father Judas Aristobulus. He was a harsh ruler and brought about a revolt by his own people by his extravagant brutality, a revolt so widespread that it took him six years to quell, albeit he was a powerful monarch and extended his territory on both sides of the Jordan and destroyed many of the Greek cities established by the Ptolomies and the Seleucids. In Transjordan, however, he was checked by the rising power of the Nabataen Arabs.

After his death, his wife Alexandra acted as regent for the two minor sons, John Hyrcanus II and Judas Aristobulus II. Alexandra survived her husband by nine years and during her regency Palestine enjoyed a period of peace and tranquility. At her death in 67 B.C., the country was plunged into civil war for a period of four years. John Hyrcanus II, the elder brother, would have willingly abdicated in favour of his younger and more dynamic brother, but he was spurred on to stand for his rights by Antipater, his Idumaean Arab minister who had been forcibly converted to the Jewish faith by Judas Aristobulus I. Antipater, because of his Arab lineage, induced Aretas III (al Hareth) King of the Arab Nabataeans to help John Hyrcanus II in the struggle for the throne. When the great Roman general Pompey arrived in 63 B.C. he found Judas Aristobulus II beseiging Jerusalem. Pompey chased him away and put a stop to the civil war and confirmed John Hyrcanus II as High Priest but deprived him of the title of King. Pompey laid tribute on Judah and restored the independence of all the territories seized by John Hyrcanus I, Judas Aristobulus I and Alexander Jannaeus, which included Galilee in the north, Idumea in the south and the Greek cities in Transjordan, or Perea as it was then called. Pompey imposed tribute on all these provinces and made them subservient to Rome only.

John Hyrcanus II ruled Judaea with his capital at Jerusalem for a period of twenty three years as a client of Rome. In the able hands of his Idumaean Arab minister Antipater, Judaea flourished. At the death of Antipater, his son Herod succeeded him as minister.

In 40 B.C. this state of complacency was shattered by the invasion of Parthia. The Parthians, under king Pacorus, aided by a renegade Roman general called Labienus and Antigonus Mattathian, the son of Judas Anstobulus II, invaded Syria and Palestine and captured Jerusalem. John Hyrcanus II was carried into captivity and Antigonus bit off his uncle's ear, thus mutilating him and debarred him from continuing to hold the office of High Priest, as the sacerdotal law required that the office of High Priest can only be held by a man without blemish. Antigonus proclaimed himself King. Herod fled first to the Nabataen Arabs to seek shelter among his own kinsmen and then to Rome where he put his case to the Roman generals and laid claim to the throne of Judaea. His chances seemed to stand him in good stead, as Antigonus forfeited his chances by allying himself with the Parthians, the enemies of Rome, and Hyrcanus was debarred from holding the office because of his mutilation. Antony and Octavian lent a willing ear to Herod's plea and in 37 B.C., when the Parthians were finally expelled from Judaea, Herod was appointed King of Judaea by the Roman Senate.

In the civil war which ensued after the murder of Julius Caesar and when Herod was still a minister, he culled favour with Cassius, one of the tyrannicides, but after their defeat at Philippi in 42 B.C., Herod quickly changed sides and ingratiated himself with Mark Antony and Octavian and managed somehow to win their confidence.

Soon after his elevation to the throne in 37 B.C. Herod married a Maccabaean Princess called Mariamne, in order to justify his claim to the throne and win the favour of Jews. He put his erstwhile master John Hyrcanus II to death for fear of an uprising in the latter's favour at a later stage. In the eyes of the Jews, however, he never ceased to be considered a foreign interloper, an Idumaean and an Arab and as such a usurper. The Jews longed for the restoration of their lawful Kings, the Maccabaean Dynasty. Herod had to rule the Jews with an iron hand and this did little to appease them. Thus in addition to being a usurper, his rule was considered odious by the Jews. However, be that as it may, the greatness and grandeur of Jerusalem belongs to Herod the Great. He rebuilt the Temple in Jerusalem on a much grander scale than that of Solomon. He constructed a large castle on the site of the Akra fortress but on a much larger scale. The castle was fortified by three massive towers, one called Phasael, after his brother, the second Mariamne, after his wife, and the third Hippicus. The castle embraces the entire western half of ancient Jerusalem. He built a formidable tower at the north end of the Temple Enclosure which he called Antonia after his friend and benefactor Mark Antony and expanded the site in the northwest section. During his reign Jerusalem covered an area of 140 acres. In other words it was fourteen times larger than the Jebusite city. With his other buildings elsewhere, we are not concerned, but mention may be made of his buildings at Sebaste (Modern Sabastiya), Caesarea, Berytus, Jericho and Hebron.

Herod also rebuilt the city walls of Jerusalem using massive marginal drafted masonry. A new wall, starting at the Tower of Antonia, was built. It ran west for about 180m., then turned south for about 100m., then west again for about 50m. then south again until it met the Macabaran wall, a length of about three hundred metres. The newly added part lay west of the Tyropaean Valley, and the two sections of the city were linked by arcaded viaducts which spanned the valley. These arcades may still be seen and they are now called Wilson's Arch and Robinson's arch after the explorers who discovered them. Jerusalem thus lay now between the Valley of Hinnom on the west and the Valley of Kedron on the east. The Tyropaean Valley now ran through the middle of the city.

Although a close friend of Mark Antony, yet after the Battle of Actium where Octavian defeated Antony, Herod managed to retain Augustus' confidence by adroit diplomacy. Only a wily diplomat of his capacity could have changed sides in his allegiance so frequently and still manage to remain on good terms with the eventual winner.

In spite of his greatness, Herod's reign was marred by many insurrections and conspiracies; even his own household was not loyal to him. He had to put to death his wife Mariamne and her two sons on well founded suspicions of treason. This measure increased his unpopularity among the Jews who looked upon Mariamne and her sons as martyrs. The rest of his reign was troubled by frequent conspiracies and suppression of plots. Before his death of a vile disease in 4 B.C. he put to death most of his brothers and children. It was during his reign that Jesus Christ was born.

At his death the Kingdom of Judaea was divided among his four surviving sons. Judaea with its capital at Jerusalem fell to the lot of his elder son Archelaus who assumed the title of ethnarch as he could not assume royalty until confirmed by Rome. The reign of Archelaus was disturbed by so many insurrections that after reigning ten years he was deposed by the Romans and banished to Vienne in Gaul. Henceforth Judaea was governed by Roman governors with the title of procurator.

During the reign of the Emperor Tiberius, Christ delivered his message of peace and good will among men. The message was misunderstood by the Jewish hierarchy who saw in him a rival to their authority. They raised a hue and cry against him which compelled the Roman procurator, Pontius Pilate, to crucify him in order to placate the mob and prevent a large scale riot. Pontius Pilate, like most Roman governors, had a great abhorrence to civil strife (called innovations by them) as generally it reflected on their capability and sometimes led to the loss of a lucrative office. Pontius Pilate was not convinced of the guilt of Christ and although he condemned Christ, he said at the time to the Jews, "His blood be upon your heads". This incident, which seemed trivial and insignificant at the time, was to have the greatest repercussions in the future. Eventually Christianity overwhelmed the Roman Empire and changed its religious and social aspect. With the triumph of Christianity, Jerusalem, which was only important in Judaea, assumed world wide importance as the centre of Christian worship, and held in great esteem throughout the entire world. Formerly the city was sacred only to the Jews. It later became the sacred city of Christendom as well.

The government of Judaea by procurators, however, was not palatable to the Jews and proved unsuccessful. Furthermore the rapacity of some procurators seemed to the Jews as odious, if not more so, as the rule of the Herods. The tax farmers and publicans were classed together with sinners and malefactors by the Evangelists, who in the narrative of the four Gospels reflect the life and manners of the time. Furthermore racial hatred and religious rivalry between the Greek Gentiles and the Jews added fuel to an already smouldering situation in the country. The Jews became exasperated at the state of affairs and organized bands of Sicarii or Zealots who were armed with daggers concealed beneath their cloaks and descended on the unwary Gentiles and progressive Jews. The Sicarii infested the countryside and rendered travel extremely hazardous and dangerous. The Emperor Caligula, in the hope of appeasing the Jews, put an end to the rule of the procurators and appointed his friend Herod Agrippa I in A.D. 41 as King of Judaea. He was a scion of Herod the Great and was formerly King of Iturea, Trachonitis and Galilee. He added Samaria to his new Kingdom. But this King died prematurely of a sun-stroke at Caesarea in A.D. 44 before he could reconcile his new subjects to the pax Romana. Nevertheless during his short reign he extended the city on the northwest side and built a wall which now lies under the present north wall of Jerusalem. The city during his reign extended over an area of 310 acres.

The rule of the procurators was restored. In A.D. 66 the Gentile population of Caesarea fell upon the Jews and massacred them without any attempt on the part of the Roman Procurator Gessius Florus to stop the pogrom. The Jews retaliated by massacring the Gentiles in Jerusalem and by beseiging the citadel in the city in which a garrison of two hundred Roman legionaires was stationed. Herod Agrippa II, the King of Galilee, mediated between the Romans and the Jews, who agreed to let the legionaires depart in peace if they left their arms behind. As the unarmed legionaires moved out in single file between rows of deriding Jews, the Sicarii set upon them and knifed every one of them in spite of the protests of the legionaires who reminded the Jews of the safe conduct given under oath.

This break of faith was a difficult pill for the Romans to swallow. An army of 30,000 men under the command of the general Gallus, the Legate or governor of Syria, advanced on Jerusalem and beseiged the city. Failing to capture it, Gallus retired; but he was waylaid on the way back at Beth-Horon and set upon by the Jews and was badly defeated. The victory at Beth-Horon gave heart to the remaining Jews, who had not joined the revolt so far, to cast their lot with the rebels and the revolt spread like wildfire throughout the country.

The Emperor Nero sent his general Vespasian with an army of fifty thousand men in A.D. 67 in order to quell the rebellion. Vespasian subdued Galilee without difficulty and captured the famous Jewish historian Josephus at Jotapata. Josephus turned renegade and accompanied Vespasian in his campaign. In A.D. 68 Vespasian reduced Peraea (Transjordan) and advanced on Jerusalem; but Nero died at this juncture and Vespasian was eventually proclaimed emperor. In A.D. 70 his son Titus resumed the seige of Jerusalem, which after going through the most harrowing ordeal was taken by assault. The Temple was destroyed in the fighting as it had been fortified by the Jews and was the focal point of their resistance. The city was utterly destroyed and a large number of Jews was crucified, while about 2,500 were led to the arena in Rome where they were made to fight wild beasts and perished in the process.

Jerusalem remained derelict and in ruins for about 65 years, when the Emperor Hadrian, after suppressing the Second Jewish Revolt, built a new city on the ruins of the old which he called Aelia Capitolina. He also built a new temple dedicated to Jupiter Capitalinus on the site of Herod's temple. The layout of the new city is partly preserved in the Madaba map. This is a map of the Near East in mosaics found in one of the Byzantine Churches at Madaba in Jordan. The plan of Jerusalem was given particular attention. Hadrian excluded the part of the city falling south of the Temple area. The cardo or main thoroughfare ran from Damascus Gate to Zion Gate, while the decumanus ran from the Jaffa Gate to the Haram area. Both streets were lined with columns and just inside the Damascus Gate there was an ornamental column which gave the gate its present name in Arabic, Bab al Amud or the Gate of the Column. Hadrian debarred the Jews from entering the city except during Passover.

Hadrian allowed the new city a measure of autonomy and henceforth it had the right to mint its own coins, a right which it continued to exercise until the reign of the Emperor Trajan Decius in the middle of the Third Century A.D.

Jerusalem was the seat of Christianity and there was a small community of Nazarenes (as the Christians were then called) in the city throughout the first three centuries of the Christian era. The Christians met in private houses and there practised the sacrament in great secrecy. There were no churches of any kind until the Church of the Holy Sepulchre was built by Queen Helena, a convert to the faith, in A.D. 328. Official sanction of the Christian faith was given by the Emperors Constantine and Galerius in their famous Edict of Milan in A.D. 312. This led to a great influx of Christian pilgrims to the city to visit the sites sanctified by Christ. The Empress Helena, Constantine's mother, was one of these pilgrims. She built a church over the site of the Crucifixion and Burial of Christ and another on the Mt. of Olives over the site of Ascension, besides many others outside Jerusalem like the Church of the Nativity in Bethlehem. Parts of Queen Helena's Church may be seen in the vaults under the present church which was built by the Crusaders. But this was only the beginning. The city of Jerusalem assumed great importance, greater than ever before. Many other churches were built by the Byzantine emperors during the next three centuries as well as hospices for pilgrims who started flocking to Jerusalem in ever increasing numbers. For three centuries the city enjoyed a period of peace and prosperity. It rose from the rank of an unimportant provincial city of the Roman Empire, of which there were thousands of others, into the rank of the Holy City of the Byzantine Empire. This led to a spate of building activity on an unprecedented scale. Near the Holy Sepulchre a Church was built dedicated to John the Baptist; while close by stood the Patriarchate, or palace of the patriarch.

On the Cardo, the Empress Eudoxia built a palace which is

shown on the Madaba map. Near the Temple area was a church dedicated to St. James. On Mt. Zion the same Empress built a church dedicated to St. Stephen, another near the Pool of Siloam and a hospice for pilgrims outside the city on the west. Churches were also built outside the city wall on the site of Gethsemane and on the Mt. of Olives. The churches were adorned with polychrome mosaic floors.

Jerusalem throve on the 'pilgrim trade' just as modern Jerusalem thrives on the tourist trade. The population of the city was a conglomerate of the original inhabitants who had flocked from the countryside after the foundation of Aelia Capitolina with a sparse mixture of Greeks and Romans.

At the Council of Chalcedan, in A.D. 450, the Bishop of Jerusalem was elevated to the rank of Patriarch and in that capacity held the highest office in the city. When Chosroes I, the Sassanian King of Persia, captured Jerusalem in A.D. 614 he carried away the Patriarch of Jerusalem into captivity as he was the highest ranking official in the city. Similarly, when the Caliph Omar captured the city it was Patriarch Sophronius who delivered the city into his hands and received from him the *firman* protecting Christians and their holy places from molestation.

7. Jerusalem Under Islamic Rule

Dr. A. L. Tibawi

It is not widely known that Arab tribes settled in and around historic Palestine before Islam, and that Islam's connection with Jerusalem was established before the Arab conquest. A great many of the Arab tribes were Christians. One of these settled in the neighbourhood of Bethlehem and became so influential that it had its chief accepted as a bishop of the Orthodox church. Pagan Arabs maintained close commercial relations with Syria and Palestine. The trade route between Mecca and Damascus branched at Petra north-west to Gaza, the market town of southern Palestine. Hashim, a great-grandfather of Muhammad, died there when he was with a merchant caravan. As a merchant, Amr Ibn al-As was familiar with the terrain and the highways of southern Palestine before he commanded the Arab army that advanced on Jerusalem and laid siege to it in 638 A.D.

Islam's first connection with the city is recorded in the first verse of chapter 17 of the Koran which reads: "Glory be to Him who carried His servant (Muhammad) by night from the Holy Mosque (at Mecca) to the Distant Mosque (al-Masjid al-Aqsa in Jerusalem), the precincts of which We have blessed, that We might show him some of Our signs".

Commentators and traditionalists developed the story of this Nocturnal Journey and embellished it with details of exquisite virtuosity. Its main features are these: escorted by the Archangel Gabriel, and mounted on a winged celestial steed called *Buraq*, Muhammad journeyed from Mecca to Jerusalem. On arrival the Buraq was tethered at a spot that has borne its name ever since, and Muhammad walked with his escort towards the holy Rock (over which later rose the Mosque of the Dome of the Rock). After leading former prophets in Prayer there, he ascended with his escort from the top of the Rock to heaven by means of a celestial ladder. In the seventh heaven to earth and the return to Mecca were accomplished during the same night before dawn.

Those with spiritual insight and poetic imagination need no reminder that this is symbolism refined to the highest degree. Early this century Asin Palacios, a Catholic priest and professor of Arabic in the University of Madrid, published a learned thesis that the story of Muhammad's Nocturnal Journey served Dante as prototype for a great many of the ideas and poetic imagery in the Divine Comedy.

In Islamic history, however, the Nocturnal Journey established Jerusalem as the third holy city after Mecca and Medina. This fact explains the Caliph Umar's ready acceptance of the request of the city's Patriarch to surrender it to him in person. It also explains why his entry into it was more that of a pilgrim than a conqueror. It, moreover, explains the magnanimous and humane terms he granted.

Before reading these terms it is necessary to cast a quick glance into the past. In 132 A.D., exactly five centuries earlier than the Islamic conquest, Hadrian obliterated the last vestige of Jewish life in Jerusalem when he had it destroyed and its site ploughed up. The Temple had already been destroyed by Titus in 70 A.D. On its site the Romans erected a pagan temple for Jupiter, and over the ruins of Jerusalem rose the Roman colony of Aelia Capitulina. Hadrian issued an edict banning the Jews from entering the city under pain of death.

Following the adoption of Christianity as the state religion of the Eastern Roman (Byzantine) Empire, and as a result of the zeal of Helena, mother of Emperor Constantine, Jerusalem was covered with Christian monuments, notably the Church of Resurrection, better known as the Church of the Holy Sepulchre. At the same time all pagan buildings, including the temple of Jupiter, were dismantled. The site of this temple (on the ruins of the Jewish Temple) was deliberately left desolate as forecast in the scriptures.

The remnants of the Jews who had survived successive disasters retired to Galilee. In 614 A.D. they saw a flicker of hope of restoration at the hands of the Persians who had overrun Syria and marched on Jerusalem. The Jews helped them as scouts and volunteers, and took part in the massacre of Christians and destruction of churches when the Persians captured Jerusalem. Fourteen years later, Heraclius recovered the city and wreaked vengeance on the Jews, and renewed Hadrian's ban. Thus there were no Jews in Jerusalem when the Patriarch Sophronius surrendered it to the Caliph Umar in 638 A.D. A clause in the covenant forbidding the Jews from living with the Christians in the city was included at the request of the Patriarch. Umar's covenant reads: "In the name of Allah, the Merciful, the Compassionate. This is the covenant which Umar, the Servant of Allah, the Commander of the Faithful, granted to the people of Aelia. He granted them safety for their lives, their possessions, their churches and their crosses . . . Their churches shall not be demolished nor diminished, nor anything of their properties. They shall not be constrained in the matter of their religion, nor shall any of them be harmed. No Jew shall live with them in Aelia. And the people of Aelia shall pay the poll-tax as the people of other cities . . . " Having concluded peace with the Christians, Umar turned to performing acts of Islamic piety. He searched for and identified, on the desolate site of the old Temple, the place of prostration

(*Masjid* in Arabic, the same as for mosque) where Muhammad prayed before ascending to heaven. This is al-Masjid al-Aqsa mentioned in the opening of chapter 17 of the Koran. Umar then joined the Muslims in cleaning the spot and led them in prayer there. By his orders a simple mosque was erected on the place which remained standing until it gave way some sixty years later to the magnificent Dome of the Rock and al-Aqsa Mosque — the latter commemorating both the place of the Prophet's prostration and perpetuating the name enshrined in the Koran. (In European usage, even at the present time, the Dome of the Rock is erroneously called "the Mosque of Umar".)

Umar's entourage included a host of companions of the Prophet, Koran readers and traditionalists, many of whom made their residence in Jerusalem, and Umar appointed one of them as governor. Umar's measures enhanced the religious importance which the city acquired during the lifetime of the Prophet. It became definitely the third holy city. Indeed according to an authentic tradition, the Prophet himself equated pilgrimage to it with that to Mecca and Medina. Furthermore, the residence in the city of renowned authorities on the Koran and traditions made it at once a seat of Islamic learning. Throughout the ages the quest for learning in Islam was combined with the duty of the pilgrimage.

The holiness of Jerusalem was the prime consideration which persuaded Muawiyah, the founder of the Umayyad dynasty, to proclaim himself caliph in Jerusalem, and not in his capital Damascus. One of his illustrious successors, Abdul-Malik, built the Dome of the Rock in 72 A.H. and al-Aqsa Mosque two years later. The two mosques and their surroundings acquired the appellation of al-Haram ash-Sharif (the Noble Sanctuary). Its walls on the east and south coincide with the city wall, but on the north and west the Sanctuary has its own walls, separating it from the city. According to an early custom the pious and the scholarly came to reside for worship and study near these two walls, and the community provided for their material needs by the institution of *waqfs* (pious foundations).

But the pious and the scholarly were a mere trickle compared to the stream of tribes that came from the Arabian Peninsula to settle in Palestine and Jerusalem. They easily assimilated with the native semitic or Arabic population. Many of the Christian Arabs were Monophysites, and the acceptance of Islam presented them with no great theological difficulty. To the Arabic-speaking the difficulty was even less. But contrary to an old myth Islam was not imposed on these or on any others by the sword. Jews and Christians who did not wish to embrace Islam were not penalised. They were in fact absorbed in the current of Islamic civilisation and participated in its development through the medium of Arabic. The survival of Judaism and Christianity, alongside Islam, in the lands of their origin, is due to a tolerant Islam. In an age of intolerance and cruelty, it did not seek to eliminate its predecessors. Not only had it no positive policy of suppression, when it was at the height of its power, it had in fact a positive one of co-existence with "the people of the Book" (the Jews and Christians).

II

When in 1099 A.D. the Crusaders captured Jerusalem it had an overwhelming Muslim majority, a minority of Christians and a handful of Jews. All the Muslims in the city, men, women and children, were butchered without mercy, even those who took refuge in the Sanctuary. The Jews were collected in their Synagogue and the Crusaders burnt it over their heads. The city was thus left without any Muslims or Jews. Nor did the conquerors treat the Eastern Christians as brothers. The Orthodox Patriarchate was suppressed and a Latin Patriarchate took its place, and a great many orthodox Christians had to become Catholic.

What is the explanation of the presence of Jews in Jerusalem, no matter how small in number, considering the stipulation on the covenant of Umar? The most valid explanation is that the atmosphere of general religious tolerance must have persuaded the Christians not to insist on the enforcement of the ban. Although there is no evidence that the stipulation was ever revoked, successive Arabs and Islamic governments must have seen no need for its enforcement and allowed it simply to lapse.

This is confirmed by what Saladin did when he recovered Jerusalem in 1187 A.D. He showed remarkable magnanimity and compassion to his enemies. He released all Franks against moderate personal ransom from which orphans, widows and the poor were exempt. He gave soldiers and civilians safe conduct to territory still held by the Crusaders. He then turned to organise the life of the city. He re-populated it with Arab Muslim tribes, and established several charitable institutions. He re-consecrated the Mamillah Cemetery outside the city to the west for the burial of the heroes of his campaigns. (The Zionists desecrated and dismantled it and made of it a public recreation ground with toilets.)

Nor did he neglect the welfare of the non-Muslims. He restored the Orthodox Patriarchate and granted the request of the Eastern Christians who had collaborated with the Crusaders to stay. As to the Jews I quote from their nineteenth century historian, Heinrich Graets, who wrote that Saladin's dominions "became a safe asylum to the oppressed Jews. Under him they rose to great prosperity and consequence. After their externination by the Crusaders, a small community was recreated in Jerusalem by Saladin's grace.

His son al-Afdal dedicated as *waqf* (pious foundation) for the benefit of North African Muslims (Magharibah), despoiled by the Crusaders, the land to the west of the wall of the Sanctuary and close to al-Aqsa Mosque. This land is hallowed in Islamic tradition by its association with the Prophet's Nocturnal

The earliest specific mention in Arabic of Islamic sources of a sizable Jewish community in Jerusalem is by an author who wrote towards the end of the fifteenth century. He was the chief justice of Jerusalem and not unsympathetic to the Jews. He wrote of the existence of a synagogue adjacent to a mosque in a Jewish quarter which formed a part of a Muslim quarter. Most of the dwelling houses of the Jews belonged either to individual Muslim owners or, more remarkable, to Islamic pious foundations. But still there is no mention of a Jewish custom of wailing or praying at any section of the western wall of the Sanctuary. This is not to deny the existence of the custom, but Journey. His steed, al-Buraq, was tethered there, and he walked over the land in order to reach the Rock. This is commemorated by the Gate of Muhammad, also called the Gate of al-Buraq (later called the Gate of al-Magharibah, the beneficiaries of the pious foundations).

As already explained the walls of the Sanctuary on the east and south coincide with those of the city. But it has its own walls on the north and west. The structure of these walls reflects the history of the city. Over Roman Foundations there are strata representing the works of successive Islamic regimes from Saladin to the Mameluks to the Ottomans. As they stand today the walls are the result of the restoration or rebuilding of Sulaiman the Magnificent in the sixteenth century.

Pious Jews believe that the lowest six courses of a portion of the western wall of the Sanctuary are remnants of the last (Herod's) Temple. But the Arabic and Islamic sources make no mention of this belief, still less of the custom of visiting the place for lamentation or prayer. Hence the name, in western literature, of 'the wailing Place' or 'the Wailing Wall' is unknown for Muslim authors. To complicate matters this is precisely the place where, according to Islamic tradition, the Buraq was tethered. Hence the place and the wall is called simply al-Buraq.

to suggest that it must have developed without ostentation or even surreptitiously.

It is necessary now to describe 'the Wailing Place' and the custom of visiting it with the tacit approval of the Muslim authorities. It was located at the doorstep of al-Aqsa Mosque, the third holy place in Islam, and it is called in Arabic the Buraq yard (Housh al-Buraq). It was in a blind alley some 30 metres long and 4 metres wide, paved with stones. It served as passage to the houses of the North Africans, beneficiaries of the Islamic pious foundations. The only access to it was from the North. The Jews were accustomed to stand on this area, in front of the exterior of the wall of the Sanctuary, for devotional purposes. It was, and is still, the only visible Jewish holy place in Jerusalem. The Christians have immeasurably more holy places. Their pilgrims visited Jerusalem before and after the Arab conquest. The famous Harun ar-Rashid is reputed to have approved the establishment of a hostel for their reception in Jerusalem at the request of his friend, Charlemagne.

There is seldom any mention of the Jews, still less of a wailing place, in the accounts of Christian pilgrims. Such mention of it by the fewer Jewish pilgrims is vague and impersonal, more in the nature of pious hopes than a description of actual performance of a devotional act. But much more significant than the flow of pilgrims was the influx of refugees. From the era of the Crusades to the fall of Granada down to the 19th Century, Jewish refugees from Christian Europe sought asylum in the lands of Islam including, of course, Palestine and Jerusalem. There is no evidence that they were ever turned back by any Muslim government. No change in this humane attitude until Zionism poisoned the atmosphere.

Ominous signs of ingratitude to the Muslim hosts began to appear from the middle of the 19th Century. Those responsible were not the acclimatised and pious Jews who became Ottoman subjects and spoke Arabic, but Jews of foreign nationality who exploited the extra-territorial privileges enjoyed by nationals of certain European powers under the system of Capitulations. Thus in 1840 a Jew under British protection submitted through the British consul an application to repave the Wailing Place. Jerusalem was then under the rule of Muhammed Ali, the governor of Egypt, as a result of his rebellion against his suzerain, the Ottoman sultan. The application was rejected on the following grounds: the passage that the applicant desired to repave was at the foot of the wall of the Noble Sanctuary, and was the place of tethering of the Buraq and is part of an Islamic pious foundation (waqf). Hence the application cannot be entertained under Islamic Law. But the scrupulous order added that the Jews were permitted to continue their visits to the place according to the old custom (*ala al-wajh al-gadim*).

In the second half of the nineteenth century, the number of Jews in Jerusalem was greatly increased. Most of the new immigrants retained their foreign nationalities in order to exploit the privileges under the Capitulations. Once more it was the Jews, who did not care very much about religion, who sought to change the *status quo* at the Wailing Wall. Religious Jews believed that the restoration of Israel depended on divine, not human, agency and they were content with what Islamic tolerance allowed them.

But not the newcomers. In 1911 they and their agents introduced chairs and other articles in the narrow passage of the Wailing Place, thus obstructing the way of the beneficiaries of the Islamic *waqf* to their homes. Accordingly the supervisor of the *waqf* lodged a formal complaint with the religious and civil authorities of the city. The administrative council recommended the prohibition of this innovation, and the governor ratified the recommendation.

Such was the position when the First World War broke out in 1914, and resulted in the British occupation of Jerusalem in December 1917 and the reaffirmation of the *status quo* in the holy places. On the second of November the British government had just issued the Balfour declaration in favour of the establishment in Palestine of a national home for the Jews, despite the fact that the country had been for centuries the national home of its Arab inhabitants, Christians and Muslims. It would be an abrupt stop here. In order to bring out certain contrasts I would crave your indulgence to isolate and underline a few aspects of the British and Israeli periods.

III

When the Balfour declaration was issued, pious Jews in Jerusalem were indifferent if not hostile to the Zionist idea. But the Zionists won over some of the rabbis with the promise to secure the Wailing Wall for Jewry. Henceforth the question became political not religious. And the Zionists lost no time in seeking to honour this promise. Only five months after the issue of the Balfour declaration Weizmann wrote formally to Balfour asking for the "Handing over of the Wailing Wall to the Jews'. At the same time Weizmann offered, through the British military governor, to buy the Wailing Place and the adjoining properties inhabited by the beneficiaries of the Islamic foundation. There was only one answer to this audacious suggestion: under Islamic law, and according to the title deeds, the *waqf* land was inalienable. This particular spot was much more so because of its association with the Prophet.

But the Jews — it is more accurate to say the Zionists — continued the provocation. In August 1929 a Zionist para-military demonstration was held at the Wailing Place and raised the cry "The Wall is ours!" This was followed by bloody disturbances. A British committee of enquiry recommended the appointment of an international commission to investigate the question of the Wailing Wall only. This was formed, with the approval of the League of Nations, of a Swedish chairman and two members, one Swiss and one Dutch.

After hearing evidence from both sides in Jerusalem, the commission reached unanimous verdicts which were ratified by the British government and the Council of the League of Nations. The verdicts were: First, confirmation that the Western Wall of the Noble Sanctuary, of which the so-called Wailing Wall is only a small section, belongs to the Muslims. Second, confirmation that the pavement, the so-called Wailing Place, in front of the Western Wall, as well as the adjacent Magharibah Quarter, also belong to the Muslims as pious foundations constituted according to Islamic law. Third, confirmation of the customary free access of the Jews to the place for devotional purposes, with permission to bring articles necessary for worship on Jewish holy days, but this permission established no rights of proprietorship. These verdicts were embodied in an order-in-council signed by King George V and were published in Jerusalem in the Official Gazette. After approval by the League of Nations they became law, both national and international.

I do not propose to dwell on the injustice of this operation of the Palestine Mandate by Britain, coercing as it did the Arab majority to acquiesce in the loss of its national rights and ultimate extinction. I only wish to remind you that when the Zionists became strong they turned against their benefactors. The pressure of their terrorism and external political pressure, particularly by the United States, compelled Britain to terminate the mandate. But it failed, as democracy dictates, to hand over the government to the Arab majority. Instead Britain left behind chaos and civil war that resulted in the survival of a foreign Zionist national home and the suppression of the indigenous Arab national home. The historic city of Jerusalem, with all the Christian and Muslim holy places inside its ancient walls, escaped by a hair's breadth.

In June 1967 the Zionist state occupied it, and immediately began its barbarous acts of destruction, usurpation, confiscation and expulsion of the population. The whole of the Magharibah Quarter on the land dedicated by Saladin's son and hallowed by its association with the Prophet was completely demolished, including two mosques and two religious schools. The land itself was seized. The exterior of the western wall of the Sanctuary, the third holy place in Islam, was appropriated. Twenty-nine acres of land to the west of the wall, including properties of Islamic pious foundations, were expropriated. Five thousand Muslim inhabitants were forcibly evicted from their homes and places of business and moved out of the city.

The annexation by the Zionist state of the historic city that did not have a single Jewish resident violated international law and disregarded two resolutions by the General Assembly and four resolutions by the Security Council.

History knows of no other refugee who usurped the haven that sheltered him, of no other guest who ousted his host, and of no other tenant who dispossessed the landlord. Israel's chauvinistic fanaticism did all this to the Arabs, Muslims and Christians in complete disregard of the laws of God and Man. Consider that this lawbreaker's only legal warrant for existence is a resolution by the General Assembly in 1947.

To conclude, Jerusalem experienced great misfortunes under non-Islamic rule. Since Umar's covenant of tolerance and coexistence it experienced massacres, usurpation of holy places and expulsion of population in the twelfth century at the hand of the Crusaders. Early this century it experienced the imposition of an unjust policy and denial of self-determination by the might of the British Empire. More recently it experienced barbarous measures reminiscent of the crusades: usurpation of Islamic pious foundations, destruction of Islamic public buildings, confiscation of public and private property and expulsion of population, all combined with a continuation of the denial of self-determination.

Finally I suggest that it was only under Islamic sovereignty that Jerusalem was the city of the three faiths. The crusaders made it an exclusively Christian city, and the Zionists are fast making it an exclusively Israeli city.

It is a dangerous Zionist illusion to believe that the Muslim world would ever acquiesce in leaving the third holy city in Islam under Israeli control. It took nearly a century to recover Jerusalem from the crusaders. It may take shorter or longer to recover it from the Zionists. But, God willing, recovered it will be. Let us pray recovery will be peaceful.

Errata

In the article on "Jerusalem Under Islamic Rule" by Dr. A. L. Tibawi (pp 141-153), please note the following corrections:

Page 142. Line 10. After the word "heaven", please add the words "he experienced the supreme joy of the Beatific Vision. The descent".

Page 143. Line 22. A fresh para begins after the word "reads" and ends with the word "cities".

Page 143. Line 31. A fresh para begins with the word "Having".

Page 146. The last word on this page "Nocturnal" is to be followed by the word "Journey", at the begining of line 12 on page 147.

Page 147. The first 11 lines should follow the para ending with the words "simply al-Buraq".

8. From British Mandate to the Present Day

Peter Mansfield

The Setting

In the last three decades of the Turkish Ottoman Empire, following the administrative reorganization of 1883, the historical Land of Palestine was divided between the Vilayet (or province) of Beirut in the north and the Sanjak (or district) of Jerusalem to the south. The Sanjak of Jerusalem was autonomous and directly linked to the Ministry of the Interior in Constantinople in view of its importance to the three major monotheistic religions. The Sanjak comprised about two-thirds of Palestine and more than three-quarters of its population. This was estimated in the 1890s at 460,000, of which the great majority were Sunni Muslims. Some 16 per cent were Christian — mainly Greek Orthodox, Latin and Greek Catholics — and about 5 per cent were Jews.

The majority of the Muslims were peasant farmers living in villages, although there was also a substantial number of bedouin, mainly in the south around Beersheba. In the towns, Muslims and Christians were merchants and craftsmen while a few belonged to the Ottoman civil service. Political leadership belonged to the Muslim notables — the large land-owning families and the *ulema* who together formed the local Ottoman ruling class as in other parts of the Empire. The Christian and Jewish communities enjoyed considerable autonomy under the

Millet system. In the early years of the 20th century the Palestinian Arabs shared in the general Arab renaissance throughout the area. Some of them sat as deputies in the Ottoman Parliament of 1908. Several Arabic newspapers were published in Palestine before 1914.

In the early 1880s the Jewish population of Palestine was about 25,000, concentrated almost exclusively in the four 'holy cities' of Jerusalem, Safed, Tiberias and Hebron. Most of these were pious Challakah Jews, which meant that they were supported by funds collected among the Jewish Diaspora for the support of Jewish studies in Palestine. A minority of Jews were also craftsmen and artisans. It was in Jerusalem that the main increase in the Jewish urban population took place in the 19th century, rising from about 3,000 (out of a total of some 11,000) in the 1830s to about 5,000 out of 15,000 in 1850, 10,600 out of 21,000 in 1872 and 30,000 Jews compared with 10,900 Christians and 7,700 Muslims in Jerusalem in 1899. From 1860 onwards new Jewish suburbs were built outside the Old City.

There were several attempts to create Jewish agricultural communities in Palestine before the early 1880s on a philanthropic basis, but it was the last two decades of the 19th century, when the pogroms of Russian Jews took place and belief in the possibility of assimilation of Jews in Eastern Europe declined, that saw the growth of *political* Zionism or Jewish nationalism. This had the aim of intensive colonization of the land by Jewish settlers and the revival of the Hebrew language and culture. By 1900 some 22 Zionist colonies had been established with financial support from Baron Edmond de Rothschild. The movement received a wholly new impetus from the publication of Theodor Herzl's *Der Judenstaat* (1896) and the establishment of organized Zionism with the first Zionist Congress in 1897. The second Aliya or wave of immigration of Jews of 1904-7 was different from the first in the important respect that it aimed to develop an autonomous and exclusive community of Jews in Palestine, relying only on Jewish labour. As a result the alarm and opposition of the Palestinan Arabs intensified. They expressed their opposition to Zionist immigration forcefully to the Ottoman authorities through the notables. Some of the resentment was against large landowners, many of them absentee families of Lebanon, who sold their lands to the Zionists. In certain cases also the Ottoman Government sold state lands to the Zionists where the peasants were unable to pay their taxes.

By the First World War the number of Zionist settlements had increased from 22 to 47 although the majority of the Jewish population remained Orthodox Challakah.

The Great Powers of Europe, collectively now so much more powerful than the declining Ottoman Empire, took a close interest in the affairs of Greater Syria and of the Holy Land in particular. France had long regarded herself as the protector of the Catholics and indeed had intervened militarily on behalf of the Maronites of Lebanon in 1860-61. Tsarist Russia considered herself protector of the Orthodox Christians and Britain of the Jews, Druze and Protestants. It was Britain which opened the first European Consulate in Jerusalem in 1839 and for many years the principal concern of the British Consul was the protection of the Jews. In 1840 Lord Palmerston, the British Prime Minister, told the British Ambassador in Constantinople that the Turkish Sultan should encourage Jewish immigration into Palestine as a check to the ambitions of Mohammed Ali of Egypt.

Britain and the Balfour Declaration

Much has been written and more has yet to be written about the three sets of conflicting promises and undertakings made between the Allies in World War I and between the Allies and Arabs and Jews. Briefly they come under three headings:

1. Promises to the Arabs to support their independence and

self-determination in all the former provinces of the Ottoman Empire in which they were a clear majority of the population. These undertakings were made in the so-called McMahon-Hussein correspondence between the British Government's representative in Cairo and the Sherif Hussein of Mecca who with British encouragement declared the Arab Revolt against the Turks in June 1916; in the Anglo-French Declaration of November 1918; in the Covenant of the League of Nations and elsewhere.

2. The secret accord between Britain and France known as the Sykes-Picot Agreement of 1916, according to which they undertook to divide most of the Arab Middle East into areas either of their direct control or spheres of influence. From this, in an amended form, was derived the Mandate system under which Britain had the Mandate from the League of Nations for Iraq and Palestine and France for Syria and Lebanon.

3. The Balfour Declaration of November 1918 which was an undertaking made in the form of a letter from the British Foreign Secretary Arthur Balfour to a leading British Zionist, Lord Rothschild, saying that "His Majesty's Government view with favour the establishment in Palestine of a national home for the Jewish people . . . it being clearly understood that nothing shall be done which may prejudice the civil and religious rights of the existing non-Jewish communities in Palestine." These 'non-Jewish communities' at the time formed some 93 per cent of the total population of about 750,000.

All three of these sets of promises are of concern to us here but primarily the last. However they were interpreted, the first two were incompatible with each other but they did not produce insoluble problems. Britain and France did not attempt to colonize the mandated territories with British or French settlers — indeed they would have been prevented from doing so under the terms of the Mandate. Therefore, although the struggle for Arab independence was often bitter and prolonged it was resolved within a generation of the collapse of the Ottoman Empire. Only Palestine was different because, as a result of the Balfour Declaration, it became the object of permanent Zionist settlement.

What were Britain's motives in making the Balfour Declaration? They were of three kinds. The first might be called 'biblical', i.e. it was derived from a literal interpretation of the Old Testament prophecies about the return of the Jews to the Promised Land which were part of the education of all Victorian Englishmen and hence of the members of the British Cabinet. (It made no difference if they were non-believers like Winston Churchill.) The second motive was an immediate war aim of securing the support of World Jewry for the Allies — and especially American Jews. The Allies feared that Russian anti-semitism would turn the Jews against them and also that Germany was preparing to pre-empt them by promising to support Zionism. The third type of motive was imperial-strategic — the belief that a pro-British Zionist Palestine would be the best protection for vital British imperial interests. As L. S. Amery, a future Colonial Secretary, wrote in a War Office memorandum in October 1918: "Strategically Palestine and Egypt go together. Not only is Palestine a necessary buffer to the Suez Canal, but conversely any defence of Palestine would have its main base at Kantara . . . *Palestine is geographically practically in the centre of the British Empire.*"

Of the real Zionist intentions, despite the qualified and guarded terms of the Balfour Declaration, there can be no doubt. Correspondence now published between the Zionist leader in Britain, Dr. Chaim Weizman, and both British officials and his own friends makes it abundantly clear that this real objective was to turn Palestine into a Jewish state or 'Jewish Commonwealth' as he usually called it, in which Jews would be the rulers and the majority. Jerusalem would of course be the capital (See *Palestine Papers 1917-1922 Seeds of Conflict*, compiled and annotated by Doreen Ingrams, London 1972). The question is how far members of the British Government both understood and approved the real Zionist motive. The answer is that while nearly all understood, some (such as Curzon and Montagu) disapproved and foresaw disaster, others believed that compromise between Zionist and Arab aspirations could be found while a third group, which included both Balfour and Lloyd George the Prime Minister, clearly intended that sooner or later Palestine should become a Jewish state. Proof of this may be found in Balfour's now famous Cabinet memorandum of 1919 — one of the frankest and most shocking documents in British imperial history. In this he freely admitted that all the statements by the Allies supporting Arab self-determination were lies because they intended to violate their promises — especially those in relation to Palestine. He added: "The four great powers are committed to Zionism and Zionism, be it right or wrong, good or bad, is rooted in age-long tradition, in present needs, in future hopes, of far profounder import than the desires and prejudices of the 700,000 Arabs who now inhabit that ancient land." From the end of World War I disaster in Palestine was virtually a certainty.

Military Administration 1917-20

Jerusalem was captured by British forces under Allenby in December 1917 and a British military administration was set up in Palestine. A general framework for British rule was provided under Article 22 of the League of Nations Covenant signed in June 1919. This recognized the provisional independence of the former Ottoman Arab provinces subject to the assistance of a mandatory power in whose selection the wishes of the communities themselves were to be consulted. These wishes were never in fact consulted except by the American King-Crane commission, with which Britain and France refused to co-operate. This found an overwhelming majority of the population were opposed to Zionism and feared the Zionists intended to dispossess the Arabs.

Although the mandate for Palestine was not approved by the League of Nations until 1922, Britain at once began preparing to implement the terms of the Balfour Declaration. In March 1918 Weizman arrived in Jerusalem at the head of a Zionist Commission. At first he was deeply depressed by what he discovered. On April 18 he wrote to his wife: "... it was sad — very sad. We have so little here — hardly a single Jewish institution to delight the eye or the heart. But instead, how much alien power, threatening and austere — Minarets and bells, cupolas reaching up to the skies; a constant reminder that Jerusalem is not a Jewish town". His heart cried out, he told his wife, when he saw the Jewish quarter, "... filth and infection, indescribable poverty, century-old ignorance and fanaticism. To organize Jerusalem, to bring some order into this hell, will take a long time and need much strength, courage and patience." The war had taken a terrible toll of all the population of Palestine. The number of Jews had fallen from about 80,000 to about 55,000.

Weizman soon realized that he had underestimated Arab opposition to his designs. He also saw that if the democratic principle of self-determination were applied, Palestine would soon become an independent Arab state. Accordingly he wrote to Balfour on 30 May 1918 that "it does not take into account the superiority of the Jew to the Arab, the fundamental difference between Arab and Jew". Balfour, as we have seen, was sympathetic. In February 1919 he wrote to the Prime Minister: "The weak point of our position of course is that in the case of Palestine *we deliberately and rightly decline to accept the principle of self-determination*. If the present inhabitants were consulted they would unquestionably give an anti-Jewish verdict. Our justification for our policy is that we regard Palestine as being absolutely exceptional, that we consider the question of the Jews outside Palestine as one of world importance."

Despite Weizman's pessimism, events did not favour the Arabs. In July 1919 a General Syrian Congress held in Damascus and attended by Palestinian delegates passed a resolution electing Amir Feisal, son of Hussein, now King of the Hejaz, King of a United Syria, including Palestine, and rejecting the Balfour Declaration. But a year later Feisal was deposed by the French while Britain pursued her own policies in Palestine. Arab opposition intensified in serious rioting in April 1920. A commission of enquiry — the first of many — attributed the riots to non-fulfilment of the promises of independence and the fear of economic and political subjection to the Zionists. In July the military administration was ended and the Zionist Herbert Samuel, who had first proposed the idea of a Jewish National Home to the Cabinet, was appointed High Commissioner at the head of a civilian administration.

The Mandate

(a) *1920-23 Impasse*

Some of the British administrators of the Palestine Mandate were pro-Zionist, some were pro-Arab; nearly all of them were primarily pro-British. Most of them, including Samuel, attempted to achieve a balance between Zionist and Arab inspirations but ultimately this proved impossible. In 1920 Samuel made a conciliatory gesture towards the Arabs by recognizing Hajj al-Amin Husseini, the popular candidate for election as Mufti of Jerusalem and hence leader of the Muslim community. But at the same time Britain proceeded with the implementation of the Balfour Declaration by announcing a quota of 16,500 Jewish immigrants for the first year. This provoked Arab opposition which was organized in the form of Christian-Muslim associations throughout the country. Further anti-Zionist rioting in May 1921 resulted in another

In July 1922 the Mandate instrument for Palestine was approved by the League Council, its preamble incorporating the Balfour Declaration and stressing the Jewish historical connection with Palestine. Article 2 made the Mandatory responsible for placing the country "under such political, economic, and administrative conditions as will secure the establishment of the Jewish National Home . . . and the development of self-governing institutions". Article 4 allowed for the establishment of a Jewish Agency to advise and cooperate with the Palestine administration in matters connected with the Jewish National Home. Article 6 required that the Palestine administration "while ensuring that the rights and position of other sections of the population are not prejudiced" under suitable conditions would facilitate Jewish immigration and "close settlement of Jews on the land". In September 1922 the East Bank of Jordan or Transjordan, although included in the British Mandate of Palestine, was excluded from the scope of the Balfour Declaration, under protest from the Zionists, and on September 29th 1923 the Mandate came officially into force.

commission of enquiry which again attributed the riots to fear of Jewish immigration. Impressed by the strength of Arab opposition the British Government issued a White Paper in June 1922 as an interpretation of its concept of a Jewish National Home. This strongly denied that Palestine as a whole should be converted into a Jewish national home or Jewish state but only that such a home would be established in Palestine. Jewish immigration would not exceed the absorptive capacity of the country and steps would be taken to set up a legislative council. These proposals were rejected by the Arabs both in principle because they were demanding the cancellation of the Balfour Declaration and on the practical ground that Jewish immigration, which had a political objective, should not be regulated by an economic criterion.

(b) *1923-29 False Calm*

In 1923 the British High Commissioner tried to win Arab cooperation by the offer first of a legislative council and then of an Arab Agency but both offers were rejected by the Arabs as falling far short of national objectives which remained the cancellation of the Balfour Declaration. Although the proposed legislative council would have had 9 Muslim Arabs, 3 Christian Arabs, 3 Jewish and 11 official members, the Arabs objected because the Jews and officials voting together would outnumber the Arabs and they opposed in principle any Jewish membership. Many still wonder whether the Arabs would not have been better advised to accept the proposal and use the council to their advantage. Certainly the Zionists were alarmed by the proposal. In the event the Arabs boycotted the elections successfully.

Nevertheless the years 1923-29 were relatively quiet. The main reason was a slump in Zionist immigration which in 1927-28 fell to zero and Arab fears were allayed. If this situation had continued, it is possible that a peaceful solution could have been found, with a substantial and active Jewish minority within a predominantly Arab independent state, even if this would not have satisfied Zionist aspirations.

Despite the economic recession suffered by the Zionists, mainly owing to a slump in Eastern Europe, they continued to consolidate themselves socially, culturally and economically in the towns and cities. In 1925 Balfour faced hostile Arab crowds when he came to Palestine for the first time for the inauguration of the Hebrew University in Jerusalem. Then in August 1929 negotiations were concluded for the formation of an enlarged Jewish Agency in which half the members were Zionist sympathisers of the Diaspora. This gave the Zionists new confidence and at the same time Jewish immigration began to pick up again.

(c) *1929-36 Prelude to Revolt*

Communal clashes which began at the Wailing Wall in August 1929 brought yet another commission of enquiry which again attributed the cause to Arab fears of immigration and Zionist domination. A British technical report established that there was no margin of land available for agricultural settlement by new immigrants and so raised in an acute form the incompatibility of British declared obligations to Zionists and Arabs. A White Paper by the British Colonial Secretary, Lord Passfield in October 1930 gave some priority to Britain's obligations to the Arabs by proposing strict limits to Jewish immigration but in the ensuing uproar in Britain the Prime Minister Ramsay Macdonald backtracked in what the Arabs termed the Black Letter to Weizman, reverting in effect to the 1922 policy. This convinced the Arabs that recommendations in their favour made in Palestine would always be overturned by Zionist influence in Britain.

In December 1931 the Mufti called a Muslim Congress in Jerusalem attended by delegates from 22 Muslim countries to warn against the dangers of Zionism and in 1933 a boycott of Zionist and British goods was proclaimed.

Meanwhile Hitler's accession to power in Germany gave a great impetus to Jewish immigration, which rose to 30,000 in 1933, 42,000 in 1934 and 61,000 in 1935, although the majority of immigrants still came from outside Germany. Although the Arabs, suffering from internal divisions and rivalry, continually failed to articulate Arab political demands effectively, the Arab political parties did combine in November 1935 to demand the cessation of Jewish immigration, the prohibition of land transfer and the establishment of democratic institutions. In December the British administration offered a legislative council of 28 members on which the Arabs would have 14 seats and the Jews 8. Although not represented in proportion to their numbers, the Arabs were prepared to consider the proposal but the Zionists attacked it bitterly as amounting to an Arab constitutional stranglehold on Palestine. The subsequent debate in the House of Commons, in which the legislative council proposal was attacked by both parties as anti-Zionist and the Arab case went largely by default, helped to touch off a smouldering Arab rebellion. Arab fears were enhanced by the knowledge that the Zionists were secretly building up arms supplies in Palestine.

(d) *1936-39 The Arab Rebellion*

In April 1936 the Arab political parties formed an Arab Higher Committee presided over by the Mufti which called a general strike. This was maintained for six months and simultaneously Arab rebels, joined by volunteers from neighbouring Arab countries, took to the hills. It amounted to a peasants' revolt on a national scale. A Royal Commission headed by Lord Peel reported in 1937, declaring the Mandate unworkable and British obligations to Arabs and Jews irreconcilable. It therefore recommended the partition of the country. The Zionist attitude towards partition was ambivalent. For the first time Britain had officially proposed an independent Jewish state. The size of the territory was much larger than current Jewish landholdings and the report even proposed the forcible transfer of the Arab population. But although Weizman was prepared to consider it, the majority of the Zionist leadership wanted wider boundaries for the Jewish state. The Arabs, on the other hand, were appalled by the prospect of the dismemberment of their country along sectarian lines and the revolt intensified.

The rebellion took on an anti-British rather than anti-Jewish character. The members of the Arab Higher Committee were arrested and deported (although Hajj Amin escaped). A technical report on partition declared it unworkable because of the huge transfer of the Arab population that would be required and the British Government withdrew the proposal. The rebellion continued into 1939 but was eventually put down with an immense show of British force. It had been the most sustained anti-colonial revolt of the first half of the 20th century. Arab casualties were conservatively estimated at 3,112 killed and 1,775 wounded. In addition 110 Arabs were hanged and over 5,000 held in detention in 1939. The Arabs of Palestine were disastrously weakened as a consequence of the revolt.

(e) *1939-45 World War II*

With the inevitable approach of war with Germany, and following the failure of a Round Table Conference on Palestine in which the Arab states participated, Britain issued its own policy statement in the White Paper of May 1939 with the aim of neutralizing Arab hostility. Starting from the assumption that the pledges of the Balfour Declaration had been largely fulfilled, the White Paper declared a limitation of Jewish immigration to 75,000 over five years after which the level would be subject to Arab approval. Palestine would become an independent state in ten years. The Arab response was lukewarm, partly because they no longer trusted Britain, also because they still considered the quota too high. The Zionists were bitterly opposed to the White Paper and turned deeply hostile to Britain. The Arabs, on the other hand, remained largely quiescent during the war and thousands cooperated with the Allied war effort.

The Zionists were in the difficult position of wanting to fight the White Paper while cooperating with Britain in the struggle against Hitler. As Britain began to try to prevent illegal Zionist immigration, underground Jewish organizations became active. As the tide of war turned away from the Middle East in 1942 and at the same time the full horror of Hitler's treatment of the Jews in Europe became revealed, anti-British terrorist actions by the Zionists intensified.

The end of the war saw the Palestinian Jewish community

vastly strengthened. Already by 1939 the Jewish population had risen to 445,000 or 30 per cent of the total. Land holdings had more than doubled (although they still amounted to less than 8 per cent of the total land area). During the war a Jewish brigade group was formed and 27,000 Palestinian Jews joined the British armed forces. A major Jewish munitions industry developed supplying the Allies and a vast network for the theft of arms from British Middle East installations was uncovered. It was equally important that Zionists gained increasing support from the USA to which they had shifted their major political effort in 1939. In May 1942 at a Zionist conference held at the Biltmore Hotel in New York, David Ben-Gurion on behalf of the Jewish Agency gained support for unrestricted Jewish immigration and a Jewish army and the establishment of Palestine as a Jewish commonwealth. American politicians competed with each other in expressing pro-Zionist views.

(f) *1947-48 Partition and War*

Exhausted by the War and aware of the difficulties ahead, Britain's newly-elected Labour Government decided to secure American co-responsibility in Palestine. An Anglo-US commission of enquiry recommended in 1946 the immediate admission of 100,000 Jews and the abolition of the 1940 limitations on land sales, thus effectively reverting to the 1922 policy. But at the same time the commission criticized the resurgence of Jewish underground forces which it estimated at 65,000. President Truman at once endorsed the recommendation for 100,000 immigrants but Britain insisted on the prior disbandment of the Jewish forces and continued to try to prevent the wave of illegal immigration, thereby incurring world-wide condemnation.

As threats by the Arab states increased against British and US interests, Arab rights in Palestine were disregarded, but with strong contrary pressure from the US, Britain decided to hand the whole problem to the UN, in despair at finding its own solution. A UN commission of enquiry recommended on August 31 in a majority report the partition of Palestine into Arab and Jewish states, which should retain an economic union, and with Jerusalem and its environs to be international. These recommendations were adopted by the UN General Assembly on November 29 1947, with the US and USSR in favour and the US exerting strong pressure on smaller states. Opposition came from the Islamic Asian states.

The Zionists welcomed the resolution, which gave them 55 per cent of the land area of Palestine and an independent state at a time when there were 678,000 Jews in Palestine compared with 1,269,000 Arabs. The Arabs were violently opposed both in principle and because there were to be almost as many Arabs as Jews in the Zionist state. Unable and unwilling to impose partition, Britain declared that it would abandon the Mandate on May 15 1948.

Communal fighting started immediately and civil war soon spread. The Arab League states pledged full support short of direct military intervention and some 3,000 volunteers from outside were organized. The Zionists mobilized their military strength and redoubled their efforts to bring in immigrants. When in March 1948 the US expressed opposition to forcible partition and called for reconsideration of the problem by the UN the Zionists redoubled their efforts to create a fait accompli. During April they launched major offensive operations which included the massacre by Irgunist terrorists of the villagers of Deir Yassin. The Arabs of Palestine, disorganized and badly led and ill-equipped in civil defence, collapsed and tens of thousands of refugees streamed in terror into the neighbouring states. The Zionist offensive, combined with psychological warfare, was highly effective in driving the Arabs away. Already before the British departure the majority of Palestinian Arabs had become refugees.

Zionist State

(1) *1948-67*

On the day that the British Mandate ended the regular armies of Syria, Transjordan, Iraq and Egypt crossed the frontiers of Palestine to help the Palestinian Arabs. Despite some earlier successes by the Arabs, including the near capture of Jerusalem, the war ended in 1949 with Arab defeat and the Zionists in possession of some 78 per cent of Palestine which they declared as the State of Israel.

Of Jerusalem only the Eastern part, including the Old City, where the 1,700 inhabitants of the Jewish Quarter surrendered to the Jordanian Army, remained in Arab hands. Although the UN had declared for the internationalization of the city, it had no means of defending it physically and never elaborated a detailed Statute for Jerusalem as it had resolved. The plan for internationalizing the city presented by the UN Mediator Count Bernadotte was rejected by both Arabs and Jews but the UN General Assembly reaffirmed on December 11th 1948 that Jerusalem should be "under effective UN control". The Palestine Conciliation Commission just appointed was instructed to prepare a detailed proposal for an international regime for Jerusalem while the Security Council was to ensure the demilitarization of the city. But the UN was quite unable to enforce these decisions — just as General Assembly resolutions requiring that the Palestinian Arabs who had left should be given the choice of returning to their homes or receiving compensation remained void.

The population of Jerusalem had risen during the Mandate from 63,000 in 1922 to 165,000 in 1948 but the Jewish proportion remained fairly constant at about 60 per cent. After 1948 the population of West Jerusalem rapidly expanded to about 170,000 in 1967. In 1950 the Knesset declared Jerusalem to be the capital of Israel and the Knesset and government ministries were established there although the great majority of countries refused to move their diplomatic missions from Tel-Aviv. In 1950 and 1952 repeated resolutions for the internationalization of the city were moved but without effect. Jerusalem was in fact partitioned as Jordan only allowed access to East Jerusalem to Palestinian Arabs living in Israel at Christmas and Easter. In 1950, following a vote by the notables of the West Bank, Jordan annexed the West Bank including East Jerusalem to the Hashemite Kingdom of Jordan.

1967 — Annexation and Absorption

The Arabs as a whole did not accept the fait accompli of the loss of nearly 80 per cent of Palestine and twenty years of armed truce interspersed with war and violent clashes ensued. The third Arab-Israeli War of June 1967 ended with Israel's occupation of the whole of the West Bank to the River Jordan. On June 29th Israel applied to East Jerusalem the Israeli "law, jurisdiction and administration." Israeli lawyers remain divided as to whether this amounts to annexation. The status of the inhabitants is also ambiguous. They have Israeli identity cards and the right to vote in Jerusalem's municipal elections but they do not have Israeli citizenship (which would give them the right to claim back property elsewhere in Palestine where many of them originate).

In 1967 Israel extended the municipal boundaries of Jerusalem southwards to the edge of Bethlehem and northwards towards Ramallah and embarked on an extensive building programme both to revive Jewish life in the Old City and to increase the Jewish population of the city as a whole by ringing Jerusalem with new suburbs. As a consequence the Jewish population has increased to some 290,000. However, the building programme has slowed down in the past 2½ years; rents are high and many Jewish families have been unable to move into the city. Israeli commentators have noted with alarm that the Arab population of the city has risen by natural increase by nearly 50 per cent during the past 12 years and the proportion of Arabs in East Jerusalem has actually risen from 26 to 28 per cent.

Conclusion

In this paper I have not dealt with the status and situation of Jerusalem in isolation but within the context first of the British Mandate and then of the Israeli and Jordanian regimes which succeeded it. I believe that this is unavoidable because the fate of Jerusalem in the first half of the 20th century was determined by the terms of the British Mandate for Palestine. This incorporated the Balfour Declaration, which in the eyes of the Zionists and also those who held most power and responsibility for implementing it, specifically denied the Arab right to self-determination. If it had not been for the British Mandate — or even if Palestine had become independent at any time between the two World Wars — there is no doubt that the State of Israel could not have been created. This does not mean that Jerusalem would have been internationalized because this was generally against the wishes of both Arabs and Jews and it is difficult to see how internationalization could have been imposed. What is certain is that Jerusalem would not have become the capital of a Zionist state although it might well have had a Jewish majority within a Palestine State which would have been predominantly Muslim and Christian Arab.

9. The Conflict on Jerusalem: Causes and Contradictions

Dr. Afzal Iqbal

Uru Salema, the city of peace, was founded almost five thousand years ago by the Jebusite Arabs, kinsmen of the Canaanites, a deeply cultured tribe. They were followed by the Philistines after whom the region came to be known as Palestine of which Jerusalem remained the capital. The Hebrew tribesmen began to infiltrate into this area in small numbers in the thirteenth century B.C. and slowly succeeded in consolidating themselves until David took control of Jerusalem in 922 B.C. He built a palace and a large garrison. Solomon set up a temple. The Hebrew rule was shortlived and did not last more than 70 years. The Babylonians took over and destroyed the Jewish temple, taking Jews into captivity. The Romans who followed destroyed part of the town including the Jewish temple. Julius Hedrian completely smashed the rest of the city and built a temple for Jupiter on the site of Solomon's temple and placed a statue of Jupiter in it. He changed the name of Jerusalem into Jolia Capitolona in A.D. 130.

When Muslims wrested the town from the Romans in 638 A.D. (17 AH) it was known as Ilya, the house of God, the name which appears in the covenant signed by Caliph Omar. Strangely the only request that Archbishop Sophronius made to Caliph Omar at the time of surrender was that the Jews should not be allowed back into Jerusalem. And thereby hangs a tale.

The fall of Jerusalem to the Muslims was not an isolated event. It was part of the pattern which emerged from Arabia in the Seventh century A.D. Rising from Mecca, the forces of Islam flashed into Syria, of which Palestine was a part, traversed the whole breadth of Northern Africa, and then leaping the strait of Gibraltor; hammered at the doors of Europe. The Muslims conquered Sicily and reached as far as the Campagna and Abruzzi in the South. Using Spain as a springboard they jumped into Provence, Northern Italy and even to Switzerland. From its stronghold in Spain and Sicily, Islam transmitted powerful cultural influences to the whole of Europe which was at that time sunk deep in superstition, ignorance and poverty. It is a paradox of history that the forces which helped generate a sense of identity and led to the Renaissance—rebirth—of Europe, should become the victim of the newly found confidence and strength. Christian Europe reacted in the eleventh century to the challenge of Islam by declaring an all-out war against it. Pope Urban in a speech on November 26, 1095, urged his followers to enter upon the road to the Holy Sepulchre, wrest it from the wicked race, and subject it to themselves. The rallying cry was 'Deus Vult' (God wills it). Thus were the Crusades launched with great fanfare. The restless, the romantic, the adventurous all joined the race. To the mass of men in France, Lorraine, Italy and Sicily, with their depressed economic and social conditions, the adventure offered an opportunity to exploit the legendary wealth of the East. To the regional rulers of Europe it came as a welcome opportunity to fulfill their territorial ambitions, and to the Pope it provided an occasion to create an edifice of artificial unity in the Church which was divided into a number of factions. When the motley hordes of Christians moved towards Syria to conquer Jerusalem, the country provided a sorry spectacle of division and impotence. Almost every town of any consequence had its own ruler. It was not surprising, therefore, that Jerusalem was not able to resist the crusaders' onslaught and fell to the Christian forces in 1099 AD. Muslims were mercilessly massacred. The Pope was informed by his lieutenants. "God was appeased by our humility. He delivered the City and its enemies to us. And if you desire to know what was done with the enemy, know that in Solomon's porch and its temple our men rode in the blood of Saracens up to the knees of their horses." For the first time in Muslim history Latin states were established on Muslim soil. Baldwin was crowned king at Bethlehem on Christmas day, 1100 AD. With the establishment of this kingdom, and with the capture of Jerusalem, the proclaimed objective of the Crusades was achieved. The war should have ended at this point but Christian Europe had other ideas. A fleet sailed to the coast of the Red Sea to conquer the Hejaz and cut off the pilgrimage routes to Mecca and Medina. The Crusaders had planned to attack the city of the Prophet and take out his holy corpse from the tomb. But this dream was not realised. The Muslim fleet inflicted a crushing defeat on the crusaders, burnt their ships and captured their crew.

Eighty seven years after Baldwin was crowned king in Bethlehem, the Muslims recaptured Jerusalem. King Richard, who, full of romantic ideas, proposed that his sister should marry Saladin's brother, Al-Malik al-Adil, and that the two should receive Jerusalem as a wedding present, thus ending the strife between Christians and Muslims. Saladin entered the town at the head of a victorious army on Friday Oct 2, 1187. It was the 27th of Rajab of 582 AH. The day marked the anniversary of the ascension of the Holy Prophet, an event which has invested Jerusalem with great significance. In sharp contrast to the havoc wrought by the crusaders after the capture of Jerusalem, Saladin repopulated the city with Muslims and Christian Arabs and welcomed the Jews back. According to Heinrech Gratez, the 18th century historian of the Jews, Saladin's empire "became a safe asylum to the oppressed Jews.

He behaved justly toward the Jew as indeed he did towards every one, even his bitterest enemies, under him the Jews rose to great prosperity and consequence."

While the crusaders were defeated in the East, they had victories to their credit in Europe. Count Roger seized Palermo in 1071, Syracuse in 1085 and Normans reconquered Sicily by 1091. This was a triumph indeed but it is hardly correct to call it a triumph of cross over Crescent. Count Roger invaded the island for the same reasons which had spurred the Hauteville brothers to many wars against the Christians, including the Pope and both the Eastern and Western emperors. He began the war as the ally of one of the rival Emirs of Sicily, employed Muslim as well as Christian auxiliaries and displayed towards Muslim, Greek and Latin adversaries alike the same admixture of cruelty, cunning, avarice and generosity. His conduct certainly fails to support the rationalisation of ecclesiastical chroniclers who extolled the Normans as ardent champions of the faith.

The Christian gains in Spain were indeed impressive, Toledo fell in 1085, Cordova followed in 1236 and Seville in 1248. With the fall of Grenada in 1492, the last vestige of Muslim power in Europe disappeared, and Ferdinand and Isabella reigned supreme. In the process about three million Muslims were banished or executed. Inquisition is a peculiarly Catholic institution, indicative of the intolerance and tyranny that was let loose in a war which was ostensibly fought for moral values of Christianity.

The simple fact which emerges from the history of Crusades is that Christian Europe was determined to wipe out Islam from the face of the earth. It exterminated the Muslims in Spain after the most ferocious and merciless persecution known to history.

The proclaimed aim of the Crusades was to wrest the Holy lands from the hands of the Muslims. This slogan had a tremendous psychological appeal for the mass of Christians whose frenzy was roused to a pitch wholly unparalleled either before or since the Crusades. Little did the common man realise that the recovery of Palestine was but a pretext on the part of the Pope and the powerful regional rulers of Europe to achieve their own individual ambitions. Little did he realise that he was being used as a mere pawn in the hands of religious and political vested interests. Different parties engaged in the crusades sought to achieve different ends. The appearance of unity on the surface was deceptive indeed. But no effort was spared to marshall all available forces for the destruction of Islam. Aggression went hand in hand with subversion. Warriors, poets, philosophers, preachers, propagandists all joined in a common endeavour to crush a cause which was seen as a danger to the feudal exploitative society backed by the Church.

There was a division of labour. While some fought in the battlefield, others manned the intellectual front, the common objective being the destruction of Islam. In the eleventh century, all Europe was mobilising to fight side by side with Spain in the *Reconquesta*. The Latin authors directed their attention to the Prophet's life with little regard for accuracy and gave free rein to the 'ignorance of triumphant imagination.' Mohammad was painted as a magician who had destroyed the Church in Africa and in the East by magic and deceit, and had made his success doubly sure by allowing sexual promiscuity. Legends from world folklore, from classical literature, from Byzantine stories of Islam and even from Muslim sources (after vicious distortion by Eastern Christians) were made to adorn the image. Guibert de Nogent acknowledged that he had no written sources and gave only the *plebeia opinio* 'It is safe to speak evil of one whose malignity exceeds whatever ill can be spoken'.

This was the basis of the criticism of Christian ideologues who crusaded without any scruples. The epics reached the greatest heights of vicious invention. The Muslims were charged with idolatrous worship. Their chief idol was Mohammad, whom, with few exceptions, the troubadours thought to be the chief god of the Saracens. His statues were of rich substances and of enormous size. Varying numbers of acolytes went with him, the figure reaching 700 in a German author of the 13th century, Der Stricker.

But with the failure of the crusades in the East came a general change in the polemical image of a diabolical foe to a more serious concept. Peter the Venerable financed a company of translators of the Quran in 1143. Roger Bacon talked of replacing military endeavour by missionary effort. In 1276, Raymond Lull founded at Miramar a college of friars for the study of Arabic. The Council of Vienne in 1312 ratified Bacon's and Lull's ideas and resolved to create chairs of Arabic and Tartar at the Universities of Paris, Louvian and Salamanca. The futility of the military method was realised and Oriental Studies emerged as an instrument of crusades.

We must revert to Jerusalem, which remains throughout this period the focal point of Christian attention, contention and conflict. The city of peace had no peace. Since the Romans, the land came under the successive rule of Byzantines, Persians, Arabs, Seljuks, Turks, Crusaders, Saracens, Memluks, Moghuls, the Ottomans, and finally the British who gifted away what did not belong to them, to the Jews for services rendered.

In the 19th century Christian Europe still considered the Muslim East as an enemy but an enemy which was doomed to defeat. Failure of the Muslim world in the technological race was attributed to Islam which became a synonym for cultural stagnation and backwardness. The attack upon Islam now became more fierce for the popular press now spread the prejudice to far more people than was possible in the age of Crusades. In the second part of the 19th century the European Jews joined the Christians in the crusade against Islam. An emissary of the Rothschilds approached Sultan Abdul Hamid with an offer to pay off Turkey's huge debts in exchange for Palestine as a homeland for the Jews.

Now Pan Islamism was considered a deadly peril, not only by the Christians by the Jews who had always enjoyed the patronage of Muslims in Spain and elsewhere. They now joined hands with Christians in order to realise their own territorial ambition. Zionism came to have the blessings of the European Christian. Strange bed follows came together. The Zionists first turned to Germany and to France for assistance but they struck a more responsive chord in Britain from whom they obtained the Balfour Declaration in 1917, one week before the capture of Jerusalem by General Allenby.

Now the Crusades were being fought with a difference. Palestine was practically in the centre of the British Empire. It was denied self-determination after the Arab revolt against the Ottomans for Great Britain needed a buffer Jewish state in Palestine to contain the Arabs in the Middle East. Since the Zionists provided the required human element to man the Palestine outpost in Europe's fight against Islam, their services were secured and solemn pledges to Arabs broken with impunity. Lord Curzon was aghast at this treachery. "There is a country with 850,000 Arabs and 30,000 Jews. I refuse to believe that the relation of the Jews which came to an end 1200 years ago, entitle them to any claims whatsoever. Depending on this basis, we do have strong claims to parts of France."

A minority of about eight percent of the population was claiming, with the protection of British bayonets, predominance over the vast Arab majority.

The Crusades continued. Jerusalem was taken "as a Christmas present for the British nation", and Allenby became "Allah en nebi". The official history published by the British Government records gleefully:

"When the time came for the great and simple act of the solemn entry of General Allenby into Jerusalem, and the Arab prophecy was fulfilled that when the Nile had flowed into Palestine, the prophet (Al Nebi) from the West should drive the Turk from Jerusalem, the inhabitants mustered courage to gather in a great crowd."

It is significant that when the British General entered Jerusalem on Dec. 11, 1917, he was flanked by the French and the Italian representatives, reminiscent of the days when Richard had a mixed European Army against Palestine. The show of unity was again empty. The element of deceit was again obvious. Allenby refused to allow the Balfour Declaration to be published in Palestine, although it was made on Nov 2, when the third battle of Ghaza was in full swing. Not only that. There was no awkwardness on the part of the British in reconciling their pledges to the Arabs, their undertakings to their own allies (the Sykes-Picot Agreement), and yet Allenby insisted that his campaign was not a crusade because like Roger in the eleventh century he was able to enlist some Muslim renegades in his army.

After Saladin's conquest of Jerusalem in 1187, Christian Europe wrested it back after a long haul in 1917. But never during this period of 730 years did the crusades come to a close. They continued on all fronts, and every conceivable effort was made to inflict a fatal blow on Islam. At one stage in the twentieth century all but one Muslim country escaped the colonial clutches of Europe and that too was a decrepit decadent state which was referred to as the sick man of Europe. It was eventually defeated and dismembered. One is simply surprised at the inherent strength and resilience of Islam that out of the debris of death and defeat, it should rise, phoenix like, and spread its wings once again. The muscles and sinews which were corroded over a period of time are flexing once again in a healthy endeavour to regain their strength. If Christian Europe could wait for seven hundred years for the prize of Jerusalem, Muslims can wait a while to redeem their honour. But this time they have to contend not only with Christians but with the Jews, who killed Christ and are now determined, in an unholy alliance, to wipe out Islam which has no quarrel either with Christianity or with Judaism, and has in fact more in common with them than is realised by most.

But the quarrel does not concern the common moral view, it is determined, among other things, by the powerful vested interests in the world as a partner in this conspiracy. All kinds of argument are being advanced in favour of a national home for the Jews in Palestine although the majority of them have been driven out from Europe, as a result of Christian persecution.

The Jews, it must be pointed out, never exercised any kind of sovereignty over the region after the termination of their authority in 586 B.C. If such a clumsy claim were to be accepted, Spain, Portugal, Sicily and parts of France, Bulgaria, Hungary, Rumania and many other countries in the world will have to be restored to Muslims.

The Vatican Ecumenical Council paid a belated homage in October 1965 to the 'Truths' that Islam had handed down concerning God, Jews, Mary and the Apostles. Some people are now coming round to the view that in containing communism Muslim 'errors' are of doubtful importance. In line with Massignon some Christians have been struck by the spiritual values of Islam and are disturbed by the historic injustices of their own people towards Islam. These feeble voices, however, have not had any tangible effect on the intensity of the conflict despite Toynbee's warning that a minority of Jews cannot ever hope to wage a successful war against the Arabs with their vast hinterland, their determination to survive. The Crusades today are not formally led by the Pope. The Christian powers, notably the United States and United Kingdom, provide the gunpowder while the Jews fight the battle. For the second time since the dawn of Islam, Jerusalem is now in enemy hands but the lesson of history seems to have been lost on those who think that they are there to stay. Time is on the side of the Arabs who are becoming increasingly powerful. Their numbers will tell. So will their resources, moral and material.

The world of Islam has always protected the Jew who has been persecuted throughout the ages by Christians. The Crusades have left a legacy of bitterness and ill will but none of it concerns the Jew. He has now pawned his future to the Christian West which cannot sustain for long a state they have created essentially to safeguard their own interests in the Middle East. The interests change. the United Kingdom has now no Empire of which Jerusalem could be a centre and a source of supplies. The need to guard the line of communications and the flow of Arab oil worries the United States more than the traditional colonial power of the area. The British burnt their boats when Anthony Eden invaded the Suez Canal; the Americans could not possibly use force to take over the Arab oil wells without provoking the USSR to retaliate. The prospects of an atomic war are too awesome to contemplate. What deters the Christian West from inflicting further injury on the world of Islam is not their understanding of it but their realisation of their own limitations to achieve their objective which remains unchanged. The old policy of divide and rule is outdated and outmoded. The world of Islam will have to be dealt with on a level of equality and sovereignty. It is the guns of Palestine and the will of the world of Islam which will determine the fate of Jerusalem. It fell to the Christians in 1099. The Muslims wrested it back in 1187. They waited for 88 years but did not forget it. Jerusalem was gifted away by the Christians in 1917 to the Jews. The Muslims can wait. Time is on their side.

The current mood of Zionism is eloquently expressed by Moshe Dayan, the Foreign Minister of Israel, who warns:

"Our forefathers reached in 1948 the frontiers recognised by the partition resolution of 1947. Our generation reached the 1949 frontiers but the generation of the six day war reached the

Suez Canal, the Jordan and the Golan Heights. However, this is not the end. The present truce lines will be followed by other new ones which will extend beyond the Jordan perhaps to Lebanon or even to Central Syria." (The Times, London, Oct. 23, 1973.)

General Sharon, the former C-in-C of Israel, adds:-

"Israel is now a great military power. It will not be affected even if the US chose to stop supplying it with Phantoms. The forces of the Arab States put together are weaker than our power. Israel can in one week run over the area extending from Khartoum to Baghdad and to Algeria."

Let the Muslim world ponder over the significance and implications of this warning. Camp David cannot provide an answer. Those who put Christ on the cross now bear it alongside with the Christian. Muslims will need all their faith, unity, and strength to combat this combined challenge.

To sum up:

(a) The immediate cause of the crusades was the repeated appeal made in 1095 A.D. to Pope Urban II by the Emperor Alexius Comnenus, whose Asiatic possessions had been overrun by the Seljuqs.

(b) The cause of the conflict has no relationship with the course of the crusades whose objective was proclaimed to be the capture of Jerusalem.

(c) The Crusades did not come to an end when Jerusalem was captured by the Christians. They proceeded to inflict further injury on the world of Islam.

(d) Jerusalem was recaptured by the Muslims but they were defeated, expelled and exterminated in the West, which succeeded in re-establishing their hegemony in Spain and Sicily.

(e) The war was waged on many fronts. Failure in the field in the East led to an intensification of the campaign of calumny and vilification of Islam and deliberate distortion.

(f) The tactics have changed over the centuries but the objective viz., the destruction of Islam, has remained unchanged.

(g) With the rise of imperialism and technological supremacy of the West the world of Islam was colonised, exploited, divided, defeated and dismembered. The Arabs were used against Turks but in flagrant violation of all solemn pledges, the British gifted away Palestine to the Zionists, in order to safeguard their own imperial interests. The creation of a buffer Jewish state in Palestine which was practically in the centre of the British Empire, was strategically desirable for Great Britain.

(h) The Arabs of Palestine are descendants of the indigenous inhabitants of the country, who have been in occupation of its since the beginning of history. They have been subjected to alien immigrants whose claim is based upon a historical connection which ceased effectively many centuries ago.

(i) Political Zionism, in collusion with British imperialism, has distorted the whole course of history. The founding fathers were mostly atheists who had no scruples in furthering their political ends by all available means. Religion was not their concern.

(j) Christians who started the crusades have joined hands with Jews in creating a powerful industrial-military centre in the heart of the Muslim world in order to dominate the whole Middle East whose oil supplies are vital to the survival of the industrial West. The Arab Israel conflict is but a consequence of Christian crusades. The history of Arab Israel conflict begins in 1917 with the Balfour Declaration. Before that no quarrel has taken place between Arabs and Jews. The contradictions of the conflict are coming into play, as they did in the thirteenth century, and expose the hollowness of proclaimed objectives.

(k) Time is on the side of the Arabs. They outnumber the Jews and Christians in the region, they have a vast hinterland, they have resources which are vital to the survival of the West. The use of force is not likely to lead to an unqualified success and peace can only be established by conceding to the people of Palestine what has always belonged to them.

(l) It is the Christians who persecuted the Jews and exterminated them in Europe and elsewhere. The Muslims have a history of tolerance and goodwill. In 1971, there were 13,951,000 Jews in the world. The largest Jewish group is in the U.S.A. (5,970,000), with the USSR next with 2,620,000. About 14 million Jews are scattered over 38 states with a population of 4 billion. How come that they have been billeted on Palestine? Jews never exercised any kind of sovereignty over the region after the termination of their authority in 586 B.C. Moslem rule has remained effective since 637 A.D. until the British occupation in 1917.

(m) There is no evidence that the West is prepared to come to terms with the world of Islam. But Christian Europe does not command the power which it once wielded. The USA was defeated in Vietnam. No power on earth can intimidate the people of Palestine to perpetual subjugation. No combination of powers can take away their inalienable right of self-determination.

(n) Jerusalem is the first Qibla of Islam. Muslims have guarded it with their blood and are not likely to surrender it. An artificially created state cannot last long in a state of conflict and confrontation. Time is on the side of Arabs who can wait.

(o) Crusades have left a legacy of hate and ill will. It's time to redress the situation for Christians cannot continue to vilify Islam and yet enlist its cooperation. In the fast shrinking world of today they cannot afford either to ignore the growing strength of Islam. It is for them to prove their credentials. They can make a beginning in Palestine. Let Crusades come to an end!

PART THREE

Jerusalem Today and Tomorrow

10. Jerusalem and International Organisations

John Reddaway

The international organisations with which we are concerned here are the League of Nations and the United Nations, including its specialised agencies and subsidiary organs. There have been—and are—other organisations, particularly religious, operating on an international plane and taking a special interest in Jerusalem. One could spend much time discussing their attitudes and activities. The role of the World Zionist Organisation, for example, in propagating the absurd idea that Jerusalem belongs to the Jews, wherever they may be throughout the world, in a peculiar way giving them a unique and exclusive title to sovereign possession of the City overriding the rights of others, including those whose ancestors have inhabited Jerusalem from time immemorial—that is a topic that could occupy hours of debate. I do not believe, however, that a widely diffused discussion embracing any and all organisations with a claim to an international character and an interest in Jerusalem is what the organisers of this Seminar had in mind; nor that such a discussion would serve any very useful purpose.

At the outset I would like to make clear my debt to others for most of the matter included in my paper. Where such respected and acknowledged authorities exist as Henry Cattan and Professor and Mrs. Tom Mallison it would be foolish not to avail oneself of their scholarship. I have drawn heavily on a recent

UN publication prepared by the Mallisons for the Committee on the Exercise of the Inalienable Rights of the Palestinian People. It is entitled "An International Law Analysis of the major United Nations Resolutions concerning the Palestine Question" and like everything the Mallisons have produced on this question is imbued not only with penetrating scholarship but also with generous sympathy and understanding for the injustice inflicted on the Palestinians. Likewise I have relied much on Henry Cattan's masterly presentation of facts and arguments in his books: "Palestine, the Arabs and Israel" and "Palestine and International Law" and also on material he presented at a seminar held in London in the autumn of 1977 on the theme of "Peace and the Palestinians". For anyone toiling in the vineyard of the Palestinian cause his writings have become an indispensable *vade mecum*. There is, I suppose, bound to be some overlap in our treatment of the topics assigned to us. But if I now trespass on his ground, I wish to make it clear that I am merely following where his footsteps lead.

With appreciation and respect I would also like to mention another recent publication which I found valuable when preparing this paper. It is "A Study on Jerusalem" by His Royal Highness Crown Prince Hassan bin Talal published by Longman. It provides a succinct, well-documented survey of the juridical status of the City of Jerusalem.

The League of Nations need not, I think, detain us long. The Mandate granted to Britain in 1922 does not contain specific mention of Jerusalem. No one at that time questioned that the City formed part and parcel of the territory of Palestine, however that was defined. It is however relevant to observe that the mandate incorporated in its preamble the text of the Balfour Declaration, including the assurance that nothing would be done to prejudice the civil and religious rights of existing non-Jewish (that is primarily Arab) communities in Palestine. In Article 6 it required the Administration of Palestine, that is the

Mandate Government, to facilitate Jewish immigration; but this was conditioned by a requirement to ensure "that the rights and position of other sections of the population are not prejudiced". Zionist apologists have tried to argue that the reference in the Declaration to "civil and religious rights" was limited and meant something less than political rights; and hence that the assertion of Jewish political sovereignty over Palestine, including Jerusalem, was not incompatible with the Declaration. The argument is untenable not only on any reasonable interpretation of the words "civil and religious" but also in view of the terms of the Mandate itself which spoke, without qualification or limitation of "the rights and position" of other sections of the population. Moreover the authors of the Declaration, that is, the then British Government, made their position clear at the time. Shortly after issuing the Declaration they sent a special message to the Sharif Hussein of Mecca that the purpose of facilitating the return of Jews to Palestine would be pursued only "in so far as is compatible with the freedom of the existing population, both economic and political". At the very time when it accepted the Mandate, the then British Government issued a White Paper in which they affirmed that they had not at any time contemplated "the disappearance or the subordination of the Arab population, language or culture in Palestine". Seventeen years later in another White Paper, the British Government of that time declared their belief "that the framers of the Mandate in which the Balfour Declaration was embodied could not have intended that Palestine should be converted into a Jewish State against the will of the Arab population of the country". These statements by British Governments were not merely a reflection of British views at those times. They were made by Britain in its capacity as the mandatory of the League. Article 5 of the mandate enjoined the Mandatory to see that no Palestine territory should be ceded to or in any way placed under the control of any other government.

In short there is nothing in the history of the Mandate to imply acceptance of the Zionist claim to sovereignty over Palestine in general or over Jerusalem in particular by either the League of Nations or its Mandatory, Britain. However wrong and unjust the Balfour Declaration and the Mandate may have been in general and in other particular respects, they do not provide grounds to support Israel's current assertion of sovereignty over Jerusalem.

Turning now to the period since 1945 when the League of Nations gave way to the United Nations, we should perhaps remind ourselves first of all that it is questionable—some would say, highly questionable—whether the United Nations, any more than the League of Nations before it, was legally competent to decide the future of Palestine and of its capital, Jerusalem. That is an argument which I imagine Henry Cattan may wish to develop. However, even if the competence of the United Nations is conceded, its power to decide this issue is clearly governed by the provisions of the UN Charter. These require that the organisation should act in conformity with the principles of justice and international law" in carrying out its stated purpose of maintaining international peace and security. Again the Charter enjoins on all member states "respect for the principle of equal rights and self-determination of peoples". Did the United Nations act in conformity with these principles in 1947 when it decreed the partition of Palestine, including a special status for Jerusalem? Here too I think I may properly leave the argument in the distinguished hands of the next speaker.

The Palestine Partition Resolution 181 of 29 November 1947 was the first statement in which the General Assembly enunciated principles concerning the international legal status of the City of Jerusalem and provides in relevant part:

"A. Special Regime

The City of Jerusalem shall be established as a *corpus*

> *separatum* under a special international regime and shall be administered by the United Nations. The Trusteeship Council shall be designated to discharge the responsibilities of the Administering Authority on behalf of the United Nations.
>
> "B. Boundaries of the City
>
> The City of Jerusalem shall include the present municipality of Jerusalem plus the surrounding villages and towns. . .".

As the Mallisons have rightly pointed out in their Analysis, to which I have already referred, the provisions which the General Assembly adopted for the establishment of Jerusalem as a *corpus separatum* were intended to ensure that this Holy City should not be under the control of any nationalism. This reflected the General Assembly's awareness of the universal character of the City deriving from its profound religious significance for the adherents of Judaism, Christianity and Islam.

The Partition Resolution provisions concerning Jerusalem were not implemented. On 11 December 1948 the General Assembly adopted resolution 194 which, in addition to provisions concerning the return of refugees, stated in paragraph 8 that the General Assembly:

> "*Resolves* that . . . the Jerusalem area . . . should be accorded special and separate treatment from the rest of Palestine and should be placed under effective United Nations control."

The basic consistency between this resolution and the Palestine Partition Resolution is that both set forth a separate status for Jerusalem and place it under United Nations control. It is significant that this later resolution was adopted *after* the seizure of the Western part of Jerusalem by the armed forces of Israel. The resolution thus constitutes a rejection by the international community of Israel's attempt to incorporate by force a large part of Jerusalem within the Jewish state.

A year later, in resolution 303 of 9 December 1949, the General Assembly refers to both resolutions 181 and 194 in the first prefatory paragraph. The first operative paragraph provides that the General Assembly decides concerning Jerusalem.

> "To restate, therefore, its intention that Jerusalem should be placed under a permanent international regime, which should envisage appropriate guarantees for the protection of the Holy Places, both within and outside Jerusalem, and to confirm specifically the following provisions of General Assembly resolution 181 (II).(1) the City of Jerusalem shall be established as a *corpus separatum* under a special international regime and shall be administered by the United Nations; (2) the Trusteeship Council shall be designated to discharge the responsibilities of the Administering Authority . . .; and (3) the City of Jerusalem shall include the present municipality of Jerusalem plus the surrounding villages and towns . . ."

The second operative paragraph of this resolution requests the Trusteeship Council to complete preparation of the Statute of Jerusalem considering "the fundamental principles of the international regime for Jerusalem set forth in General Assembly resolution 181 (II)" and to proceed immediately with its implementation". The Statute, which was approved by the Trusteeship Council on 4 April 1950, provided for, *inter alia*, protection for the Holy Places and for human rights and fundamental freedoms for all persons in the City. There has been no change in the basic international juridical status envisaged for Jerusalem in the three General Assembly resolutions just considered.

In the interval between the General Assembly resolutions of December 1948 and December 1949 Israel had applied for membership of the United Nations and after considerable debate was admitted to membership in May, 1949. The General

Assembly resolution 273 of 11 May 1949 noted that the Security Council judged Israel to be a peace-loving State able and willing to carry out the obligations contained in the Charter; that the Security Council had recommended that the General Assembly admit Israel; and that the State of Israel had declared that it "unreservedly accepts the obligations of the UN Charter and undertakes to honour them". The Assembly then recalled its resolutions 181 (that is, the partition resolution) and 194 (that is, the resolution of December 1948 dealing with the return of refugees and re-affirming a separate status for Jerusalem under UN control). Finally in this preamble to its resolution, the General Assembly took note of "the declaration and explanations made by the representative of the Government of Israel before the Ad Hoc Political Committee in respect of the implementation of the said resolutions." It was with this preamble and on this basis that the General Assembly then decided to admit Israel to membership of the United Nations.

Two points are worth emphasising here. First, there is the reference to the partition resolution and to the later resolution re-affirming the special status for Jerusalem. Second, there is the reference to "the declaration and explanations" provided by the representative of Israel. This representative was Mr. Abba Eban, who later became Foreign Minister of Israel. Among the explanations he had given to the Ad Hoc Political Committee was the following:

> "I do not think that Article 2, paragraph 7, of the Charter, which relates to domestic jurisdiction, could possibly affect the Jerusalem problem, since the legal status of Jerusalem is different from that of the territory in which Israel is sovereign—"

It seems clear that at this point of time the whole international community, even including the new state of Israel, accepted the concept of a "*corpus separatum*" for Jerusalem. Subsequent events, however, call into question the sincerity of Israel's acceptance. Once it had gained admission to the United Nations, it soon began demonstrating in the UN Palestine Conciliation Commission a stubborn refusal to withdraw from any of the territory, including Jerusalem, which it had seized by force of arms during the conflict in 1947 and 1948.

Soon after the hostilities ended in June 1967, the Government of Israel incorporated, through Israeli municipal law, that portion of Jerusalem previously controlled by Jordan. On 4 July 1967, the General Assembly adopted resolution 2253 which provided that the General Assembly

> "*Deeply concerned* at the situation prevailing in Jerusalem as a result of the measures taken by Israel to change the status of the City,
>
> 1. *Considers* that these measures are invalid.
>
> 2. *Calls upon* Israel to rescind all measures already taken and to desist forthwith from taking any action which would alter the status of Jerusalem."

The resolution ended by requesting the Secretary-General to report on its implementation within a week.

Ten days later, the General Assembly adopted resolution 2254 which, after recalling and noting Israel's non-compliance with resolution 2253, stated that the General Assembly:

> "1. *Deplores* the failure of Israel to implement General Assembly resolution 2253 (ES-V);
>
> "2. *Reiterates* its call to Israel in that resolution to rescind all measures already taken and to desist forthwith from taking any action which would alter the status of Jerusalem."

As the Mallisons have pointed out in their Analysis, there is an apparent ambiguity in these two resolutions. The preambular paragraph of resolution 2253 refers to "the status of the City" and the second operative paragraph of each of the two resolutions refers to "the status of Jerusalem". These terms may be interpreted as referring either to the juridical status of

Jerusalem as a *corpus separatum* or, since there is no mention in these post-1967 resolutions of resolutions 181, 194 or 303, to the *de facto* status of the City as it existed under partial Jordanian and partial Israeli control prior to the intense hostilities of June 1967. The broad phrase "all measures already taken" which appears in the second operative paragraph of each of the foregoing resolutions may be interpreted as meaning that the State of Israel is called upon to rescind its measures, without specific reference to the time when the measures were taken. So interpreted, the Israeli measures to be rescinded would include those taken after the conquest of the Western part of Jerusalem in the hostilities of 1947-1948 as well as those taken after the conquest of the Eastern part of the City in 1967.

On 16 December 1976 the General Assembly adopted a further resolution reaffirming that —

> "all legislative and administrative measures taken by Israel, including the expropriation of land and properties thereon and the transfer of populations, which purport to change the legal status of Jerusalem, are invalid and cannot change that status."

In October 1977 the General Assembly adopted a further resolution condemning Israeli settlements and again calling for an immediate halt to any action which would result in changing the legal status, geographical nature or demographic composition of the occupied territories, including Jerusalem. It went on to call for strict Israeli compliance with the 1949 Geneva Convention on the protection of civilians in time of war.

Similar resolutions have been adopted by the General Assembly in succeeding years.

The major Security Council resolutions concerning Jerusalem were not adopted until 1968 and 1969. Security Council resolution 252 of 21 may 1968, after recalling General Assembly resolutions 2253 and 2254, provides in its first three operative paragraphs that the Security Council:

"1. *Deplores* the failure of Israel to comply with the General Assembly resolutions mentioned above;

"2. *Considers* that all legislative and adminstrative measures and actions taken by Israel, including expropriation of land and properties thereon, which tend to change the legal status of Jerusalem, are invalid and cannot change that status;

"3. *Urgently calls upon* Israel to rescind all such measures already taken and to desist forthwith from taking any futher action which tends to change the status of Jerusalem".

The first quoted paragraph manifests Security Council concurrence with the broad terms of General Assembly resolutions 2253 and 2254. The second quoted paragraph refers to the invalidity of "all legislative and administrative measures and actions taken by Israel" without limitation of time. The most significant feature of the second paragraph is the setting forth of "the legal status of Jerusalem" as the standard and providing that actions which tend to change it are invalid. The only legal status that has been provided for Jerusalem is the one establishing it as a *corpus separatum*. The use of the term "legal" status suggests that it is *not* the *de facto* status obtaining before June 1967 that the Security Council has in mind.

Israel failed to comply with the terms of resolution 252, and on 3 July 1969, the Security Council adopted unanimously resolution 267 which recalled its resolution 252 and General Assembly resolutions 2253 and 2254. Its first five operative paragraphs provide that the Council:

"1. *Reaffirms* its resolution 252 (1968);

"2. *Deplores* the failure of Israel to show any regard for the resolutions of the General Assembly and the Security Council mentioned above;

"3. *Censures* in the strongest terms all measures taken to change the status of the City of Jerusalem;

"4. *Confirms* that all legislative and administrative measures and actions taken by Israel which purport to alter the status of Jerusalem, including expropriation of land and properties thereon, are invalid and cannot change that status;

"5. *Urgently calls* once more upon Israel to rescind forthwith all measures taken by it which may tend to change the status of the City of Jerusalem, and in future to refrain from all actions likely to have such an effect".

The first quoted paragraph reaffirms resolution 252 which includes the norm of "the legal status of Jerusalem" which is the *corpus separatum*. The fourth quoted paragraph confirms the invalidity of "all Israeli measures and actions which purport to alter the status of Jerusalem", again without reference to time.

Although resolutions 252 and 267 reflect similar legal principles, the latter contain some particularly strict language. For instance, paragraph 3 of resolution 252 simply urges that the State of Israel "rescind all such measures already taken", whereas paragraph 5 of resolution 267 explicitly states that such rescission must be made "forthwith". Moreover, paragraph 5 of resolution 267 urges Israel not only to rescind measures which may tend to change the status, but also to refrain comprehensively "from all actions likely to have such an effect". And paragraph 3 of the later resolution "censures in the strongest terms all measures taken to change the status of the City" — unusually severe language.

Security council resolution 298 was adopted on 25 September 1971. Here the Security Council appears to have become apprised of the ambiguity in the use of the term "status" and to have tried to limit it to the *de facto* interpretation. Its first preambular paragraph recalls Security Council resolutions 252 and 267 as well as General Assembly resolutions 2253 and 2254 and describes them as "concerning measures and actions by Israel designed to change the status of the Israeli-occupied section of Jerusalem". It appears to be the intention of the Security Council to restrict by this language the scope of the recalled resolutions to the post-1967 situation. Although it is within the authority of the council to interpret its own resolutions, it is beyond its power to impose limitations on the meaning of General Assembly resolutions. The third preambular paragraph of resolution 298 reaffirms "the principle that acquisition of territory by military conquest is inadmissible" and no time frame is set forth for the application of this principle. It could thus be interpreted as referring to Israel's military conquests of 1947-48 as well as of 1967.

The first four operative paragraphs of resolution 298 provide that the Security Council.

> "1. *Reaffirms* its resolutions 252 (1968) and 267 (1969)
>
> "2. *Deplores* the failure of Israel to respect the previous resolutions adopted by the United Nations concerning measures and actions by Israel purporting to affect the status of the City of Jerusalem;
>
> "3. *Confirms* in the clearest possible terms that all legislative and administrative actions taken by Israel to change the status of the City of Jerusalem including expropriation of land and properties, transfer of population and legislation aimed at the incorporation of the occupied section, are totally invalid and cannot change that status;
>
> "4. *Urgently calls upon* Israel to rescind all previous measures and actions and to take no further steps in the occupied section of Jerusalem which may purport to change the status of the City or which would prejudice the rights of the inhabitants and the interests of the international community, or a just and lasting peace".

The second operative paragraph deplores the failure of Israel to respect the prior resolutions of the United Nations, thereby including both General Assembly and Security Council resolutions. The second and fourth operative paragraphs refer to "the status of the City". The third operative paragraph, in comprehensive terms, states that "all legislative and administrative actions taken by Israel" aimed at "the incorporation of the occupied section" are totally invalid and ineffective in changing the status of the City. The fourth paragraph calls upon Israel to rescind "all previous measures and actions" to change the City's status and prejudice other important interests. The term "occupied section" in these operative paragraphs, as well as in the first and last paragraphs of the Preamble, apparently refers to the section of Jerusalem which was occupied by Israel following the intense hostilities of June 1967. These references also raise the implication that in the view of the Security Council there may be an unoccupied section of Jerusalem. However, it must be noted that the first operative paragraph of resolution 298 in reaffirming resolution 252 retains its standard of "the legal status of Jerusalem", which is the *corpus separatum*.

On 11 November 1976 the Security Council issued what was described as "a consensus statement on the situation in the Israeli occupied Arab territories". This description would seem to limit the scope and effect of the statement to the post-June 1967 state of affairs. However, again the language used in regard to the status of Jerusalem is ambiguous.

> "Having expressed grave anxiety and concern over the serious situation in the occupied territories as a result of continued Israeli occupation, the Security Council re-affirms that the Fourth Geneva Convention is applicable to the Arab territories occupied by Israel since 1967. It declares that measures taken by Israel to alter the demographic composition or geographical nature of the occupied territories have no legal validity, cannot prejudice the outcome of the search for peace and constitute an obstacle to peace."

The Security Council then turns to Jerusalem and says:

> "It considers once more that all legislative and administrative measures and actions taken by Israel, including expropriation of land and properties thereon and the transfer of populations which tend to change the legal status of Jerusalem, are invalid and cannot change that status, and urgently calls upon Israel once more to rescind all such measures already taken and to desist forthwith from taking any further action which tends to change the status of Jerusalem. In this connection the Council deplores the failure of Israel to show any regard for Security Council resolutions 237 (1967) of 14 June 1967, 252 (1968) of 21 May 1968 and 298 (1971) of 25 September 1971 and General Assembly resolutions 2253 (ES-V) and 2254 (ES-V) of 4 and 14 July 1967."

Here there is no reference to merely "the occupied section" of Jerusalem except in so far as this may be inferred from the general description of the statement as a whole.

Thus there is apparent lack of clarity in the post-1967 General Assembly resolutions and in the Security Council resolutions as to whether the status of Jerusalem referred to in particular instances is the legal status of the *corpus separatum* provided for in General Assembly resolutions 181, 194 and 303, and in the specific reference to "the legal status" in Security Council resolution 252, or to the factual status of the pre-June 1967 divided City.

Before leaving this question of the meaning to be attached to the terms "the status of Jerusalem" and "the legal status of Jerusalem" in resolutions of the General Assembly and the Security Council adopted since 1967, perhaps I may record the conclusion reached by the Mallisons in their Analysis. Having set out the facts (and I have followed closely their presentation) they conclude—

> "In examining the Security Council resolutions along with

> those of the General Assembly, it appears that there is, at the least, an implicit intent to preserve the principle of the *corpus separatum* even though these resolutions, following the intense hostilities of June 1967, put special emphasis upon the post-1967 Israeli actions."

As an appendage—more curious perhaps than significant—to this discussion I might perhaps recall an incident that occurred in Washington in 1977. On 26 May of that year President Carter declared that the "binding policies" of the United States, which he said derived from Security Council resolutions, included "the right of the Palestinians to have a homeland and to be compensated for losses they have suffered". He was immediately challenged by Israel on the grounds that these matters were not included in Security Council resolutions 242 and 338 and that Dr. Kissinger had agreed at the time of the Second Sinai Agreement that the United States would be bound only by those resolutions. An embarrassed State Department had to exculpate the President by admitting that he had been mistaken in attributing these policies to Security Council resolutions but adding that they *were* covered in General Assembly resolutions 181 of 1947 (the partition resolution) and 194 of 1948 (the resolution providing for the return of refugees and re-affirming the separate status of Jerusalem)—in fact the resolutions that Israel had specifically undertaken to observe at the time of its admission to the United Nation). Now the interesting thing here is that the United States Government thus went on record—albeit in a roundabout and grudging way—as acknowledging that the partition resolution, providing for a *corpus separatum* of Jerusalem and for an Arab as well as a Jewish state in Palestine, still has validity in American eyes.

A potentially important new development occurred in March of this year when the Security Council adopted a resolution which, after reaffirming the Council's previous condemnation of Israel's settlement policy and Israel's failure to abide by earlier Security Council resolutions,—

> "3. *Calls once more upon* Israel, as the occupying Power, to abide scrupulously by the 1949 Fourth Geneva convention, to rescind its previous measures and to desist from taking any action which would result in changing the legal status and geographical nature and materially affecting the demographic composition of the Arab territories occupied since 1967, including Jerusalem, and, in particular, not to transfer parts of its own civilian population into the occupied Arab territories;
>
> "4. *Establishes* a commission consisting of three members of the Security Council, to be appointed by the President of the Council after consultation with the members of the Council, to examine the situation relating to settlements in the Arab territories occupied since 1967, including Jerusalem".

The three-man Commission was duly established, the members being provided by Bolivia, Portugal and Zambia. It visited the Middle East in May, but Israel refused to have any contact with the Commission or to allow it to visit the occupied territories. The Commission reported in July. The paragraph dealing with Jerusalem in its recommendations reads—

> "As to Jerusalem, the Council should also call upon the Government of Israel to implement faithfully Security Council resolutions adopted on that question as from 1967. Moreover, recalling that Jerusalem is a most sacred place for the three great monotheistic faiths throughout the world, i.e. Christian, Jewish and Moslem, the Security Council might wish to consider steps to protect and preserve the unique spiritual and religious dimension of the Holy Places in that city, taking into account the views of high-ranking representatives of the three religions."

On 20 July 1979 the Security Council, having received the report, adopted a resolution calling on—

> "the Government and people of Israel to cease, on an urgent basis, the establishment, construction and planning of settlements in the Arab territories occupied since 1967, including Jerusalem".

The specialised agencies and subsidiary organs of the United Nations are guided by the resolutions of the Security Council and the General Assembly in regard to political questions, such as the status of Jerusalem. Thus, for example, the two UN bodies located in Jerusalem, UNRWA (the United Nations Relief and Works Agency for Palestine Refugees) and UNTSO (the United Nations Truce Supervision Organisation) have always taken care to avoid action that might give an appearance of acceding to Israel's claim to sovereignty over the City, both that part which Israel seized in 1947-48 and that seized in 1967. The same goes for other UN bodies.

From 1971 onwards Unesco has been expressing its concern about the preservation of religious and cultural sites in Jerusalem and about Israeli interference with them. In 1972 the Unesco General Conference adopted a resolution in which it urgently calls upon Israel—

> "(a) to take the necessary measures for the scrupulous preservation of all sites, buildings and other cultural properties, especially in the Old City of Jerusalem.
>
> (c) to desist from any archeological excavation—the transfer of cultural properties, and any alterations of their features and historical character, particularly with regard to Christian and Islamic religious sites;"

The resolution was ignored by Israel.

The UN Human Rights Commission has also concerned itself with the question of Jerusalem and adopted a number of resolutions on similar lines to those of the General Assembly and

Security Council. For example, in its resolution of 15 February 1977 the Commission—

"*Reaffirms* that all such measures taken by Israel to change the physical character, demographic composition or status of the occupied Arab territories or any part thereof, including Jerusalem, are null and void, and calls upon Israel to rescind all such measures already taken and to desist forthwith from taking any further action which tends to change the status of the occupied Arab territories, including Jerusalem."

In the last four years increased attention has been given to the Palestine Question and to Jerusalem, as an important aspect of that question, as a result of the General Assembly's decision in 1975 to establish the Committee on the Exercise of the Inalienable Rights of the Palestinian People. In 1978 this was followed by the establishment, again on the authority of the General Assembly, of a Special Unit on Palestinian Rights. The Committee and the Special Unit have produced much valuable material, particularly on the right of return of the Palestinian people and their right to self-determination. References to Jerusalem appear of course in this material but, as far as I am aware, neither the Committee nor the Special Unit has yet undertaken any special study of the question of Jerusalem. Perhaps this is something to which they could usefully turn their attention.

Having set out what I understand to be the position in legal terms adopted by the United Nations on the question of Jerusalem and having shown that, as far as the record goes, the concept of Jerusalem as a *corpus separatum* still stands as the solution approved by the international community, I would propose concluding my remarks with some rather more down-to-earth observations based on my own acquaintance with the question since I first came to know the City some twenty years ago and particularly since Israel seized the whole of Jerusalem in 1967 and began its frenzied attempt to incorporate it into the

Zionist state. As Crown Prince Hassan has observed in his study on Jerusalem:

> "It is manifest that the acutely difficult question of the future status of Jerusalem is not likely to be resolved by exclusive attention to the legal issues".

Of course we need to examine and understand those issues, which (as Prince Hassan says) "in themselves present formidable difficulties". But in the end it is political action, not legal analysis, that must provide the solution.

I hope it will not be taken amiss if I speak with more warmth than I would usually employ on such an occasion and in such company. The cause and justification, if any is needed, is the anguish, the indignation that I feel as I contemplate the outrageous reality of what is happening in Jerusalem and contrast the well-meaning, highly principled sentiments expressed in so many UN resolutions on Jerusalem with the wretched failure of the international community over so many years to do anything effective towards carrying them out.

Ten years ago, at the time when the Security Council had just adopted its strongly worded resolution 267 castigating Israel for its attempts to change the status of Jerusalem, *The Times* of London commented in these terms—

> "During the Security Council debate on the latest resolution the American Ambassador, Mr. Yost, said that his Government did not consider the problem of Jerusalem should be dealt with piecemeal. America opposes proposals that sanctions should be invoked against Israel to force her to revoke the various changes in the status of the city and its administration she has carried out since the June war. This means, in effect, that no sanctions will be taken. The Egyptian representative in New York said after the resolution had passed that 'more than ever before, Israel stands alone'. He is deluding himself if he thinks this significant. However much the rest of the world may

> deplore some of Israel's actions, this disapproval will not extend to applying the sort of pressure that would be needed to get her to change her policy towards Jerusalem. It is, after all, of secondary importance, and if ever a serious attempt to impose a solution is to be made, it should be directed at the essential."

I remember thinking at the time that I wished I could take Ambassador Yost and the author of the article in *The Times* and confront them with the reality of what was going on in Jerusalem. With the Arab families in tears and despair as the Israeli bulldozers smashed their homes. With the vandalism with which historic Arab buildings were being torn down to make way for tastefully designed flats where rich part-time Israelis from America and elsewhere could spend a few months each year dwelling in Jerusalem. With the brutal overpowering presence of the fortess blocks of flats with which Israel was then beginning to surround the Arab side of Jerusalem.

Now, ten years later, I would again like to take them to see what has resulted from the policy of refusing "to deal piecemeal" with the problem of Jerusalem, of failing to apply the sort of pressure that would be needed to get Israel to change its policy towards Jerusalem and of treating the problem of Jerusalem, of failing to apply the sort of pressure that would be needed to get Israel to change its policy towards Jerusalem and of treating the problem of Jerusalem as, "after all, of secondary importance". The cruel eviction of the Arab inhabitants of the so-called Jewish Quarter was completed years ago. The new flats which have replaced the Arab homes and other buildings now destroyed are finished and exclusively occupied by Jews. The circumvallation of Arab Jerusalem by Israeli fortresses in the form of apartment blocks occupied exclusively by Jewish settlers is far advanced and is being pushed ahead at a frantic pace, regardless of cost or even housing need. Many of the occupants of the new apartments are said to be not new immigrants at all but Israelis who had established residences within Israel and have now been transferred to the Arab side of Jerusalem to reinforce the occupation.

The effect of these wasted years, during which nothing has been done to give effect to General Assembly and Security Council resolutions calling on Israel to desist from its attempt to change the status of Jerusalem, has been to render peace much, much more difficult to achieve. If ever the international community does decide to act, it will be far more difficult now to get Israel out of the Old City and the adjacent Arab area than it would have been within the first few years after 1967. And with every year that passes the task becomes more difficult, as Israel raises yet more obstacles to withdrawal and to peace. Those who took the view after 1967 that the Jerusalem problem could not be tackled piecemeal have much to answer for. The truth is that nothing would have done more to promote a general settlement than firm, decisive international action to tackle the specific problem of Jerusalem. If that had been done, everything else would have at once become more manageable.

If the passage of twelve years has made it more difficult for the United Nations to secure its limited objective of getting Israel to withdraw from the part of Jerusalem which it occupied in 1967, it is obvious that the passage of over thirty years has made it even more difficult for the United Nations to secure its original, wider objective of establishing a *corpus separatum* of Jerusalem under international control. The lesson to be drawn from the whole history of the United Nation's involvement in the search for peace in the Middle East is that procrastination has been the undoing of international peace-making. There has been plenty of good intentions and right principles and sensible statements. But always procrastination has proved the thief of peace. For a time after each war in the Middle East—in 1948, in 1967 and in 1973—there has been a chance of peace, if only it were pursued with firmness of purpose. And each time it has been frittered away. It is tragic that this should be so.

Must there be yet another war, more bloody and destructive than ever before, in order to open the way for a new, perhaps a last, chance of peace? I pray not. Even now, though it is so late, the United Nations could bring peace to the Middle Eact if only it would avail itself of the machinery provided in the UN Charter for dealing with precisely the kind of defiance of international authority which Israel has persistently shown, and never more so than today. Enforcement action against Israel under Chapter VII of the Charter is amply justified. Indeed those provisions of the Charter were expressly designed to deal with just such a case as that with which Israel now confronts the world, where the government of a country, being a member state of the United Nations, defies international authority and endangers world peace. Without this any UN intervention is futile and bound to fail in the face of Israel's intransigence. Enforcement is the key to peace.

It is easy to say that there is no point in seeking sanctions against Israel because the United States will veto any such proposal in the Security Council. But that is no excuse for others to fail to bring the opposition. Until they do, there is no hope that Washington will even begin to consider the case for enforcement action against Israel. Until they do, the sensible, moderate elements in Israel who advocate withdrawal from the occupied territories in return for peace will be "voices crying in the wilderness". Every government, every organisation and individual throughout the world, sincerely concerned for peace should be proclaiming loud and clear on every possible occasion the simple, evident truth that there will be no peace in Jerusalem, no peace in the Middle East, until it is enforced on Israel.

11. Jerusalem and the Palestine Question in International Law

Dr. Henry Cattan

PART I

JERUSALEM

1. The problem of Jerusalem

Since its foundation some thirty-eight centuries ago, Jerusalem has been a holy city. First for the Canaanites who founded it, then for the Israelities, the Pagans, the Christians and lastly for the Arabs and Moslems generally. The city contains their holy places and all in turn have ruled it and revered it. Jerusalem has a deep historic and religious significance to one thousand million Christians, seven hundred million Moslems and fourteen million Jews.

Jerusalem was the source of many wars in the past: between Canaanites and their neighbours, between Greeks and Persians, Jews and Romans, Christians and Moslems and lastly between Arabs and Jews. On several occasions, it was beseiged, destroyed and its inhabitants massacred. The last of the fateful events in the life of Jerusalem occurred in our time: in 1948 the Jews seized modern Jerusalem, displaced all its Arab inhabitants, and in 1967 they captured the Old City and displaced part of its residents.

Israel's occupation and annexation of Jerusalem, its proclamation of the city as its historical capital, its uprooting and displacement of the Arab inhabitants and the judaization of its character and population have created a grave international problem which has dangerous religious undertones.

For its annexation of Jerusalem and its proclamation of the city as its capital, Israel has invoked the pretext that in biblical times, some thirty centuries ago, Jerusalem was the capital of a Jewish kingdom.

In the next section we shall examine Israel's claim to Jerusalem in the light of history and international law.

2. Israel's claim to Jerusalem

Israel's claim of a right to annex Jerusalem on the ground that the city is its historical capital is spurious in fact and in law.

A. *Falsity in fact*

Two overriding considerations completely refute the claim made by the present State of Israel of an historical connection with the Jewish Kingdom established thirty centuries ago and which disappeared without any trace less than five centuries later. These are:

First, the continuity of the Palestinian presence in Jerusalem since its foundation by their ancestors, the Canaanites, in contrast with the transient presence of the Jews in the city during biblical times.

Second, the absence of any racial link between the Israelis of today and the Israelites of the Bible.

Contrary to politically inspired, but historically inaccurate assertions, Jerusalem was founded not by the Jews, but by the Canaanites[1] (the ancestors of the Palestinians), around 1800 BC. It was inhabited by the Jebusites, a Canaanite subgroup. In 1000 or may be in 1006 BC, the city was captured by David who made it the capital of a Jewish kingdom. It remained under Jewish rule until 587 BC when it was captured by the Babylonians and was retained by them until 538 BC. Thereafter the city was ruled by a succession of peoples: the Persians (538-332 BC), the Greeks (332-164 BC), the Jews during the Maccabean revolt (164-63 BC), the Pagan Romans (63 BC-323 AD), the Christian Romans (323-614), the Persians (614-628), the Christians again (628-637), the Arabs (637-1517) except during the three periods in which they lost control of the city to the Turks (1072-1092), to the Christians (1099-1187) who established there the Latin Kingdom of Jerusalem, and to the Christians again (1229-1239). From 1517 until 1917 the city was under Turkish rule. Then followed the British occupation and mandate (1917-1948), the seizure in 1948 by Israel of the New City and by Transjordan of the Old City, and finally the capture by Israel in 1967 of the Old City in whose hands it still remains today.

Despite the successive occupations of Jerusalem by the biblical Israelites, the Greeks, the Romans, the Crusaders and the Turks, Jerusalem retained a predominantly Palestinian Arab character as it also retained its indigenous Canaanite and Palestinian Arab population. Unlike the Israelites who came and went, so to speak, Palestinian presence in Jerusalem has been continuous and uninterrupted. Even when David seized the city, he did not, like the Israelis thirty centuries later, displace the original inhabitants. The "Jebusites were allowed to remain in their city, but not in the fortress; he (David) permitted them to settle in the east of the town, on Mount Moriah."[2] Similarly, none of the subsequent invaders, Persians, Romans, Moslems, Crusaders, displaced the non-Jewish inhabitants of the city, i.e. the Palestinians.

It is to be remarked that the Palestinians gave its Arab Character to Jerusalem long before the rise of Islam and the Moslem conquest.[3] The Arabs generally, including the Palestinians, were a pre-Islamic people who had their history, traditions and culture. Upon the rise of Islam, most Arabs adopted the new religion. Hence it is an error to imagine, as some people do, that the Arab inhabitants of Jerusalem and of Palestine generally, came to the country only at the time of the Moslem conquest in the seventh century. The Palestinian Arabs were the indigenous and original inhabitants of Palestine.

So again, the Turkish conquest of Jerusalem in the sixteenth century did not entail any colonization by the Turks or any displacement of the Palestinian Arab population of the city. During the four centuries of Turkish rule, the Turkish demographic element consisted only of a few officials and was less than one per cent of the population of Jerusalem.

In contrast, unlike the Palestinians who remained in Jerusalem as its indigenous inhabitants throughout its vicissitudes until 1948, the Jews who came to the country as invaders were driven away from Jerusalem by other invaders. In 587 BC, they were deported by the Babylonians who burned Solomon's Temple, and carried them into captivity. Following their first revolt against the Romans in AD 70, Titus destroyed Jerusalem and Solomon's Temple. After its destruction by Titus, Jerusalem "never again revived as a Jewish city."[4] But after their second revolt against the Romans in AD 132-135, Jerusalem was again destroyed and the Jews were either killed or dispersed to the four corners of the Roman Empire. When the new city of Jerusalem was rebuilt by Hadrian after AD 135 no Jews were allowed to live in it. The prohibition of the presence of the Jews in Jerusalem was relaxed by the Moslem Arabs after their capture of the city in the seventh century. But despite this liberal measure few Jews lived in Jerusalem until the middle of the ninteenth century. In AD 1180, a Jewish traveller, Petahia of Ratisbon, found one co-religionist only in Jerusalem and in AD 1267 a Spanish rabbi, Moise Ben Nahman, found two Jewish families in Jerusalem.[5]

Only in the nineteenth century did the Jewish population of Jerusalem, under the impetus of Zionism, both religious and political, begin to increase. In 1838, there were 3,000 Jews in Jerusalem out of a total population of 11,000.[6] In 1922, according to the census of the Government of Palestine, the Jewish population of the urban area of Jerusalem numbered 33,971 out of a total population of 62,578. The Jewish population substantially increased during the British mandate so that in 1946 the number of Jews living in the *corpus separatum* of Jerusalem as delineated by the UN had reached 99,690 out of a total population of 205,230.

The second consideration which refutes Israel's claim of an historical connection with the Jewish Kingdom that existed in biblical times is the fact, recognised by Jewish historians, that the Jewish settlers who emigrated to Palestine since the middle of the nineteenth century are not the descendants of the Israelites of the Bible who were twice deported from Jerusalem. In fact, the Israelis who presently live in Jerusalem and the rest of Palestine have no racial link with the biblical Israelites. Joseph Reinach explains that most of today's Jews in Palestine have no connection with this country:

> "The Jews of Palestinian origin constitute an insignificant minority. Like Christians and Moslems, the Jews have engaged with great zeal in the conversion of people to their faith. Before the Christian era, the Jews had converted to the monotheistic religion of Moses, other Semites (or Arabs), Jewish proselytism was not less active in Asia, in the whole of North Africa, in Italy, in Spain and in Gaul. Converted Romans and Gauls no doubt predominated in the Jewish communities mentioned in chronicles of Gregoire de Tours. There were many converted Iberians among the Jews who were expelled from Spain by Ferdinand the Catholic and who spread to Italy, France, the East and Smyrna. The great majority of Russian, Polish and Galician Jews descend from the Khazars, a Tartar people of Southern Russia who were converted in a body to Judaism at the time of Charlemagne. To speak of a Jewish race, one must be either ignorant or of bad faith. There was a Semitic or Arab race; but there never was a Jewish race."[8]

B. *Falsity in law*

The Israeli claim to Jerusalem on historical grounds is also spurious in law.

The Kingdom established by David around 1000 or 1006 BC lasted seventy-three years. After the death of his son Solomon, the Israelite tribes revolted and the Kingdom was split into the Kingdom of Israel in the north with its capital at Sichem in Samaria and the Kingdom of Judah in the south with its capital at Jerusalem. These two Kingdoms were continuously at war with each other and with their neighbours. The Kingdom of Israel was destroyed by the Assyrians in 721 BC and its people carried into oblivion while the Kingdom of Judah was destroyed by the Babylonians in 587 BC and its inhabitants carried into capitivity. This represented the end of any Jewish rule in Palestine. Georges Friedmann observes:

> "The twelve tribes were deported to the Caucasus, Armenia and in particular Babylonia, and disappeared; and with them the Jewish people in the plenitude of their existence as a simultaneously ethnic, national and religious community also disappeared for ever."[9]

It is clear then that the Kingdom established by David as well as its two successors the Kingdom of Israel and the Kingdom of Judah have all disappeared with their peoples into the dust of history. The Jewish presence in Palestine which originated in the invasion of the land of Canaan around 1200 BC and which ended with the deportation of the invaders by the Assyrians and the Babylonians was a transient biblical episode in the life of the country.

None of these Jewish bibilical monarchies can be said to be the predecessor of the State of Israel which was established in 1948 under a resolution of the UN. There exists neither continuity in the existence of such monarchies, nor any identity of population to link them to the present State of Israel.

Moreover, the Jews were not the only people who ruled Jerusalem, nor was their rule the longest in time. We have seen that many people ruled Jerusalem during the thirty-eight centuries of its known existence: the Canaanites and other Pagans for the longest period of time, the Jews for almost five centuries, the Christians, taking into account the period of the British mandate, for over four centuries, and the Moslems (Arabs and Turks) for almost twelve centuries. And the conclusion is that if an historic connection is to be accepted as the basis of a territorial claim, the better title belongs no doubt to the Palestinians, the Arabs and the Moslems.

On the the other hand, the state of Israel is not, and cannot claim to be, the successor of those biblical monarchies. State succession occurs in international law when, as a result of cession, conquest or dismemberment, a state *follows* its predecessor in the possession of its territory. Israel which was established in 1948 did not follow any of the biblical monarchies in the possession of the territory of Palestine. It is separated from them by twenty-five centuries. There exists no rule of international law that recognizes a right of succession by a state created in the twentieth century to a state that existed twenty-five or thirty centuries earlier.

In conclusion, there exists no legal basis whatsoever for Israel's annexation of Jerusalem and its proclaiming the city its capital under the pretext that in distant history it was for a time the capital of a Jewish monarchy. It is the Palestinians, in fact, who have had a long and more continuous historical connection than any other people with Jerusalem. Israel's claim to Jerusalem is mere deception and political exploitation of an historical episode.

3. Israel's illegal actions in Jerusalem

Briefly, the illegal actions committed by Israel in Jerusalem may be summarized as follows:

(i) Occupation and annexation of most of modern Jerusalem in 1948-1950 and of the Old City in 1967.

(ii) Alteration of the demographic structure of Jerusalem, first, by barring the repatriation of some fifty to sixty thousand Palestine refugees (now over one hundred thousand) who were forced to leave their homes in 1948 by reason of terror, hostilities or deportation and, second, by swamping the city with Jewish settlers brought to it for political reasons. The result has been that, compared with official population figures towards the end of the mandate, the Jewish population of the city today has trebled rising from less than 100,000 to 275,000 while the Arab population comprising Moslems and Christians has been reduced from 105,000 to 70,000.

(iii) Violations of the human rights of the inhabitants as will be explained in greater detail in Part II with respect to occupied Palestine generally.

(iv) Confiscation and pillage of all Arab homes numbering over ten thousand in the twelve Arab quarters in modern Jerusalem which were seized by Jewish forces in 1948.

(v) Destruction in 1967 of several hundred houses including the historic Mughrabi quarter in the Old City, for the creation of a car park near the Wailing Wall, and the confiscation of large tracts of land around Jerusalem for the creation of Jewish settlements.

(vi) Archaeological excavations underneath and around the Haram Al-Sharif endangering one of the three most holy places of Islam.

(vii) Desecrations of, and threats to Holy Places, and interference with religious rights and freedoms.[10]

Israel's actions in Jerusalem violate Palestinian sovereignty, international law, the Geneva Convention (1949) and UN Resolutions.

Sovereignty over the territory of Palestine, including Jerusalem, has remained with the Palestinians despite the vicissitudes that have beset the country. By occupying and annexing Jerusalem, Israel has violated the sovereignty of the Palestinians.[11]

Under international law the status of Israel in Jerusalem is that of a military occupier. A military occupier cannot annex occupied territory, or destroy property outside hostilities, or confiscate or expropriate, or alter the demographic structure of occupied territory. These obligations are also contained in the Geneva Convention relative to the Protection of Civilian Persons in Time of War, of 12 August 1949, which forbids pillage, transfer or deportation of persons and destruction of property.

Israel has violated each and every one of these prohibitions.

Finally, Israel's occupation and annexation of Jerusalem, whether of modern Jerusalem in 1948-1950, or of the Old City in 1967, violate Resolution 181 (II) of 29 November 1947. This Resolution, it will be recalled, established the City of Jerusalem as a *corpus separatum* under a special international regime to be administered by the UN.

Despite that Resolution 181 (II) was not effectively implemented by reason of the military occupation of modern Jerusalem by Israel and of the Old City by Transjordan in 1948, yet it was not abrogated. In fact, the international regime which it laid down was reaffirmed by the General Assembly *after* the occupation of Jerusalem by Resolutions 194 (III) of 11 December 1948 and 303 (IV) of 9 December 1949.

Israel cannot invoke its breach of Resolution 181 (II) as a pretext for arguing that it is not bound by it. Israel is bound by this Resolution like all other states. Moreover, Israel was admitted to UN membership only after it gave assurances regarding its respect for the status of Jerusalem as defined by the General Assembly.[12] The only party that is not bound by Resolution 181 (II) is the people of Palestine because, unlike Israel or any other state, the Palestinians alone possessed sovereign and vested territorial rights in Palestine prior to the adoption of the Resolution of 29 November 1947. The Palestinians have not assented to the partition of their country and they cannot be divested of their rights by any UN Resolution.

Israel's illegal actions in Jerusalem, in particular those committed since June 1967, were condemned by the UN.

Following Israel's capture of the Old City in 1967, the General Assembly of the UN promptly condemned Israel's action. In its Resolutions dated 4 and 14 July 1967, it expressed its concern over the situation resulting from the measures taken by Israel to change the status of Jerusalem, declared these measures invalid and called upon Israel to rescind them and desist forthwith from taking any action which would alter the status of the city.

Then on 21 May 1968 the Security Council deplored in Resolution 252 Israel's failure to comply with the General Assembly's Resolutions of 4 and 14 July 1967 and declared that it:

> "2. *Considers* that all legislative and administrative measures and actions taken by Israel, including expropriation of land and properties thereon, which tend to change the status of Jerusalem, are invalid and cannot change that status."

The condemnation of the measures taken by Israel in Jerusalem was again reiterated by the Security Council in its Resolutions dated 3 July 1969, 15 September 1969 and 25 September 1971. In this last Resolution, the Security Council stated that it:

> "3. *Confirms* in the clearest possible terms that all legislative and administrative actions taken by Israel to change the status of the City of Jerusalem, including expropriation of land and properties, transfer of populations and legislation aimed at the incorporation of

the occupied section, are totally invalid and cannot change that status."

These condemnations were followed by a number of other condemnations of Israel's actions in the occupied territories, including Jerusalem, by the General Assembly, the Commission on Human Rights and UNESCO. Since 1968 UNESCO adopted several resolutions, the last being that of 28 November 1978, which called on Israel to desist from archaeological excavations in the city of Jerusalem and from altering its features or its cultural and historical character.

In two recent Resolutions, the Security Council again deplored Israel's actions in Jerusalem. In Resolution 446 adopted on 22 March 1979 the Security Council declared that it:

> "2. *Strongly deplores* the failure of Israel to abide by Security Council Resolutions 237 (1967) of 14 June 1967, 252 (1968) of 21 May 1968 and 298 (1971) of 25 September 1971 and the consensus statement by the President of the Security Council on 11 November 1976 and General Assembly Resolutions 2253 (ES-V) and 2254 (ES-V) of 4 and 14 July 1967, 32/5 of 28 October 1977 and 33/113 of 18 December 1978.
>
> "3. *Calls once more upon* Israel, as the occupying Power, to abide scrupulously by the 1949 Fourth Geneva Convention to rescind its previous measures and to desist from taking any action which would result in changing the legal status and geographical nature and materially affecting the demographic composition of the Arab territories occupied since 1967, including Jerusalem, and, in particular, not to transfer parts of its own civilian population into the occupied Arab territories."

Then in Resolution 452 dated 20 July 1979, the Security Council reconfirmed "pertinent Security Council Resolutions concerning Jerusalem and, in particular, the need to protect and preserve the unique spiritual and religious dimension of the Holy Places in that city."

4. Non-recognition of the annexation of Jerusalem, including its modern section, by the international community

Apart from re-emphasizing the internationalization of Jerusalem *after* Israel's occupation of the modern quarters of Jerusalem in May 1948 by its Resolutions dated 11 December 1948 and 9 December 1949, the General Assembly remained silent until 1967 over the question of the annexation of Jerusalem. It was only following Israel's seizure and annexation of the Old City in June 1967 that an outcry was raised at the UN. Since then, as we have seen, one Resolution after another has condemned Israel's actions in Jerusalem.

The silence of the UN over the issue of annexation until 1967 should not, however, be taken to mean that the world acquiesced in Israel's annexation of modern Jerusalem. On the contrary, such annexation was disavowed and rejected since 1948 by most of the nations of the world. The world's disapproval of the annexation of modern Jerusalem rested on the internationalization laid down by the UN for the entirety of the City of Jerusalem and its environs.

President Truman, the architect of the partition of Palestine, questioned in 1949, at the time of the abortive Lausanne Conference, Israel's transgression of its boundaries and its disregard of the General Assembly's Resolutions of 29 November 1947 and 11 December 1948 concerning territory, the internationalization of Jerusalem and refugees.[13]

Then in 1953 when Israel transferred its Foreign Ministry to Jerusalem and urged countries with which it had diplomatic relations to move their embassies to it, the Western powers protested Israel's action and refused its request. Secretary of State Dulles emphasized that Jerusalem is, above all, the holy place of the Christian, Moslem and Jewish faiths and that the world religious community has claims in Jerusalem which take precedence over the political claims of any particular nations.[14]

The US Government replied to the Israeli request for transfer of its embassy to Jerusalem as follows:

> "The United States does not plan to transfer its embassy from Tel-Aviv to Jerusalem. It is felt that this would be inconsistent with the international nature of Jerusalem."[15]

Secretary of State Dulles also declared at the time that the presently standing UN Resolution about Jerusalem contemplates that it should be, to a large extent at least, an international city rather than a purely national city.[16]

The Government of the UK took a similar position. In a written reply to the House of Commons made on 27 November 1967 the British Foreign Office said:

> "While Her Majesty's Government have, since 1949, recognised the *de facto* authority of Israel and Jordan in the parts of Jerusalem which they occupied, they, in common with many other governments, have not recognised *de jure* Israeli or Jordanian sovereignty over any part of the area defined in General Assembly Resolution 303 (IV) of the 9th of December 1949, which called for an international status for a designated area of Jerusalem.
>
> "In the light of this United Nations Resolution HM Government have held that the status of this area could be determined only in the context of a settlement in the Middle East.
>
> "It would in present circumstances be inconsistent with this position to take any action, such as the recognition of Jerusalem as the capital of Israel, or the establishment of Her Majesty's Embassy there, which would imply recognition of Israel's sovereignty in West Jerusalem."

In 1967, following Israel's annexation of the Old City, the US again reaffirmed its attitude of non-recognition of the annexation. It then declared:

> "The United States have never recognised such unilateral actions by any of the States in the area as governing the international status of Jerusalem."[17]

Two years later, US Ambassador Yost told the Security Council on 1 July 1969:

> "Jerusalem is a sacred shrine to three of the world's largest and oldest religious faiths: Islam, Christianity and Judaism. By virtue of that fact, the United States has always considered that Jerusalem enjoys a unique international standing."

In addition to the US and the UK, all the Great Powers and most nations have rejected Israel's annexation of Jerusalem, including its modern section, and have refused to transfer their embassies to it. Only the Netherlands and some Latin American and African countries (before their severance of diplomatic relations with Israel) had embassies in Jerusalem. Save for such exceptions, the international community disavowed the Israeli action in Jerusalem.

The non-recognition of the measures taken by Israel in Jerusalem was affirmed by several resolutions adopted by the Conference of Islamic States which convened in 1969 after the fire at the Mosque of Al-Aqsa. The Conference set up a permanent Organization to pursue and follow up its activities. The establishment of the Organization of the Islamic Conference was the first collective Arab and Islamic reaction to Israel's occupation of Jerusalem and to the danger which it represents to the Holy Places of Islam. In fact, Israel's occupation of the Holy City has unified the Islamic world and largely contributed to the political revival of Islam which we are witnessing in the world at the present time. At its Xth Conference at Rabat (8-12 May 1979) the Islamic Conference of forty Arab and Islamic States adopted several resolutions on Jerusalem. In Resolution 3/10 the Conference decided, *inter alia*, that:

— The liberation of the Holy City and its restoration to Arab and Islamic sovereignty was a collective Islamic responsibility.

— Member States should invite those states that have their embassies in Israel to resist Israeli pressure to move them to the Holy City.

— Adequate measures be taken to ensure the implementation of the Resolutions adopted by the UN on Jerusalem since 1947.

The Vatican also did not recognise Israel's annexation of Jerusalem. In his Encyclical *In Multiplicibus* of 24 October 1948 Pope Pius XII expressed the hope that "an international regime, juridically established and guaranteed" should be applied to Jerusalem and its environs. The same was repeated in the Pope's Encyclical *Redemptoria Nostri* dated 15 April 1949. Since then, in several declarations, the Vatican has favoured a special statute for Jerusalem. More recently, in his address to the General Assembly of the UN on 2 October 1979, Pope John Paul II declared:

> "I also hope for a special statute that, under international guarantee — as my predecessor Paul VI indicated — would respect the particular nature of Jerusalem, a heritage sacred to the veneration of millions of believers of the three monotheistic religions, Judaism, Christianity and Islam."

The non-recognition of the annexation of Jerusalem, whether of its Old City or of its modern section, thus being almost universal, it is, therefore, a matter of surprise that Egypt, despite its stand that the Old City be restored to Arab sovereignty, should have deviated from the attitude adopted by almost all other nations of the world. Article III of the Egyptian-Israeli Treaty of Peace with Israel of 26 March 1979 provided that the Parties "recognize and will respect each other's sovereignty, territorial integrity and political independence." This meant that Egypt recognized Israel's "territorial integrity" which, in Israel's estimation, included, in addition to the territories seized in 1948 and 1949 in excess of its boundaries as fixed by the UN, modern Jerusalem which it annexed in 1950 and the Old City which it annexed in 1967. Such recognition was made by Egypt without any reservations. By a stretch of the imagination, one might perhaps consider that in signing the Treaty of Peace, President Sadat had a mental reservation about the Old City, but he had none, it seems, with respect to modern Jerusalem, which stands on an equal legal footing as the Old City. Thus Egypt's attitude in this matter ignores the international status of Jerusalem as laid down by the UN in 1947 and stands in contrast with the position taken by the great majority of states in refusing since 1948 to acquiesce in Israel's annexation of modern Jerusalem or of its Old City. Nonetheless, since recognition is not under international law translative of title, it goes without saying that Israel did not gain any rights or title by virtue of Egypt's recognition of its territorial integrity, nor did such Egyptian recognition affect or impair the legal status of Jerusalem.

5. Israel's obligation to withdraw from the corpus separatum of Jerusalem

Let us first examine the legal status of Jerusalem.

Already in Turkish times, Jerusalem was given a special status. Under the administrative re-organization of 1887-1888, Jerusalem and its surrounding area enjoyed an "autonomous" or "independent" status, which meant that the city was linked directly to Constantinople, the capital of the Turkish Empire, instead of being dependent upon the governor of a province.[18]

In 1947, at the same time as it proclaimed the termination of the British mandate over Palestine, the General Assembly recommended that the City of Jerusalem shall be established as a *corpus separatum* under a special international regime and shall be administered by the UN. The boundaries of the *corpus separatum* were delineated in the Resolution and included the

City of Jerusalem plus certain villages and towns including Bethlehem. Although, as we have seen, this Resolution was not implemented as a result of the military occupation of Jerusalem by Israel and Transjordan, still it remained on the statute book and was reaffirmed by two subsequent Resolutions in 1948 and 1949. Moreover, as we have noted, most states have invoked its provisions to reject for the whole City Israel's annexation of modern Jerusalem in 1950 and of the Old City in 1967.

After the 1967 annexation, the UN adopted several Resolutions which have condemned Israel's actions in Jerusalem, and in particular, all measures that tend to change "the status of Jerusalem."[19] Other Resolutions have made reference to "the legal status of Jerusalem": Security Council Resolution 252 of 21 May 1968 and General Assembly Resolution 32/5 of 28 October 1977. More recently, in its Resolution 452 of 20 July 1979 the Security Council spoke of "the specific status of Jerusalem."

The legal status of Jerusalem extends to the two sections of the city, i.e., the Old City and modern Jerusalem. There have been various appellations of these two sections, particularly since the division of the city in 1948 into two military sectors, one controlled by Israel, and the other by Transjordan. All such appellations as "Jewish Jerusalem", "Arab Jerusalem", "East Jerusalem" and "West Jerusalem" are misleading since they reflect the military picture as established in 1948. In view of the confusion that exists in the mind of some people regarding these various appellations, and, in particular, with respect to the character of modern Jerusalem which they erroneously consider to be the Jewish section of the City, it seems incumbent to give a few words of explanation about this section of the City.

Until 1862 Jerusalem was a walled city and all its inhabitants, mainly Palestinian Arabs, lived within its walls. As a result of the growth of the population, the walled city could no more contain the increasing number of its inhabitants and both Arabs and Jews began building homes outside the walls. In 1948, the large majority of the inhabitants of Jerusalem, both Arabs and Jews, lived outside the Old City. The Arabs had fifteen residential quarters in the modern section of Jerusalem outside the walls, twelve of which were seized by Israel in May 1948.

The modern section of Jerusalem had, therefore, a mixed population of Arabs and Jews. The greatest number of the Arabs of Jerusalem lived in this section and almost all the refugees from Jerusalem in 1948 came from its modern section. In addition, the Arab inhabitants owned three-quarters of the properties of the modern section.

The fact that modern Jerusalem contains the homes of the Palestinian Arabs displaced in 1948 is not the only matter of concern. This part of the City has also a religious significance to Moslems and Christians by reason of the large number of religious sites it contains, including a number of Christian churches and religious institutions as well as the historic Islamic cemetery of Mamillah, part of which was converted by Israel for a car park. In addition, the vicinity of Jerusalem contains a great number of Holy Places located in Bethlehem (Church of the Nativity, the Milk Grotto and Shepherds Fields), in Bethany and in Ain Karem (birthplace of John the Baptist). All these Holy Places, as well as others (the Mount of Olives, the Tomb of the Virgin, the Garden of Gethsemane, the Garden Tomb) fall within the area of the *corpus separatum* of Jerusalem as defined by the UN in 1947.

Hence to speak of modern Jerusalem as being the Jewish section of the City shows a total ignorance of the facts. Similarly, to speak of the Old City as "Arab Jerusalem" — as if it were the only part of the City which is Arab — shows equal ignorance of the facts. A realization of the basic fact that the Arab character of Jerusalem extends to modern Jerusalem will reveal the insanity of a proposal often made to divide Jerusalem between Arabs and Jews, giving the Arabs the Old City and the

Jews modern Jerusalem. Apart from its incompatibility with the international status of the city such a proposal would prevent the return to their homes of the Palestinians displaced from the Arab quarters of modern Jerusalem in 1948, and, in consequence, would preclude the restoration of the Arab character of the City.

The legal status of the Old City and of modern Jerusalem is identical and the wrong caused by the Israeli annexation is the same in both sections. Both sections were occupied and annexed by Israel without right. To condemn and disavow what was seized and annexed in 1967 and overlook and sanction what was seized and annexed in 1948 is an error and a contradiction. The City of Jerusalem is indivisible and what is wrong in one part is also wrong in the other part.

Accordingly, Israel is bound, in accordance with international law and UN Resolutions, to withdraw from the entirety of the *corpus separatum* of Jerusalem as defined by the UN in 1947.

6. Implementation of relevant UN Resolutions

If Jerusalem and the precious holy places it contains are to be saved for the world's three great religions, it is imperative that Israel should be made to withdraw from the City and also that all relevant UN Resolutions on Jerusalem be implemented. This, as we have seen, is also the wish expressed by forty states at the Islamic Conference of Rabat in May 1979 for the implementation of the Resolutions adopted by the UN since 1947.

It goes without saying that implementation of the UN Resolutions on Jerusalem will not be easy. On the contrary, one must assume that such implementation will be very difficult. The task, however, is not impossible because the international community cannot be expected to bend the knee before a handful of political fanatics and an even smaller handful of religious zealots whose Zionist experiment could plunge the world into a war of religion.

The various relevant UN Resolutions that would require implementation appear to be the following:

(1) The Resolution of the General Assembly which recommended a special international regime for the City of Jerusalem. It is evident that, in view of the changes made by Israel in the demographic structure of Jerusalem, such a Resolution cannot be implemented in its original form. The principle of internationalization only should be retained but the machinery of government and administration of the City should be replaced by a new formula that would ensure the equal representation of each of the three communities concerned: Moslem, Christian and Jewish.

(2) The Resolutions which have called for the repatriation of the Palestine refugees to their homes, payment of compensation for the property of those choosing not to return and payment of compensation for loss of or damage to property.

(3) The Resolutions adopted since 1967 which have declared the invalidity of the measures taken by Israel to change the status of Jerusalem and called for their rescission. These measures concern:

— the massive introduction of Jewish settlers into Jerusalem.

— all confiscations, expropriations and other forms of misappropriation of Arab property.

— all other measures that tend to change the status of Jerusalem.

Although the measures which the UN declared to be null and void and called for their rescission are those that were taken by Israel in Jerusalem since 1967 and concern mainly the Old City and the environs of Jerusalem, it seems logical and imperative that the nullity should be extended to similar measures taken by

Israel in modern Jerusalem since 1948. The reason for their nullity is absolutely the same in both cases.

PART II

THE PALESTINE QUESTION

1. Essence of the problem

The Palestine problem is one of the most crucial and explosive issues in the world. Since it originated, it was the source of regional conflict with international repercussions: it has created one of the most acute refugee problems of present times (two thirds of the population of Palestine), it was the cause of four wars, it has unsettled the Middle East and more than once it came near to causing a confrontation between super powers. The last Arab-Israeli war was a principal factor in the quadrupling of the price of oil which resulted in the upheaval in the world's economy that we are witnessing today.

The essence of the problem lies in the usurpation of Palestine, a purely Arab land for two thousand years, by alien Jewish settlers who immigrated into the country against the will of its original inhabitants, proclaimed a racist Jewish state, uprooted the majority of the indigenous population and subjugated the remainder, all in violation of international law, UN resolutions and the most elementary principles of civilisation.

No other colonialist enterprise, no other conflict in modern times — such as the conflicts in Ireland, Rhodesia, South Africa, or even past conflicts, to mention only Algeria, the occupation of Alsace-Lorraine and Ethiopia — resembles the Palestine situation. All these other conflicts or colonialist adventures never involved the uprooting of the original inhabitants and their replacement by aliens. In all cases the indigenous population continued to live in its homeland. Not so in the case of Palestine where most of the inhabitants — two-thirds of the population — were uprooted and dispersed in foreign lands. The Zionist racist objective of establishing in Palestine an exclusively Jewish state by displacing its inhabitants and dispossessing them of their homes and lands is at the root of the Palestine problem. Sir John Glubb has rightly observed:

> "It is quite essential vividly to grasp the unique conditions of the struggle in Palestine. We have witnessed many wars in this century, in which one country seeks to impose its power on others. But in no war, I think, for many centuries past, has the objective been to remove a nation from its country and to introduce another and entirely different race to occupy its lands, houses and cities and live there. This peculiarity lends to the Palestine struggle a desperate quality which bears no resemblance to any other war in modern history."[20]

Clearly then the Palestine problem is the outcome of a series of wrongs done to the people of Palestine. The first and paramount of these wrongs was the violation of their sovereignty over their country. It is necessary, therefore, to discuss at the outset the question of Palestinian sovereignty because, though the issue may have been clouded by the fateful events of the last few decades, it remains the key issue and constitutes the basic guidelines for a solution.

2. Palestinian sovereignty

In Turkish times, the Palestinians were Turkish citizens and enjoyed equal civil and political rights with the Turks. The principle of equality of rights between Turkish citizens, regardless of race, creed or religion, was affirmed by the Turkish Constitution of 23 December 1876. The Palestinians had the right to vote and to be elected and were, in fact, elected as deputies to the Turkish Chamber of Deputies. Accordingly, they shared sovereignty over the Turkish territories comprised within the Turkish empire, regardless of whether such territories were Turkish or Arab provinces.

During the First World War Palestine was detached from Turkey in 1917 by the British military occupation. Such occupation did not have as objective the acquisition of territory and this explains why Article 22 of the Covenant of the League of Nations (1919) recognized the existence of the Palestinians, like other peoples detached from the Turkish Empire, as "an independent nation", subject to the rendering of advice and assistance by a mandatory until such time as they are able to stand alone. The legal effect under international law of the detachment of Palestine from the Turkish Empire and of the recognition of its people as an independent nation by Article 22 of the Covenant was to make of this country a separate and independent international entity or, in other words, a state in which was vested legal sovereignty over Palestine.

The grant of a mandate over Palestine to the British Government in 1922 did not divest the Palestinians of their sovereignty. According to the opinion of most jurists, sovereignty over Palestine during the period of the mandate vested in the indigenous inhabitants.[21]

Likewise, the Resolution of the General Assembly of the UN of 29 November 1947 which recommended the termination of the mandate and the partition of Palestine into Arab and Jewish States recognized Palestinian sovereignty over the territory earmarked for the Arab State. In so far as the Resolution envisaged the establishment of a Jewish State on part of the territory of Palestine, it did not, and could not, divest the Palestinians of their right of sovereignty over the territory earmarked for the Jewish State. The incompetence of the General Assembly to partition Palestine is now almost generally recognized or, at least, its competence to do so is seriously doubted by international jurists.

Accordingly, Israel did not by its occupation of the territory earmarked for the Jewish State by the Resolution, and much less by its seizure of territories in excess of the boundaries fixed for the Jewish State, acquire legal sovereignty over such territories. Its legal position is that of a military occupier: not having acquiesced in the partition of their country, the Palestinians have not lost their sovereignty over Palestine. They have only been deprived of its exercise, as in the case of the Poles whose country was partitioned and annexed by other states between 1795 and 1919, or the Ethiopians when their country was seized and annexed by Italy in 1936, to cite only two examples.

The sovereignty of the Palestinians has now been recognized by several UN Resolutions which have reaffirmed the inalienable rights of the Palestinians. Mention may be made of the following Resolutions:

Resolution 2532 (XXIV) of 10 December 1969 reaffirmed the inalienable rights of the Palestinians.

Resolution 2628 (XXV) of 4 November 1979 recognized that respect for the rights of the Palestinians is an indispensable element in the establishment of a just and lasting peace in the Middle East.

Resolution 2787 (XXVI) of 6 December 1971 reaffirmed the inalienable rights, *inter alia*, of the Palestinian people to freedom, equality and self-determination.

Resolution 2949 (XXVII) of 8 December 1972 recognized that respect for the rights of the Palestinians is an indispensable element in the establishment of a just and lasting peace in the Middle East.

Resolution 3089 of 7 December 1973 expressed once more its grave concern that the people of Palestine has been deprived by Israel from enjoying its inalienable rights and from exercising its right of self-determination.

Resolution 3236 (XXIX) of 22 November 1974 reaffirmed the inalienable rights of the Palestinian people in Palestine, including the rights of self-determination without external interference and the right to national independence and sovereignty.

Resolution 3375 (XXX) of 10 November 1975 requested the Security Council to adopt the necessary measures to enable the Palestinian people to exercise its inalienable rights and called for the participation of the Palestine Liberation Organization in the efforts for peace in the Middle East.

Resolution 33/20 of 25 November 1977 expressed deep concern that the Arab territories occupied since 1967 have continued, for more than ten years, to be under illegal Israeli occupation and that the Palestinian people, after three decades, are still deprived of the exercise of their inalienable rights.

Resolution 33/29 of 7 December 1978 reaffirmed the urgent necessity of the establishment of a just peace, based on full respect for the principles of the Charter of the UN as well as for its Resolutions concerning the problem of the Middle East, including the question of Palestine, and declared that a lasting settlement of the Middle East problem

> "must be based on a comprehensive solution, under the auspices of the UN, which takes into account all aspects of the Arab-Israeli conflict, in particular the attainment by the Palestinian people of all its inalienable national rights and the Israeli withdrawal from all the occupied Palestinian and other territories."

Therefore, the solution of the Palestine problem does not lie in the grant to the Palestinians of any new rights of self-government to be determined by Messrs. Begin, Carter and Sadat under the name of "autonomy" or otherwise. The solution simply lies in removing the impediment to the exercise of Palestinian sovereignty that arises from Israel's illegal military occupation.

3. Wrongs done to the people of Palestine

In the Palestine situation, there was an extraordinary accumulation of wrongs committed not only in violation of Palestinian sovereignty, but also of principles of justice and international law. A summary outline of those wrongs is given hereinafter.

Balfour Declaration

The Balfour Declaration of 2 November 1917 is at the root of the Palestine situation.

Regardless of its real meaning as to whether it meant an autonomous political entity or simply a cultural and religious home for the Jews, regardless of the safeguard which, in any event, was completely disregarded — and regardless also of its conflict with the prior pledges made to the Arabs concerning the independence of Palestine and other Arab countries, the Balfour Declaration was an aggression against the Palestinians and constituted a gross violation of their natural rights and sovereignty. The Declaration was aptly described as a document in which "one nation solemnly promised to a second nation the country of a third."[22]

Under what principle of law or justice could the British Government promise Zionist Jews the establishment of a national home in Palestine has never been explained. Legally and morally, the Balfour Declaration, having been made by a state which possessed no sovereignty or dominion over Palestine, was null and void and could not confer on the Jews any territorial or political rights. The British Government could not give what it did not possess. Yet despite its invalidity and ineffectiveness in creating any rights in favour of the Jews, it was exploited by the Zionists to impose and implement a colonialist programme which caused an irreparable wrong to the people of Palestine.

In defence of the British people, it is only fair to mention that the Balfour Declaration never received the approval of the House of Commons or the House of Lords, but was the act of the British Government.[23] In fact a motion in the House of Lords declaring the Palestine mandate to be unacceptable (by reason of its inclusion of the Balfour Declaration) was carried on 21 June 1922 by 60 to 29. This meant, in effect, the abrogation of the Declaration.[24] But the British Government took it upon itself, without legislative concurrence or approval, to accept the mandate with the Balfour Declaration included therein as one of its terms.

The Balfour Declaration did not receive either the approval of the international community. After the First World War ended and the Allied Powers laid the framework for peace, they adopted in Article 22 of Covenant of the League of Nations (which was incorporated in the Treaty of Versailles in 1919) the principles that were to govern the future of the peoples detached from Turkey as a result of the war. The Palestinians were among the peoples concerned. Article 22 provided that "the well-being and development of such peoples form a sacred trust of civilization" and that "their existence as independent nations can be provisionally recognized subject to the rendering of administrative advice and assistance by a Mandatory until such time as they are able to stand alone." One may doubt whether the people of Palestine were in need of administrative advice and assistance, because their level of culture and experience in self-government while they formed part of Turkey was not inferior to other peoples. One may suspect that the Allied Powers, not wishing to disavow openly their stated objective of not making any territorial gains from the war, masked the creation of spheres of influence in favour of Great Britain and France in the Middle East under the guise of the mandate system. Be that as it may, the apparent intentions of Article 22 of the Covenant appeared honest and free of mischief since it took no account of the Balfour Declaration, proclaimed the provisional independence of the peoples concerned and merely provided for a temporary trusteeship whose aims were the well-being and development of such peoples and eventually their attainment of full and complete independence.

This, however, did not take into account the power of the Zionist lobby which succeeded in making the Balfour Declaration one of the two objectives, if not the main objective, of the mandate.

British mandate

The British mandate over Palestine was not made in conformity with the underlying objective envisaged by Article 22 of the Covenant of the League of Nations of giving administrative aid and assistance to the people of the country in order to achieve complete independence. The draft mandate "was formulated by the Zionist Organization"[25] and its terms were settled by the British Government "in consultation with Zionist representatives."[26] In contrast, the parties most concerned and affected, the Palestinians, were not even consulted, in violation of the most elementary principles of justice.

The mandate so drafted had two objectives. First "to give effect to the provisions of Article 22 of the Covenant of the League of Nations" and to develop self-governing institutions and, second, to put into effect the Balfour Declaration. As to the first of these objectives, Palestine was administered by the British Government throughout as a colonial possession and there was no trace of any self-governing institutions in the country when the mandate ended in 1948. On the other hand, the Balfour Declaration was implemented by permitting a massive Jewish immigration which substantially altered the demographic structure in Palestine. As a result, from 8 to 10 per cent of the total population of Palestine at the date of the Balfour Declaration (55,000), the number of Jews in Palestine increased to become one-third of the population towards the end of the mandate (608,230 in 1946). Such a substantial and forcible alteration of the demographic structure with all its political implications and consequences caused a grave prejudice to "the rights and position" of the Palestinians, contrary to the terms of the mandate and furthermore created the conditions that precipitated the catastrophe which followed its termination.

We witness at present the disastrous consequences of this unnatural implantation of an alien people in Palestine against the will of its indigenous inhabitants. These consequences were foreseen at the time by some lucid British statesmen. Speaking in the House of Lords in 1922 in opposition to the inclusion of the Balfour Declaration in the mandate, Lord Islington pointed out that its provisions were inconsistent with Article 22 of the Covenant of the League of Nations and then continued:

> "the mandate imposes on Great Britain the responsibility of trusteeship for a Zionist political predominance where 90 per cent of the population are non-Zionist and non-Jewish . . . This local race is flying in the very face of the whole of the tendencies of the age. It is an unnatural experiment . . . It is literally inviting subsequent catastrophe."[27]

Answering this criticism, Lord Balfour, author of the Declaration, declared: "I do not think I need dwell upon this imaginary wrong which the Jewish Home is going to inflict upon the local Arabs."[28]

Lord Sydenham replied to Lord Balfour in prophetic words:

> "but the harm done by dumping down an alien population upon an Arab country — Arab all round in the hinterland — may never be remedied . . . what we have done is, by concessions not to the Jewish people but to a Zionist extreme section, to start a running sore in the East, and no one can tell how far that sore will extend."[29]

That sore has now grown to become a political cancer which is destroying the tissues of the Middle East.

The mandate over Palestine, by its inclusion of the Balfour Declaration as one of its two objectives, and its implementation in a manner that made the Declaration its sole objective, clearly violated the rights of the Palestinians as well as the Covenant of the League of Nations. In fact, the mandate became the vehicle for opening the gates of Palestine to a massive Jewish immigration and realising the Zionist colonization of Palestine. In the words of Lord Islington, "the Palestine mandate is a real distortion of the mandatory system" and, one may add, a perversion of its raison d'etre.

General Assembly's Resolution for the partition of Palestine

Another grievous wrong was done to the people of Palestine by the General Assembly's Resolution for the partition of Palestine of 29 November 1947. This Resolution bristles with irregularities, illegalities and injustices. Briefly, mention may be made of the following:

(i) The now generally recognized incompetence of the General Assembly of the UN to recommend the partition of Palestine.

(ii) The denial of justice arising from the refusal of the General Assembly of the repeated Arab requests to refer the legal issues affecting the Palestine Question, including the question of the Assembly's competence, to the International Court of Justice for an advisory opinion. The political forces that were working in favour of partition were not anxious to have their efforts hampered by an adverse judicial ruling and the request for an advisory opinion on the question of the General Assembly's competence was defeated by 21 votes to 20. Pitman Potter has observed that the rejection of the Arab request to refer the question of UN jurisdiction over the Palestine Question to the International Court of Justice "tends to confirm the avoidance of international law."[30]

(iii) The violation of the sovereignty of the people of Palestine and of the Covenant of the League of Nations by the partition resolution.

(iv) The scandalous undue influence exercised by President

Truman on some Member States to secure their votes in favour of partition.

(v) The revolting injustice of the partition Resolution which attributed 57% of the area of Palestine, including its best lands, to the Jewish State despite that the Jews owned less than 6% of the area of the country while it left to the Palestinians only 43% of their own homeland, comprising mostly barren hills.[31]

Proclamation of the State of Israel and its tragic sequels

The wrong caused to the Palestinians by the partition Resolution was consummated by the proclamation of the State of Israel on 14 May 1948, the eve of the termination of the British mandate. This proclamation which was made by the National Council, "representing the Jewish people in Palestine and the World Zionist Movement" on the basis of "the natural and historic right of the Jewish people and of the Resolution of the General Assembly of the United Nations", is tainted with an inherent illegitimacy. Two-thirds of the Jews of Palestine at the time of the proclamation were foreign immigrants who had not even acquired Palestinian nationality. The so-called natural and historic right of the Jewish people to Palestine was legally and factually a phoney and a spurious claim. The Resolution of the General Assembly for the partition of Palestine had no legal basis. In consequence, the proclamation of the State of Israel was a usurpation of political power and territory made in violation of international law and the rights of the Palestinian.

The proclamation of the State of Israel triggered on the following day a war between the new state and the neighbouring Arab States. Both the Palestinians and the Arab States had declared their opposition to the partition of Palestine and had indicated their intention to oppose such partition. But, unlike the Jews, there was no preparation on their part for this war. The Palestinians possessed no arms and no military forces as they had been disarmed by the Mandatory during the mandate on account of their opposition to Jewish immigration and the

Balfour Declaration. As to the Arab States who participated in this war, they were completely unprepared for it, exactly as happened in the wars that followed in 1956 and 1967. The Arab armies which moved into Palestine in May 1948 were token forces that totalled about 20,000, without any central command and no concerted aim. These token and scattered Arab forces were expected to fight the combined Jewish forces of the Naganah, the Irgun and the Stern Gang, all trained and seasoned, which numbered over 100,000 men. As a result, most of the territory of Palestine (80%) including a large part of the territory earmarked by the UN for the proposed Arab State and for the *corpus separatum* of Jerusalem, was seized by Israeli forces and about one million Palestinians (now over two and a half millions) were displaced either by hostilities, terrorism or actual deportation. And after the hostilities ceased and Armistice Agreements were signed, Israel stubbornly refused, as it still refuses, to allow their repatriation.

Not content with displacing the Palestinians, Israel dispossessed the refugees of all the property they left behind, movable or immovable. Movables were plundered. Houses and lands were confiscated. This meant that Israel seized and took over whole Arab cities and towns, (like Jaffa, Acre, Nazareth, Lydda, Ramleh and Beersheba, including the Arab quarters in Jerusalem and Haifa) and hundreds of villages. Arab homes were used to house Jewish settlers and Arab lands were used to create Jewish settlements.

The Palestinians who remained under Israeli rule, numbering in 1948 less than 300,000 (about 600,000 today), were subjected to a regime of oppression, treated as second-class citizens and deprived of their human rights. Despite Israel's claim of a "beneficent" rule for the Palestinians under its dominion, there is no doubt that the underlying objective of Israeli policy was, and still is, to make life difficult for the

Palestinians, politically and economically, so as to force them to emigrate.

Those were the tragic sequels of the proclamation of the State of Israel. The actions of the Israeli Government since it came into existence aimed at nothing less than the fulfilment of the Zionist programme for taking over Palestine without its people. The next step which Israel took in further implementation of its programme was the war which it waged in June 1967.

Israel's aggression of 1967 and its equally tragic sequels

Despite the falsehoods propagated by Israel in June 1967 to deceive world opinion and even the Security Council,[32] the war of June 1967 was a clear aggression by Israel against Egypt, Syria, and Jordan which had been planned and prepared in advance for the purpose of fulfilling another chapter — presumably not the last — of the Zionist programme. All that was needed was the pretext and this was furnished by President Nasser's closure of the Straits of Tiran to Israeli navigation. The fact that twelve years after, Israel still remains in occupation of the territories seized — to the exception of Sinai which it has partly evacuated — and that Begin keeps repeating that Israel intends to keep and colonize Judea and Samaria, constitute cogent evidence of such underlying purpose.

During this war Israel seized the remainder of Palestine, that is, the small morsel (20% of Palestine) that was left over to the Palestinians after 1948, as it also seized the Old City of Jerusalem, as well as Sinai and the Golan. It also annexed the Old City and surrounding area of Jerusalem, as we have seen.

Israel also uprooted and displaced more than 410,000 Palestinians. The Security Council and the General Assembly called for the repatriation of these new refugees. Some 14,000 were allowed to return, but at the same time as this token repatriation was allowed, Israel forced 17,000 Palestinians to leave the occupied territories and to seek refuge on the East Bank of the Jordan.

Israel's occupation of the remaining part of Palestine in 1967 meant that 1,100,000 Palestinians in the West bank and Gaza were brought under Israeli domination. In its treatment of the Palestinians in the occupied territories, Israel violated and still violates their human rights and the Geneva Convention of 1949. In December 1968, the General Assembly established a Special Committee to investigate Israeli practices affecting the human rights of the civilian population in the occupied territories. The Committee was not allowed by Israel to visit such territories. This notwithstanding, the Committee conducted its enquiries and reported to the General Assembly on Israeli policies and practices that violated human rights. In the words of the Committee, these violations indicated that "the occupying power is pursuing a conscious and deliberate policy calculated to depopulate the area."[33] The General Assembly condemned Israel's actions and called upon it to respect the Geneva Convention (1949) and the Universal Declaration of Human Rights. But all without avail. Since then, the Special Committee has been reporting on Israel's violations and the General Assembly condemning them, also without result. The General Assembly condemned, *inter alia*, the following grave breaches of the Geneva Convention:

— Annexation;
— Establishment of settlements and transfer of an alien population thereto;
— Confiscation and expropriation of Arab property;
— Destruction and demolition of Arab houses;
— Mass arrests and administrative detention;
— Torture of persons under detention;
— Pillaging of archaeological property;
— Interference with religious freedoms.[34]

An eloquent testimony as to the violations of human rights in the occupied territories was given by Mr. Michael Adams to the International Colloquium on the Rights of the Palestinians held in Rome on 24-26 September 1979. Michael Adams said, *inter alia*,:

> "Consider now the situation of the Palestinians living in the West Bank and the Gaza Strip. For more than twelve years they have been subjected to an alien dominion against which they have no protection. In every detail, the pattern of their daily lives is dictated by the occupation regime. Waking and sleeping they are at the mercy of a military authority which has the power —and uses it freely — to invade their homes, to arrest them, to detain them without trial, to deport them, to demolish their homes and to impose collective punishments on whole communities which impose severe physical hardship. Their publications are censored, they may not engage in political activities, their rights to assemble together for any purpose are rigorously controlled. Their schools and universities are subjected to arbitrary interference which takes no account of the principle of academic freedom. Their lands are confiscated without warning and under the specious pretext of military "security", only to be handed over to Israeli settlers as part of a bare-faced programme of colonization which has been repeatedly condemned as illegal by the highest international authority. Even the water supplies on which the Palestinian farmers depend are being diverted by the Israeli authorities to serve the interests of the Israeli settlers at the expense of the indigenous owners of the land."

Colonization of the occupied territories

The seizure, confiscation and expropriation of land by the Israeli authorities in the occupied territories has proceeded since 1967 without the slightest regard to international law, to the Geneva Convention or to UN condemnations of such actions. Seventy-nine settlements, including seventeen which encircle Jerusalem, were established in the West Bank and more than one-quarter of the area of the West Bank was taken over for the creation of settlements or for "security reasons". State land, or more precisely, what Israel wrongly considers as such, as it is more often common land of a village or uncultivated private land, is taken over without formality for the creation of settlements as if Israel were, in fact, the legal successor to state land in the occupied territory. Of course, a military occupier is not a legal successor in international law. In the case of privately-owned land, the device used is the recourse to its seizure and confiscation for "security reasons". The scandalous recourse by the Israeli government to "security reasons" as a pretext for the confiscation of private Arab land was exposed by the Israeli High Court of Justice on 22 October last when it held that the land seized for the creation of the new settlement of Elon Moreh near Nablus was taken for "political reasons" and not for "security needs" as claimed by the government. The High Court further rejected the contention made by the promoters of the settlement (Gush Emunim) that the Jews possess a "biblical right" to settle in the West Bank. The Court ordered the dismantling of the settlement.

A Commission was established by the Security Council in 1979 under Resolution 446 to examine the situation relating to the creation of settlements in the Arab territories occupied since 1967. But the Commission was denied access by Israel to the West Bank. Nonetheless the Commission reported its finding on the Israeli settlements policy and the extent of land seized.

The Commission stated in its Report to the Security Council (S/13450) that it found:

> "evidence that the Israeli Government is engaged in a wilful, systematic and large-scale process of establishing settlements in the occupied territories for which it should bear full responsibility." (*para*. 228).

Further, the Commission is of the view that:

"a correlation exists between the establishment of Israeli

settlements and the displacement of the Arab population." (*para*. 229).

Since 1967, the Commission found that:

"the Arab population has been reduced by 32 per cent in Jerusalem and the West Bank."

Finally, the Commission considers that:

"The pattern of that settlement policy, as a consequence, is causing profound and irreversible changes of a geographical and demographic nature in those territories." (*para*. 233).

The taking of land for the creation of settlements has been accompanied by an equally serious plunder, namely, that of water resources. Wells are sunk by the authorities to pump out the scarce water of the West Bank, with the result that Arab sources of water are dried up or severely depleted. To Arab farmers, this leads to one of two results: either to emigrate or to accept to be employed as labourers on their own ancestral lands.

Israel's policy of establishing settlements on Arab land is nothing but a colonization of the worst kind and a creeping annexation of the occupied territories thereby disproving any intention of their eventual evacuation.

Terrorist raids on Palestinian refugee camps

Armed with most sophisticated arms and aircraft supplied generously by the US, the Israeli Government has undertaken since 1949 numerous terrorist raids against Palestinian refugee camps and against neighbouring Arab States, more often under the pretence of attacking or retaliating against Palestinian guerillas. Thousands of men, women and children were killed or maimed in these raids. Between 1949 and 1968, Israel has perpetrated hundreds of savage attacks on Palestinian refugee camps in Syria, Jordan and Lebanon and was condemned by the Security Council for more than forty attacks, almost all causing heavy loss of life. Among these condemnations mention may be made of Israel's attacks on Huleh (1953), Qibya (1953),

Nahalin (1954), Gaza (1955), the Syrian outpost on Lake Tiberias (1955), the Syrian villages in the Lake Tiberias area (1968 and 1962), the villages of Samou (1966), Karameh (1968), Salt (1968) in Jordan, and on Palestinian refugee camps and on villages in Lebanon.

Between 1969 and 1974, Israel was condemned by the Security Council on four occasions for large-scale air attacks on Lebanese villages and Palestinian refugee camps.[27] There were many other attacks that were not brought up to the attention of the Security Council, in the absence of a formal complaint by the Lebanese Government.

Since the outbreak of the civil war in Lebanon in 1975, Israeli air raids and shelling of Palestinian refugee camps increased considerably causing thousands of casualties. This is not the place to discuss the role played by Israel in the tragic events of Lebanon and its contribution to the conflagration which occurred in that country against the Palestinians. One might its military operations against the Palestinians. One might perhaps wonder why since then there was a scarcity of Security Council condemnations of Israeli attacks which were on the increase. For this there are two reasons; first, Lebanon was too immersed in chaos to complain to the Security Council about Israeli violations of its sovereignty—except in March 1978 when Israel invaded South Lebanon—and, second, the US Government became less prone, presumably for internal reasons, to vote at the Security Council in formal condemnation of Israel's actions. This reserve in formal condemnation, however, has not prevented the US Government from denouncing Israel's massive and indiscriminate air raids last July against civilians in Lebanon. In these raids Israeli aircraft hit roads "filled with motorists returning from excursions to the beaches and the mountains". The US Government also complained against the use by Israel in Lebanon of US arms given to it for defensive purposes, though no action was actually taken to prevent Israel's use of such arms. And when Israeli air raids and shelling devastated South Lebanon and caused hundreds of thousands of Lebanese and Palestinians to abandon their villages and their camps to flee north, Andrew Young, US Ambassador to the UN, told the Security Council on 29 August 1979:

> "We condemn the policy of artillery shelling and preemptive attacks on Lebanese towns, villages and refugee camps which Israel and the armed Lebanese groups Israel supports have followed in recent months."

The pretext invoked by Israel to justify its raids was a so-called right of reprisal. This excuse has been repeatedly rejected by the Security Council in several of its condemnations of Israel's actions. But when Israel's reprisals received universal condemnation, it switched to another pretext, namely, that of "preventive strikes against guerilla bases."

Such an excuse is completely false and fallacious in every respect. A preventive strike is not permitted under international law or by the Charter of the UN. A so-called preventive strike is both a criminal aggresion against the victims and a violation of the sovereignty of the state in which it occurs. Moreover, a strike against Palestinian refugee camps in Lebanon in response to the explosion of a bomb in Tel-Aviv or Jerusalem or an attack on an Israeli plane somewhere in Europe can in no case be described as preventive action. On the other hand, Israel's claim that its strikes are directed against Palestinian guerilla bases is completely false. The accounts of witnesses as well as newspaper reports and photographs belie such an excuse and prove beyond the shadow of doubt that in all cases the targets were Palestinian refugee camps with their old men, women and children, not only in South Lebanon, but also around Tyre, Sidon and even Beirut and Tripoli in the north. But even if one were to concede that Israel's aim is to strike at Palestinian guerillas—which is far from being the case—such aim is simply a continuation of its aggressions against the Palestinians, who are merely exercising their inherent and legitimate right, recognized by the law of nations, to pursue the struggle for the liberation of their homeland.

One cannot resist the conclusion that the shelling and bombing of Palestinian refugee camps, with their frequency and the destructive weapons used, are not so much aimed at Palestinian guerillas and attacks on Palestinian refugee camps are purely and simply acts of terrorism and genocide.

Camp David Accords

To crown the long list of wrongs done to the Palestinians, Messrs. Begin, Sadat and Carter have now added the Camp David Accords of 17 September 1978.

Before examining the Accords it is illuminating to consider briefly the guiding principles which dominated the negotiations that preceded their conclusion.

After the euphoria that resulted from his spectacular visit to Jerusalem had subsided and even cooled in the face of Israeli intransigence, President Sadat abandoned the peace programme which he outlined to the Knesset on 20 November 1977. This programme, it will be recalled, included two basic points:

1. Total Israeli withdrawal from Arab land occupied in 1967, including what Sadat described as "Arab Jerusalem", because such withdrawal, he said, was elementary, not negotiable and not subject to argument.

2. Realization of the fundamental rights of the Palestinian people and of their right of self-determination, including that of establishing their own state.

After abandonment of his peace proposals, President Sadat limited himself to the recovery of Egyptian territory and vehemently declared: Egypt will insist on Israel's withdrawal from "every inch" of Sinai, on the dismantling of every settlement established by Israel and on the departure of all

Israeli settlers. To which Begin, in a language reminiscent of one of the characters of Shakespeare, retorted that Israel would not return "one grain of sand" of the Sinai desert without receiving something in return.

When a complete deadlock occurred, it was resolved, with US assistance, by the parties finding what they thought was a suitable terrain for compromise: Palestinian rights and Palestinian territory (West Bank and Gaza).

Accordingly, the Accords and the Peace Treaty between Egypt and Israel provided for the return to Egypt of "every inch" of Sinai, the dismantling of all Israeli settlements and the departure of all Israeli settlers. The price paid in return for the sand of Sinai was Egyptian acceptance of the Israeli plan of "autonomy" for the West Bank and Gaza, a plan which meant Israel's retention of these territories, its continued subjection of their inhabitants and the permanent exile of the Palestine refugees.

Therefore, the beautiful and deceptive rhetoric that figures in the preamble of the Accords such as the reference to the Charter of the UN and accepted norms of international law should be discounted because it merely conceals a sordid deal whereby Egypt would recover Sinai and the Palestinians would pay the price.

What is the autonomy plan which is envisaged by the Camp David Accords?

The autonomy plan is an Israeli proposal first made by Begin in December 1977. It does not mean real autonomy, nor does it mean self-government. It involves the establishment of an administrative body that would be described in English legal terminology as a local council or in continental countries as a municipality. The autonomy plan, as outlined by Begin, contemplates the establishment of an administrative authority without legislative or sovereign powers under Israeli overlordship, the continuation of Israeli military occupation subject only to the "relocation" of Israeli armed forces and the continuation of the creation of Israeli settlements. Begin made it quite clear that Israel would claim sovereignty over the West Bank and Gaza which he prefers to describe as Judea and Samaria (so as to impress these territories with a Jewish historical association), that the self-governing authority to be established could in no circumstance evolve into a Palestinian State, and that Jerusalem must be considered to be Israeli territory and hence not subject to the autonomy plan.

One cannot guess what is really in President Sadat's mind about the autonomy for the Palestinians which he subscribed to, but the third partner of the trio who concocted the Camp David Accords has clearly and publicly set significant limits on the scope of the proposed autonomy and indicated, like Begin, his firm opposition to the creation of a Palestinian State. In a recent interview with newspaper editors, President Carter, who apparently knows best what is in the best interest of the Palestinians, Israel and the Arab States, but not of his own country, declared:

> "I am against any creation of a separate Palestinian state. I don't think it would be good for the Palestinians. I don't think it would be good for Israel. I don't think it would be good for the Arab neighbours of such a state."[28]

Can there be any doubt that the Israeli proposal on autonomy is nothing but a sham and a subterfuge designed to throw dust in people's eyes so as to conceal Israel's usurpation of the small morsel of the land of Palestine that was left over to the Palestinians after the War of 1948? Its effect would be to throw all UN Resolutions on the destinies of the people of Palestine and to condemn the Palestine refugees to permanent exile from their homeland.

It is perhaps unnecessary to stress that neither Israel, nor Egypt, nor the US who have arrogated to themselves the power to decide the future of the occupied territories possess any power to do so. Israel is a military occupier. There exists no rule of international law which confers on a military occupier any power to decide the political and constitutional future of the inhabitants of occupied territories. It would, in fact, be an irony that the original inhabitants of Palestine should receive their autonomy at the hand of alien immigrants who usurped their homeland and it is shameful for any Arab statesman to participate in negotiations to that effect.

Similarly, Egypt has no right, capacity or mandate from the Palestinians enabling it to decide their future or to barter away their inalienable rights. Even putting the most favourable construction on President Sadat's intentions, the very fact of his acceptance to negotiate with Israel an anachronistic and colonialist concept of autonomy for the Palestinians in their own country—or more precisely—in a small morsel of their country, constitutes a grave violation of their natural rights since it puts in question their full sovereignty over their homeland.

As to the US, one cannot see by what right it purports to settle the future of the Palestinians. The US Government has as much a right to decide the future of the Palestinians as the Palestinians have a right to decide the future of US citizens.

We have seen that in Turkish times the Palestinians formed part of a sovereign state and enjoyed full national rights. It is preposterous for three outside powers to negotiate among them the quantum of rights to be accorded to the Palestinians. It is irrelevant whether such rights are those that Begin is willing to concede, or those that Sadat is trying to obtain, or those—minus a Palestinian State—which the US is prepared to accord because the very idea itself of granting autonomy to the Palestinians suggests that they are just emerging from a barbarous stage when, in fact, they enjoy a level of culture and civilization as high, if not higher, as that enjoyed by those who want to bestow on them the blessings of autonomy. Granting such autonomy to the Palestinians is both an insult and a retrograde step which will put them, at least, one century behind. The Palestinians are in no need of being granted autonomy in their own country over which they are and have always been sovereign. All they need is the withdrawal of the aggressor.

Accordingly, the Camp David Accords constitute an aggression against the national rights of the Palestinians, violate international law and UN Resolutions and must be considered to be null and void and of no effect in so far as the Palestinians and Palestinian territory are concerned. The great wrong done to the Palestinians by the Camp David Accords is that they delay the aggressor's withdrawal.

The preceding outline contains a rough sketch of the wrongs inflicted on the people of Palestine. These wrongs have violated not only international law but also the principles of justice. The concept of justice is not an empty one. The Charter of the UN prescribes in Article 1 that the purposes of the UN are, *inter alia,* to bring about by peaceful means, and "in conformity with the principles of justice and international law", adjustment or settlement of international disputes or situations which might lead to a breach of the peace. It is significant that the Charter makes mention of the principles of justice before international law. "If we may judge by the working of Article 1, paragraph 1 of the Charter, the 'principles of justice' are something distinct from 'international law'."[29] Kelsen also points out that: "If justice is identical with international law, one of the two terms is superfluous."[30] All were agreed during the debate that preceded the adoption of the Charter at San Francisco in 1945 that "the concept of justice is a norm of fundamental importance". [31] At the first meeting of commission 1 (UNCIO Doc. 1006, 1/6) its President declared during the discussion of the Preamble and Article I of the Charter: "We feel the need to emphasize that our first object was to be strong to maintain peace, to maintain peace by our common effort and at all costs, at all costs with one exception—not at the cost of justice."

The concept of justice is universal, and, unlike international law, is much less subject to divergence of opinion or interpretation. The concept of justice introduces into the international sphere a gauge of moral and technical values which are not conspicuous in the field of international law in its strict sense.

Is it in conformity with principles of justice that two-thirds of the Palestinians should be uprooted from their homeland and should be denied their human right to return to their homes, and that the remaining one-third should live in their country subjugated by an alien people, oppressed and deprived even of their human rights?

The principles of justice have not been taken into account in the only solution that has so far been suggested—by Resolution 242—for a settlement of the Palestine problem, namely, Israeli withdrawal from territories occupied in 1967. Can one in all conscience consider that the restitution of one-fifth of Palestine measures up to the enormity of the wrong done to the Palestinians? Such a pretended solution would solve very little: it would leave four-fifths of the land of Palestine in the hands of the usurper and it would also leave the refugee problem completely unresolved since four-fifths of the people of Palestine would be condemned to continue to live as refugees away from their country and their homes.

The unnatural implantation of alien Jews in Palestine and the displacement and dispossession of its indigenous inhabitants in violation of the most elementary principles of law and justice have created the Palestine problem. This problem is of such depth in infamy that it will resist patching and palliatives and will continue to be the most explosive problem of modern times until it receives a solution—not any kind of solution—but one that will correct, at least substantially, the injustice done to the people of Palestine.

[1]Josephus Flavius, *The Great Roman-Jewish War, AD 66-70*, p. 250, Gloucester, Mass., 1970.

[2]Henrich Graetz, *History of the Jews*, Vol. I, p. 114, Philadelphia 1956.

[3]Araf El-Aref, *A History of Jerusalem*, p. 833 (Arabic), Al Andalus Library, Jerusalem, 1961.

[4]Albert M. Hyamson, *Palestine Old and New*, p. 83, Methuen, London 1928.

[5]M. Franco, *Histoire des Israelites de I'Empire Ottoman*, pp. 4, 5 and 195, Dulacher, Paris, 1897.

[6]C.M. Watson, *The Story of Jerusalem*, p. 278, Dent, London, 1912.

[7]Official Records of the 2nd Session of the General Assembly *Ad Hoc* Committee on the Palestine Question, p. 304.

[8]Translation from *Journal des Debats*, 30 March 1919, cited by Philippe de Saint Robert in *Le Jeu de la France en Mediterranee*, p. 222, Julliard, 1970.

[9]Georges Friedmann, *The End of the Jewish People?*, p. 266, Doubleday Anchor Books, 1968.

[10]For details see UN Document A/6793; Rouhi Al-Khatib, *The Judaization of Jerusalem*, Beirut, 1970 and Henry Cattan, *Palestine and International Law*, pp. 188-190, 2nd ed., Longman, 1976

[11]The question of sovereignty will be discussed in Part II with reference to Palestine generally.

[12]Henry Cattan, pp. 252-255.

[13]James G. McDonald, *My Mission to Israel*, pp. 181-182, Simon and Schuster, New York, 1951.

[14]*Department of State Bulletin*, 15 June 1953, p. 832.

[15]*Department of State Bulletin*, 20 July 1953, p. 82.

[16]*Ibid.*, 10 August 1953, p. 177.

[17]*Ibid.*, 28 June 1967, p. 57.

[18]A. Heidelborn, *Droit Public et Administratif de I'Empire Ottoman*, p. 7, Vienna-Leipzig, 1908.

[19]See, in particular, General Assembly Resolutions 2253 of 14 July 1967 and Security Council Resolutions 267 of 3 July 1969, 271 of 15 September 1969 and 298 of 25 September 1971.

[20]Sir John Glubb, *The Middle East Crisis*, p. 41, Hodder and Stoughton, London, 1967.

[21]D.F.W. Van Rees, *Les Mandats Internationaux*, p. 20, Rousseau, Paris, 1927 and Henry Cattan, *Palestine and International Law*, 2nd ed., pp. 105-130, Longman, 1976.

[22]Arthur Koestler, *Promise and Fulfilment*, p. 4, Macmillan, New York.

[23]The Official British documents relating to the Balfour Declaration and to

British policy with respect to Palestine were compiled by Doreen Ingrams, *Palestine Papers 1917-1922, Seeds of Conflict*, John Murray, London 1972.

[24]*Hansard's Reports*, House of Lords, 21 June 1922, p. 1034.

[25]J.C. Hurewitz, *Diplomacy in the Near and Middle East*, Vol. 11, p. 45, Van Nostrand, New York, 1956.

[26]H.W.V. Temperly, *History of the Peace Conference of Paris*, Vol. VI, p. 174, Hodder and Stoughton, 1924. See also John Marlowe, *The Seat of Pilate*, pp. 60-62, Cresset Press, London, 1959.

[27]*Hansard's Reports*, pp. 998-1004.

[28]*Hansard's Reports*, p. 1015.

[29]*Hansard's Reports*, p. 1025.

[30]Pitman B. Potter, "The Palestine Problem Before the United Nations", *American Journal of International Law*, 1948, p. 860.

[31]For a discussion of the General Assembly's Resolution for the partition of Palestine, see Henry Cattan, pp. 69-90.

[32]At the very moment that Israeli bombers were destroying Egyptian aircraft on the ground on the morning of 5 June 1967, the Israeli Ambassador to the UN, on the instructions of Abba Eban, Israel's Foreign Minister, awoke the President of the Security Council to tell him falsely that Egyptian air and land forces had attacked Israel.

[33]UN Document A/8089, 26 October 1970.

[34]G.A. Resolution dated 18 December 1978.

[35]S.C. Resolutions 270 (1969), 280 (1970), 316 (1972) and 347 (1974).

[36]*The New York Times*, 11 August 1979.

[37]P.E. Corbett, *Law and Society in the Relations of States*, p. 286 Harcourt, New York, 1951.

[38]Hans Kelsen, *The Law of the United Nations*, p. 18, Praeger, New York, 1950.

[39]*Ibid.*, p. 17.

12. The Future of Jerusalem

Khalid Al Hasan

Jerusalem is so beautiful, and those who lived there and those who happen to visit Jerusalem have to recognise that it has a special landscape — even the air smells special. Those who would like to be sure of what I say, let them go to Palestine through Jordan and they will see that the moment they cross the river, the smell of the air and the sound differ. Jerusalem is the sweetheart of God, the sweetheart of Prophets, sweetheart of mankind, of those who believe in justice, peace and freedom in the world.

After my speech in the opening session*, I was offered many thanks, and some said: "You were moderate", and "Thanks for your moderation". I would also like to say here that we do not like to hear that word. Moderation and extremism are not the description of national causes. It is not a love affair, it is not a business transaction: to be moderate or extremist. In national affairs, specially in affairs related to human, social and religious values, it is only right and wrong that measure the act and the speech. If it is a necessity to use arms and instead we use words, it is not moderation: it is *wrong*. And when the necessity is to use words and we use arms, it is not extremism: it is *wrong*.

So we believe in wrong and right. True, when we talk to

---

*Reproduced at Appendix VI.

politicians they ask us to be realistic. To be realistic is something, and to be moderate in your national cause is another thing. To be realistic is to know that, as in our case, we cannot achieve what we want now. This is a reality. So we have to programme our struggle accordingly.

Israel is, so they tell us, a fact. It is not a fact: it is a *de facto:* by the act of force, because facts are always the *de facto* of right. Sadat, President Sadat, is described in the West as "the most moderate". In their terms of understanding, he is moderate because he talks the language of the West, because he has shifted from Arabism to Westernism, because he thinks the same way the West thinks about dealing with this problem and any other problem.

I was also asked what I mean by 'mini-state', and I have heard that the word 'mini' is not that good a word. To us *any part* of Palestine is 'mini'. Two states in Palestine are two 'mini-states'. When Palestine is united, the word 'mini' will be deleted. I used the word 'mini' just to express how, for the sake of peace, without putting aside our main goals of uniting Palestine, we are ready to act, to have a smaller state instead of having *all* the state because we have decided — as a strategy — that we will have all of Palestine all together: Christians, Jews and Muslims.

I would also like to say that I am not going to read all the speech that I have written, because a lot of it has already been said by the distinguished speakers from whom I have learned a great deal. Therefore, I am not going to repeat what you have heard, but I would like to approach the main subjects of what I was going to talk about today from a special point of view.

A 'lie' in religion and in civilised society is something rejected. But let us see how the 'lie' was used to mislead the innocent people of the West in order to justify the acts of their Governments against our people.

The House of Commons in the early 1920's adopted the Zionist slogan "We have to give the land without a people to a people without a land". At that time the population of Palestine was just about 1 million: out of them less than 50,000 were Jews and more than 50% of them came from Europe during the last 10 to 15 years of the 19th century. The others were Palestinian, Christians and Moslems. The Jews were here in Europe and they *had* a land — they *even* had a citizenship.

Colonel Meinotzagen, in his book *The Diary of the Middle East*, says that on 17th September 1919 a meeting was held in Sinai. It included the British Prime Minister and General Allenby and himself, who was acting at that time as the Political Adviser to General Allenby. The discussion that took place is written in his book. He says, "We discussed the future of Palestine in the following terms: that the First World War will emerge with two chickens — the Arab nationalism and the Jewish nationalism, and we have to decide from now which chicken to take care of". Then he says, "We have also agreed that science and technology are becoming a main factor in the war strategy, so, in the future, it is not the number of soldiers that will count, it is the standard of technology that will win the war. And the Jews that will come from Europe — they are Europeans, they know our technology and by establishing a state in Palestine we will have the power that will be able to support our ambitions in the Middle East". This is also another 'lie', not in the terms of colonialism. It is another lie in the terms of understanding people — and we have seen recently in Iran that the people, when they are united and have a good leadership, can beat easily a big army and sophisticated weapons (as the Shah used to have).

Colonel Meinotzagen also told a big lie about Jewish nationalism. I think, (and I was educated in Western schools — those schools of the Mandated authority in Palestine) we were taught that nationalism is related to race and not related to anything else. There is the British nationalism, the German nationalism, the Italian nationalism, the Arab nationalism. We, the Arabs, use the word *Ummah* and the word *Shaab*. The literary translation of the word *Ummah* is "related to ideology", and *Shaab* is "related to race". All those who have a minimum knowledge about race and race philosophy, could easily say that the Jews of the world are not a race. They do not belong to one race — they belong to many races. In addition to that, the purity of race does not any more exist in our modern world.

Yet another lie which was told to the people of the West was "We have to support, we have to help the Jews acquire a homeland where they can live peacefully".

If Germany is considered one of the greatest persecutors of the Jewish race, what is the explanation of the fact that all the Jewish societies and organisations in Germany were attacked and closed down and also the Jewish papers, while the Zionist organisations were allowed to continue even during the beginning of the War? What is the explanation of the financial agreements between the leaders of the Zionist movement and Hitler that they could pay money from outside and take instead of it German products, while it was said at the same time all over the world that the Jews were boycotting the German products? Even when we come here to England we will see that those who were known to be anti-Jewish because of religious or racial feelings, used to say (as it is written in the documents that started to appear): "By adopting Zionism we get rid of the Jews from our society and we will have a Jewish commonwealth in Palestine".

From these few examples, we can understand the volume of 'lies' which formed the base to try and convince the public opinion in the West that the policy of the Government of Britain, (and before that of Germany and other countries and later on the United States) — in creating Israel was for the benefit of ensuring a peaceful life for the Jews. But the facts point to the contrary, as I have explained.

Charles Webster, in his book, writes that Britain's partnership with the Jews helped its strategic interests in Palestine and consequently affected British plans in Europe and the Middle East after the First World War. He goes on to say that following Britain's promises to Egypt to grant Egypt independence, it became imperative to have a British presence on the other bank of the Suez Canal. This is the real cause, this is the real reason, why Britain supported the creation of a Jewish state. As for the United States, it delayed its approval of the Mandate for two years until Britain and France gave promise and agreed that the United States would have equal commercial rights in the Middle East; and then it became a partner in the major oil companies in the Middle East.

After securing European and American support for the idea of the creation of a Jewish state, the Zionist movement realised that a part, or even the whole of Palestine would not be enough for the establishment of a viable self-sufficient state. Therefore it used the element of religion to realise the following:

First, the mobilisation of the Jews round a strong ideology.

Second, the idea of expansionism to create Greater Israel, comprising a large enough number of Jews with a large area of territory which would enable it to be independent and self-sufficient without having to continuously rely on foreign aid and protection, thus becoming a partner rather than a simple tool of European and American imperialism, and eventually a strong independent power able to control the Middle East. Therefore the Constitution of Israel did not define the boundaries of the state, and a resolution adopted by the Knesset binding the State to a strategy of a Greater Israel was passed and is still 'valid'. It is good to talk about the future of Jerusalem on the term of reference of 'peace', but this term of reference could be saleable if there is peace in Palestine, and somebody is violating the rights of the Jews or anybody else to have a freedom of religion and the freedom of access to Jerusalem.

This is not the case. The case is purely political. Moshe

Dayan himself said, in a private talk in Paris, to some of the Socialists: "Jerusalem is a bunch of stones. Let those religious people wail whenever they want".

But this is not our point. Our society is not a religious society.

Lord Caradon is doing his best to find a solution for the future of Jerusalem. He wrote so many articles about that, and I do hope that when he comes to the conclusion it will not be a classic of British drafting, which always ends with dispute about the translation of the text, as happened with Resolution 242!

Israel does not want Jerusalem for religious reasons, although religion is used as a strong umbrella to convince the Christians, to create or to restore or to exaggerate the complex of guilt of Christianity towards the Jews. And that is why when you listen to the BBC, you will always find something from the Old Testament in order to let all the Christians in the U.K. remember that they have a duty towards the Jews.

So, religion is used as a tool. It is not the base and it is not the aim.

One of the problems we are facing is what I call 'The Term of Reference'. There is no term of reference to approach the Palestinian people and international society. Every ten years they have a special 'term of reference' and between the decades — I mean the beginning of a decade and the end of a decade — they deal with what they call 'realities' until a new physical state is realised by aggression and then they will say "Well, look, the old term of reference is out of date. Now we have new realities. So let us deal with the new realities".

This happened in 1947.
This happened in 1956.
This happened in 1967.
This happened in the Camp David accords.

And I do not know what is going to happen in the future.

Another problem of the 'Term of Reference' is that when one talks about the 'historical right' one is faced with the following:

"Well, you know, but — these are religious rights". When you say: "Alright, let us adopt religious rights as a term of reference", they will say: "Well, there are political dimensions to the problem".

As a matter of fact we are not able to find a starting point in dealing with the West. And I say here 'the West' because 'the West' is supporting Israel and it was 'the West' which started the problem and 'the West' that can solve the problem in one way or another.

Therefore I have found it my duty to give a brief survey of all the 'terms of reference' that can be used to prove that not only Jerusalem, but also Palestine, is an Arab state through history, through religion, through nationalism, through civilisation, and through the future.

This does not mean in any way that the Jews who are there cannot stay there. But before I start talking about these things I have also to mention something: that Palestine is very beautiful — but it is a very poor country. The three million who are there now — 600,000 of them are Palestinian Muslims and Christians — cannot live on the resources of Palestine alone. I think this is one of the reasons why Palestine's borders were made the way they were made: exactly the same was done to Lebanon and to Jordan, becuase of the strategic location of these three countries on the Eastern part of the Mediterranean. Palestine, whether an Arab or a Jewish or an American or any other state, can only survive if the Middle East was open to it: the same as Lebanon and the same as Trans-Jordan. If the Middle East is not opened, then it has to have foreign aid. Without this it cannot survive. And this explains why the Americans are paying four billion dollars to 'The Government of Israel' — that is, about *$1,000 a year* for each single Jew — otherwise the state will collapse. And this means that it is artificial. It is also the same with Lebanon. If the borders of Syria are closed and the planes are not allowed to pass through the Syrian sky, Lebanon will starve in less than a year. It is the Middle East markets which make the Lebanon survive — and it is the same with Jordan. And this was done purposely.

But here we have to realise that history has *never* told us that any state could survive for ever depending on foreign aid. Therefore, and taking into consideration the process of history, we are very sure of the future. The future is that Israel will not be able to receive the amount of foreign aid it is receiving now, and we are sure that the Middle East will never be opened in front of Zionism — because Zionism is an act of war. Recognising Zionism means recognising the right of others to take your land and 'pump' you out — and I do not think anybody will recognise that.

And here let us take examples from the history of the West. In the Second World War the Allies won: they were not fighting against the German people, they were fighting against the Nazi ideology. And when they won the war, the first thing they did in Germany, Italy and Japan was to change the Constitution and the system of education and the means of the media, in order to bring back to the people of Germany and Italy and Japan the terms of liberal democracy. Otherwise winning the war would have been in vain.

I do not know why they ask us to do exactly the opposite of what they do for themselves. Are we all not the people who believe that the values of social ideology are the main thing in our life for which we fight and for which we die? Has not that happened in the First and the Second World War? People were dying for the sake of democracy and freedom: they were not dying to take the land of Germany. Because when the wars were over, the Germans remained on their land. Germany, because of political powers, was parted into two countries. Until now the German people refuse to believe, or to accept, that Bonn is their capital! They insist that Berlin is their capital. Until now they believe that they should reunite their country. And when they came to recognise each other, it was included in the agreement that reuniting Germany is something legal — and it is included also in the Constitution of West Germany. Berlin was split into two, for two. Why don't they agree on uniting Berlin? What have the Americans and the British and the French and the Russians to do in Berlin? Why do they want to keep Berlin as two Berlins, while they love to talk about the unity of Jerusalem under the Israeli occupation?

I think that now we are facing a new era of our international life. In the past, because of the lack of communications there were clashes of culture between Europe and the Islamic world which led to so many wars, especially when both misinterpreted the culture of the other. Now, the world is becoming small. Books are everywhere. Radio is everywhere. TV is everywhere. And the international culture era is about to become a reality. Therefore we should not keep these bars between our cultures. Let the cultures of the world digest each other, understand each other, so that the time may come when we can understand each other mutually and stop attacking and inciting hatred as it happened with the Palestinian problem, and as it is happening now with the Iranian Revolution.

The world is becoming small and the exchange of culture will make an Englishman and a German and an Arab talk together — and understand each other — in a better way. But our problem is with those who are on the pyramid of authority. When I talk to Lord Caradon now he is called a friend, but if he became a Prime Minister he would talk a different language.

When we come to the rights, and let us start with the religious rights: as far as Jerusalem is concerned, it is historically known that Jerusalem was sacred since it was established — and it was established more than two thousand years before Judaism was known. Abraham came from Iraq to Palestine: he was welcomed — because he is the Father of the Prophets — and at that time Judaism had not yet become a reality or even a name.

The only established connection between Judaism, as a religion, and Jerusalem came when the Kingdom of Israel was established through invasion. It merely lasted 78 years as a united state and about three hundred years as a divided one, but Judaism originated in Egypt and came into Palestine. During the Jewish rule of Jerusalem no others were allowed into the city — as a matter of fact, when the city was conquered all were killed and those who were not, managed to run away. When the Romans came, and when the Greeks came, and when the Persians came — and the Babylonians and the Chaldean, and the Assyrians — they each had a monopoly over Jerusalem. At the time of the Crusades, the Jews and the Arabs, the Muslims, were not allowed to stay in Jerusalem; also, as we heard yesterday, the Orthodox Christians. While in fact, the Arabs guaranteed the freedom of residence and praying in Jerusalem 30 years before Judaism, and 1,300 years after the fall of the Roman rule. They have never been know to forbid anyone from practising their religious freedom in Jerusalem. When the Christians came — the European Christians — they fought each other because of the various sects of Christianity. And, at the time of the Arab rule, this fight continued to exist and they always used to go to the Arab ruler — to the Muslim ruler — to put an end to the struggle and to bring them to an agreement.

A significant event we should always think about: the way Jerusalem was handed over to the Muslims by the leadership of Christianity at that time. It was handed over by peace. They insisted that the Khalifa himself should receive the keys of the city. An agreement was signed, and you heard about it yesterday. But one point I should like to mention: that, when the Caliph Omar Ibn El-Khatab was in Al Kiyama Church and he wanted to pray, the priests of the Church asked him to do so inside the Church. He said "No. If I am going to do it, maybe a crazy Muslim in the future will come and say 'Omar prayed here — so the Church is a Mosque'." This was done by Omar.

What happened when the Zionists occupied Jerusalem?

I think you all know that two years ago the Court — the Supreme Court of Israel — said that the Jews have the right to pray in the Al-Aqsa Mosque. Look at the difference. Look at the way the Zionists behaved when they entered the Al-Aqsa Mosque — with mini-skirts (and that is why the word 'mini' is not liked by some of the people), with mini-skirts, without any respect to the holy traditions, and some of them tried to practise sex in the Mosque. These are facts. And that is why the people of Jerusalem are always demonstrating against them. And when I talked about the Crusades, I did not mean the people: I meant those princes, those nobles, who were really coming out not for religious reasons but to run away from their European disputes about authority and power in Europe.

This single example that I gave, in addition to what you heard yesterday, will prove two things:

(1) that the freedom of religion was practised for *all* only under the Arabs;

(2) there are no physical religious rights for Judaism in Jerusalem.

There are hundreds of mosques and churches but there is not a single place holy to Judaism in the sense of the holiness of the Aqsa to Islam and of the Holy Sepulchre (Al Kiyama) to Christianity. Not even the 'Wailing Wall', as you have heard yesterday: a mission which was formed under the Mandate, with the request of the League of Nations to investigate the property of that wall, gave the resolution that *all* the wall *and* the land and the *stones* of the wall *and* the platform adjacent to the wall is *purely Muslim property*. It has nothing to do with Jews and Judaism.

After 1967, they started to dig *under* the Aqsa Mosque in order to find a proof that there was a temple there — they have been digging for the last 10 years and they found nothing. Even Moshe Sharett himself, on 4th August 1967, said: "The Wailing

Wall is not a Holy Place — it is only a *memory* to the Jews. Give me a single Holy Place for the Jews in *all Palestine* — not only in Jerusalem: there is none. But it is full of Christian and Muslim churches, cemeteries, mosques — and memories."

We are not against having *memories* — and we respect that — but there is a big difference between memories used to justify a right of property, and using them to practise prayers.

When we come to the historical rights, it was very well explained yesterday, and I could not say more. But I would like to say one little thing: that if *invasion* (you have heard yesterday that the Jews came to Palestine by the act of *invasion*; they conquered Jerusalem, they conquered Palestine, and even when they ruled they were a minority, the Palestinians remained there — the Jews after that left: as a matter of fact they were Egyptian Jews who came after 400 years of living in Egypt) was a *historical* right — what about the *historical* right of the Romans and the Greeks, and the British, and the French, and the Russians in Palestine and the area? What about our rights in Spain; and Spain is full of our churches and our mosques and our culture? Is it not a fact that when an invader is conquered by a new invader, he loses his rights? This is the rule of history, the process of history. The Chaldeans came and went and the Assyrians came and went, the Romans, the Greeks, the Persians, the Egyptians, the Turks, the British, the French — they all came and went: but the Palestinians remained because it is their own historical right to be *in Palestine*. So, uprooting them is not right, and that is why the Western technology of law has invented the word 'legitimate' instead of the word 'legal'. The 'legitimate' right is the right that we agree upon, the 'legal' right is the right of the law.

So, historically speaking, they have not been there — they were always a minority — they have been given the chances of history to come back and they did not come back — and, as it was said by either Ben-Gurion or Weitzman, they used to come to Jerusalem, they only used to find the true religious people offering their prayer and living in poverty, while the other rich Jews were enjoying life in Alexandria and Babylon at that time, and Athens and Rome and London later on.

Who forbade the Jews from Palestine under the Arab rule? — Nobody.

Under the Turkish rule? — Nobody.

They were only forbidden in the old days of history when captivity was a rule of law.

So, I think, in addition to what you heard yesterday, they have not got even one historical right.

When we come to the Bible — and this is the breakthrough to Christian people in Western Europe — they refer always to 'the Promise' in the Bible: the promise was given to Abraham and his descendants. Abraham had two sons — Isaac and Ismail. from Ismail came Idnan, and from Idnan came the whole Arab tribes in addition to Kha'tan who belonged to another Arab origin. Out of Ishak (Isaac) came the Twelve Sons. So, if we want to adopt the promise of the Bible, I think it is the Arab Jews and the Arab Christians and the Arab Muslims who have the right to that promise, and when we say that "let all the Arabs, Jews, Christians and Muslims live together in Palestine in one democratic state", I think we give the real explanation and translation to 'The Promise'.

They claim that Hager was not a free woman, she was a slave and accordingly those who came from Hager were not legitimate. If this is true, then Abraham is not a Prophet, because Prophets do not practice promiscuity; they do not practice slavery. To be a Prophet is to believe in mankind and brotherhood and equality. The Zionists have neither a religious right nor a historical right in Palestine. What they really have is the right of power, through the Western powers, and not through their own.

Now that they are in Palestine, the people of Palestine are as follows:

67% Arab Jews and
35% European Jews (Tartar Jews) and
600,000 Arab Palestinians.

I do not know if you do know that the Arab Jews are considered in practice 'Second Class Citizens'. Out of 120 members of the Knesset, the Arab Jews are only about 10%, and out of the 20 members of the Cabinet there are only 2 Arab Jews. I do not think this represents democracy or representation. As for the Palestinian Arabs, who are about 600,000, they are not even considered citizens. They cannot have their political parties, they can do nothing as citizens, for now and then the Government will come and uproot the people from a village to another place. They have been horrified to discover — and thanks to our women — that the numbers of Arabs in Galilee is 52% now; so they wanted to uproot the greater part of them to the South, to keep a Jewish majority in Galilee. Out of the 37% of the youths who are entitled to join universities in Israel from among the Arab Jews, only 1% went to a University, while from the other part — the super part — the Nazi-thinking racial part — it is more than 52% that go to universities.

We, the Palestinians, the refugees outside the occupied areas — out of the slums — we managed to graduate more than 11,000 medical doctors and 21,000 engineers and 60,000 teachers, teaching all over the Arab world.

Can you tell me: how many Arabs inside Israel managed to be doctors? According to statistics: only one dentist. The Arabs are not allowed to go to the Schools of Science. They can go to the Schools of History and learn the Hebrew History, but they are not allowed to go to the Schools of Science: they do not want them to be educated, they do not want them to be graduated. With this kind of discrimination and this kind of violating not only the human rights of the people but also the human rights of the individual and of the mind — if the mind is human — I do not think they are entitled to have the sovereignty of anything holy: because they manage to destroy holiness through their behaviour. They are against civilisation as Zionists. They are against other cultures as Zionists. And when you come to an argument with one of them and you disagree with them, it is plainly that he will tell you "Look you are not a Zionist, you can't understand": this is the final argument.

Maybe someone will say: "What you are talking about is a political problem; and when you say it is a political problem, why are you talking so much about morality and values and all these things?" Well, when we talk about Jerusalem we talk about a religious value, a human value, and a social value; and when we talk about value, we have to put aside politics. Either one can be a politician — or one can talk about values. And, to our understanding, values should always have the priority because it is the values that we live for and the values that we die for. It is not the soil — it is the value, the social value, that we fight for. You will find that a lot of Britishers emigrated to the United States and Australia and Canada — why do not they emigrate to the Gulf, to Iraq for instance or to Syria? Is it because the land in the United States is more beautiful? Or is it because when they go there they go to practise the same values that they have in England? So, they do not feel that they are strangers one hundred percent. But if they want to go to Saudi Arabia, for instance, they will find themselves unable to continue living there because the values conflict with their own — so they only go there to work, they do not go there to live unless they have been attracted by that culture, and, in that case, they have become a different people.

I do not want to talk too much about these things: I think I have expressed myself enough. But adding to what I said today, and to what all of us heard yesterday, I would like to say that *we support* and call for one Jerusalem, for one Palestine: we could not have one Jerusalem for two Palestines. And because all the historical rights, the religious rights, the rights of the social values and practices, are on our side — and we proved to be not only the owners but the guardians of values, even if they were not our own values — so, *Jerusalem should be an Arab city*. We are going to fight for that.

Freedom of religion was never our problem, and I agree to what was said today — that it is the state of war that did not allow the Israelis to come to the 'Wailing Wall', and it was not because they were Jews. We have all the rights, and without solving the problem of Palestine there is no talking about the practicality of offering a solution for the problem of Jerusalem. But if we are going to programme our struggle and we will accept a state on part of Palestine, then Jerusalem will also be two Jerusalems until Palestine is united. I agree with what Lord Caradon said — that no-one should live in Jerusalem as a subject. But what kind of subject: we are all subjects of a state? If he means that a Jew is subject to an Arab — we are also against that; in the same way that we are against an Arab being subject to a Jew. Of course, to be subject to the country, to the state, to the social values, to the old religious values that we all believe in, is a law.

Therefore the solution of the future of Jerusalem, if we want to start with it, means that we have to start with the Palestinian problem. There is no united Jerusalem under Zionist rule. There is no future for Palestine under Zionism. Our 120,000 people who remained in Palestine after 1948 have doubled five times in 30 years. In another 30 years they will be three million. Immigration to Israel is decreasing and emigration from Israel is increasing — because everything there is artificial. And I say that we are very sure of the future even by peaceful means when we have our national state — but all what we are asking for, what we are urging the Super Powers to do is to let the real future become a reality in as short a time as possible, to avoid more victims, more hatred, more sacrifice, so that we can be the symbol of peace not only in Palestine and the Middle East — but for the whole world.

As I once said in London in 1975, "We do not want to throw anybody to the sea, but also we do not want to be thrown to the desert". So, we should come back from our 'desert' — the desert of statelessness — to the 'oasis' of belonging, of citizenship, of being human beings that live with all our brothers in peace: in united Palestine.

Two nights ago, I think, I saw a film here about one of the Indian religious sects. The hero of the film, when asked "What can you do?", used to say: "I can think; I can be patient; I can fast". And we, the Palestinians, we can think; we *are* patient; we *are* fasting; and we have the *will* to continue our struggle until we realise our human goals not only for us, but for those who have been subjects of Zionism — which is based on the philosophy of war and discrimination. Let us help the truth to be known to the public opinion in England and elsewhere, where the Governments will be forced by this public opinion to go back again to the track of right and not to the track of selfish economic benefits.

Lastly I would like to say something about what is happening now in Iran.

Because we are an oppressed people and because we are peace-lovers and the events in Iran may develop to an international tragedy, therefore I hope that this gathering will urge Mr. Carter not to use military force and to be patient, as he used to ask all the others to be patient when they are involved in international crises. And we hope that Khomeini and Carter, both of them, will be able to solve the question of the hostages as soon as possible, avoiding any kind of military confrontation, otherwise all the Middle East will come to a flare-up. The Americans should understand one thing: when we started to talk about our mediation, the whole people of the area were against us. This demonstrated the fact how much the policy of the West is hated by the people over there. This is the lesson that should be learned from the hostages: not just the pride of a Super-Power or the violation of certain laws, while we find that violation of *all* the laws is practised in Palestine.

Appendix I

Welcome Address by H.E. Mr. Salem Azzam, Secretary General, Islamic Council of Europe, at the Inaugural Session of the International Seminar on Jerusalem in London on 3rd December 1979.

Excellencies, Ladies and Gentlemen,

It is my great pleasure to welcome you to this International Seminar on Jerusalem.

The fact that this Seminar has been sponsored by the Ministry of Information, Saudi Arabia, underlines the determination of the government and the people of Saudi Arabia to spare no effort for the liberation of Jerusalem and Palestine. It is a matter of great satisfaction and gratification for us.

We also pay tribute to the late King Faisal bin Abdul Aziz, whose services to the cause of Jerusalem, Palestine and Islamic solidarity will always be remembered with respect and gratitude. May Allah rest his soul in peace.

I would also like to thank His Excellency Mohammad Abdo Yamani, Minister of Information, Saudi Arabia, and His Excellency Habib Chatti, Secretary General of the Organisation of Islamic Conference, for their cooperation.

Distinguished guests,

The continued denial of the legitimate rights of the people of Palestine poses a grave threat to world peace. What has happened in Palestine is a great human tragedy — the tragedy of more than one million men, women and children driven out mercilessly from their land, where they had lived for thousands of years. It is the sad story of a whole new generation of Palestinians born and bred in refugee camps. It is, unfortunately, the story of the trading of principles for political and economic gains by powerful vested interests.

And yet, before the Zionists appeared on the scene, Palestinians of all religious faiths — Muslims, Christians and Jews — had lived together in peace and harmony over the centuries. Their troubles only began with the Zionist infiltration into Jerusalem and Palestine — an infiltration which was actively aided and abetted by colonial powers.

The situation is, and will continue to remain, extremely explosive and a serious threat to world peace. It can be defused only, *and only*, by the restoration of the usurped rights of the people of Palestine through the establishment of a Palestinian state and the return of Jerusalem to its former status. It is the duty of all just and fair-minded peoples, governments and organisations the world over to throw their full weight on the side of what is right. We must remember that, ultimately, right *shall* prevail and the forces of tyranny and oppression will sooner than later disappear. This important lesson of history no one should forget.

Honourable guests,

Unfortunately there are some misguided elements who do not want to learn lessons from history. Some of them recently hatched a conspiracy at Camp David. Instead of solving any problem it has only added fuel to the fire. It is an ugly and crude attempt to legitimise aggression. It is a sell-out of the sacred city of Jerusalem and of the rights of the people of Palestine. We strongly denounce this conspiracy and consider it illegal, immoral, null and void. We are not surprised that the United Nations General Assembly has just passed a resolution condemning the Camp David agreements and declaring that those agreements "have no validity insofar as they purport to determine the future of the Palestinian people and of the Palestinian territory . . . "

I also take this opportunity of paying tribute to all those valiant men, women and children who stood up against the dark forces of oppression and tyranny and gave the supreme sacrifice of their lives for the cause of Jerusalem and Palestine. I have no doubt that their sacrifices will not go in vain.

In this Seminar, eminent and distinguished scholars, statesmen, lawyers and public figures from various parts of the world, including those of Muslim, Catholic, Protestant and Jewish faith, will look objectively and truthfully at the religious, historical, political, legal and social aspects of Jerusalem and Palestine, and present the true facts of the case.

It is our earnest hope that their deliberations shall help in projecting the problem in its proper perspective and make a significant contribution towards finding a just solution to the Jerusalem and Palestine case.

May God bless you all.

Appendix II

Message from His Majesty Hassan II, King of Morocco, for the International Seminar on Jerusalem in London, read on his behalf by H.E. Mr. Mohammed Boucetta, Foreign Minister of Morocco, at the Inaugural Session of the Seminar on 3rd December 1979.

It is for us a source of pleasure and satisfaction that the British capital should play host to an international symposium on the city of Al Qods and that we should address this meeting in our capacity as King of a Muslim country devoting its capabilities and energy for the recovery of this holy city. It is also in our capacity as King of a Muslim country devoting its capabilities and energy for the recovery of this holy city. It is also in our address your distinguished assembly.

This international symposium, which takes place in one of Europe's largest capitals, provides us with a good opportunity to address ourselves to the question of Al Qods in its historical, legal and political aspects. It is also an occasion for us to inform the international public opinion of the various acts of profanation committed by Israel and Zionism in defiance of the world's conscience, the rights of the Palestinian people, and the feelings and sacred values of the Islamic and Christian communities.

The City of Al Qods, which is the converging point of Muslim prayers, the crossroad of religions and the place where God's messages were revealed, is now facing Judaization and a policy of settlement which distorts the religious and historical features of the city. Consequently, the whole of humanity, and particularly the Muslim and Christian communities are now in duty bound to oppose firmly such Israeli schemes and preserve the heritage bequeathed to the city by the Muslim and Christian civilisations.

It is the primary task of the symposium, which gathers a fine elite of scholars and politicians, to stimulate awareness within the international public opinion about the religious and historical ties binding this city with Islam and Arabism, and also to make it clear that it is impossible to reach any settlement in the Middle East which does not provide for the return of Al Qods to Arab and Islamic sovereignty, as was the case before 1967; thus reasserting that the question of Al Qods is at the heart of the Palestinian problem and the Middle East conflict.

Al Qods symbolises the encounter of Islam and the other revealed religions. It is also the cradle of all civilisations. The city was run by Muslims for 13 centuries, and history bears witness to their tolerance and respect for other religions. Muslims alone are capable of ensuring that this continues to be the case. They should be the guardians and custodians of these sacred shrines because it is they who believe in the religions of the three Prophets, which are deeply rooted in Al Qods.

The Muslim world, through its Kings and Heads of State, proclaimed during the First Summit Conference held in Rabat in 1969 its determination to secure the restoration of Arab sovereignty over Al Qods, and its rejection of any settlement of the Palestinian problem which does not ensure the return of the holy city to its Arab-Islamic status prior to the 1967 occupation, a status which enabled it through the centuries to safeguard the freedom of worship and the sacred character of the holy shrines. The Islamic Conference, in recognition of the particular significance of Al Qods in the hearts of Muslims, decided to set up a standing committee called "Al Qods Committee", and entrusted it with the task of protecting the city and following up the implementation of the relevant resolutions of international organisations. During the 10th Conference held in the city of

Fez, the Foreign Ministers of Islamic countries unanimously decided to entrust us with the Presidency of Al Qods Committee. It is a very heavy task which we are determined to perform to the best of our ability.

The Committee held its first meeting under our Chairmanship in Fez last July. It made a number of recommendations, the most important of which stresses the need to recognise the importance of information, lay down a programme to publicise the question of Al Qods, and organise international gatherings involving a selection of scholars and politicians. It is in response to these recommendations that this Symposium is being held on an initiative by the Kingdom of Saudi Arabia, and with the assistance of the Islamic Conference Secretariat and the Islamic Council of Europe. Our meeting is also in line with the stands taken by the Kingdom of Saudi Arabia under the guidance of its great Monarch, His Majesty King Khaled, and His Royal Highness Prince Fahd, in defending Al Qods and the holy shrines.

In performing our duties as Chairman of Al Qods Committee, we have sent a letter to His Excellency President Giscard D'Estaing as President of the European Council, and another letter to Pope John Paul II, in which we explained that the city of Al Qods was being Judaized and we called for joint action to ensure that the city, which is deeply cherished by millions of believers of different faiths, is again the cradle of cooperation and brotherhood amongst men instead of being a cause of differences and hostilities.

The Arab population of Al Qods incurred all kinds of sufferings and tragic experiences. Since the Occupation in 1967, Israel has been involved in the progressive extermination of those people and the expropriation of their land and property. Israel attempts to undermine the legacy of their ancestors, profanate their sacred values, and distort the landmarks of their city as part of a scheme aimed at Judaizing the holy Al Qods. Israeli authorities are still exerting all kind of pressure and terrorism on Arab owners in an attempt to make them give up their property.

The Moroccan community in the city has greatly suffered from such practices. Thus, since the occupation of the city, Israel has been pulling down the Moroccan district, which is adjacent to the western wall of Al Aqsa Mosque, in addition to demolishing Moroccan houses which are part of the Mosque's assets in the Jewish sector of the old city. The Zaouia Abu Ghawth sanctuary and the adjoining mosque are the remaining Moroccan property facing such destruction.

The international community, through the United Nations Organisation, the Security Council and Unesco, has condemned and rejected such deeds. It has also called for the annulment of all similar steps taken by Israel in the past. However, as Israel shows only contempt for world and Islamic public opinion, and as she continues in her policy of Judaization and distortion of the city, turning a deaf ear to resolutions and appeals by the community, it has become the duty of the world public opinion, and particularly this elite of scholars and politicians, to oppose such practices by all available means and to condemn present Israeli attempts to distort the features of the holy city and disrupt its housing structure.

The international community is also duty bound to support the Palestinian people's resistance, and particularly the inhabitants of Al Qods, in order that the city enjoys again its former special status and the Palestinian people recover their legitimate and inalienable rights including self-determination and the establishment of an independent state on their land.

May God grant you success and guidance in your work.

Appendix III

Address by H.E. Mr. Habib Chatti, Secretary General, Organisation of Islamic Conference, Jeddah, at the Inaugural Session of the International Seminar on Jerusalem in London on 3rd December 1979.

Your Excellencies and Eminences,
Mr. Secretary General, The Islamic Council of Europe,
Gentlemen,
May the peace, mercy and blessing of God be upon you.

It is an honour and a pleasure for me, at the beginning of my activities at the head of the General Secretariat of the Organisation of the Islamic Conference, to be present today at the inauguration of this symposium alongside men who occupy the highest positions of responsibility in their own countries, and at the head of whom is His Royal Highness, Prince Fahd Ben Abdul Aziz.

Your presence here is undoubtedly to re-affirm your sincere wish to throw light upon a cause which, in the eyes of the entire Muslim world, is one of the greatest and most vital current problems.

It is also a cause of satisfaction that this honourable gathering today should comprise prominent personalities who have come to this European capital in order to raise before world public opinion, once more, a problem in whose legal, political, historical and human characteristics you are the most knowledgeable people.

It is a problem which, unfortunately, continues to be the victim of a conspiracy of silence and cover-up. The problem of

Holy Jerusalem in particular, and that of Palestine in general, is still encompassed, in most international mass-media, by a wall through which it was until now unable to pass to world public opinion. World public opinion is still held, in its understanding of this problem, by what the Zionist organs may concoct in their continuous distortion of the facts, utilizing for this end all of their diverse and advanced means.

Your Excellencies, Eminences, and Honourable Gentlemen,

Allow me not to go into the details of the various aspects of the problem and the stages through which it has passed, since I am confident that the studies of the esteemed researchers present here today will have all the details pertaining to this just cause. It is incumbent upon us all to exert, for this just cause, a great deal of effort and of sacrifice so that the truth — whose echoes will reverberate in this hall — may find its way to world public opinion.

Our presentation of this problem, once more, before world public opinion, and Your Excellencies' kind participation with us in this exercise, confirms our belief that the situation to which this problem has been relegated is one of the most dangerous situations that threatens the destiny of those very values for the establishment, preservation and defence of which humanity, with the people of this great continent at its forefront, has fought through the ages.

This symposium of ours is being held at a time in which the Palestine Liberation Organisation, the sole legal representative of the people of Palestine enjoys increasing sympathy from some countries in the European continent which, in 1947, had approved the international resolution forcing an Israeli entity inside the heart of the Arab nation in general, and in noble Palestine in particular.

While we take note of this sympathy as a pointer to the

increasing awareness of these countries we re-iterate the fact that the positions adopted earlier by these countries were in clear contradiction with the obligations they had already undertaken in the various international charters, and especially those that outlaw the use of force and territorial expansion at the expense of other people.

Did not these states as well as others undertake to abide by the Charter of the United Nations which expressly prescribes, in Chapter six, Article 3 and 4, the prohibition of the use or threat of force, in international relations, against the territorial integrity and political independence of any state; or in any form that is not in conformity with the aims of the United Nations?

Where is Palestine today? Where are its lands, its glorious history and its people?

At least, where are the lands and the sovereignty of that state which the United Nations had legally recognized on the very day in which Israel was created; the day in which the United Nations had adopted its partition resolution in 1947?

Excellencies, Eminences and Gentlemen,

Thirty years have now passed since that day in which was perpetrated this great injustice, which condemned the Palestinian people to destitution and deprivation of their inalienable rights. And since no one disputes today that each and every people has its right to self-determination, it is one of the paradoxes of these times that the Palestinian people cannot exercise this right. It is truly strange to deprive the Mayor of a Palestinian city the right to live upon the soil of his ancestors; to imprison him and then to put him on trial for the 'crime' of defending his own identity and the freedom of his people.

It is vital for the peoples of the world, today, more than at any other time, to protect the principles which they have developed and established, and at the forefront of which is the respect of human rights. I will not be informing this august gathering of anything new when I say that the aggression now being perpetrated against the original inhabitants in Palestine and Holy Jerusalem, and the measures aiming at the disfiguration, transformation and destruction of the famous, religious landmarks of Holy Jerusalem are proof of Israel's persistence in jeopardizing these rights.

The injustice, oppression and discrimination that I have just referred to have already been confirmed by the testimonies and confessions made inside Israel itself and by persons whose sincerity and integrity are above suspicion.

Excellencies and Honourable Gentlemen,

Allow me now to raise a question that I have always repeated in the international arena. It is this: What did Israel do with the huge and ever-widening number of international resolutions on Holy Jerusalem?

Israel has thrown all these international resolutions overboard and did not even hesitate only a few days after the 1967 war, to go against the entire world, by introducing a new law enacted by the Israeli Knesset entitled: 'The Administrative and Organisation Law' which authorizes the Israeli Government to enforce its laws upon any area or land which it may want to annex.

Through this de facto situation which it had unjustly imposed, Israel wanted to annex the city of Holy Jerusalem into its territorial domain, after it had occupied it by sheer force.

Then it began to implement a plan whose outlines were forumulated a very long time ago. Asher Grinsberg had exposed his cards by saying that the Jews had the right to re-build Palestine; and that this right should be understood as implying the reestablishment of the ancient rights of the Jews and as abolishing the rights of the present inhabitants who had, by mistake, resided upon land that did not belong to them!

Hertzel had expressed, on his first visit to Holy Jerusalem, the same greed when he said: "If I am still alive when the day of our occupation of Jerusalem comes, I will destroy every Holy place that is not Jewish, and I will burn down the monuments that had existed for centuries".

Israel resorted to execute a policy aiming at the elimination of Arab and Islamic presence in Holy Jerusalem through:

—Expulsion of the inhabitants and expropriation of their property;

—Destruction of their buildings; for example the fire at the Al-Aqsa Mosque;

—Aggression on the historical and civilization landmarks of the Holy City, and

—Then settlement of Jews in it with total disregard to all the international Charters.

Excellencies, Eminences and Honourable Gentlemen,

Both ancient and modern history — especially in the contemporary times through which we have all lived — testifies to the fact that it is impossible for any power, no matter how it may heedlessly persist in its delusion, to destroy the determination of people to preserve their original identity; an identity which is represented by its heritage, from which it in fact emanates, and which is considered to be tributaries of human civilization, as well as of its moral and spiritual values.

The Arab Palestinian people, gentlemen, has been thoughout history the honest guardian of the human heritage, and the witness to all the heavenly revelations in our Holy Jerusalem.

The reward given to this people, however, has been to condemn it, for the past thirty years, to live in destitution, under persecution and deprivation of its homeland.

World public opinion must understand that Israel's defiance

of the international community, as well as its non-compliance with all the resolutions adopted by the General Assembly of the United Nations, the Security Council and UNESCO, undoubtedly constitute a dangerous situation which may prevent these institutions from playing the role for which they were created, and which basically aim at the protection of humanity from danger, war and destruction.

Perhaps this is what the Security Council had expressed in its Resolution no. 271, issued on 15th December, 1969 and which said:

> "The Security Council, while feeling sorrow for the grave damage resulting from the fire of the Al-Aqsa Mosque in Jerusalem on 21st August, 1969, which has taken place under Israeli military occupation,
>
> "Aware of the loss sustained by human civilisation,
>
> "Confirms that any act of destruction or profanation of the Holy Places, buildings or religious locations in Jerusalem; or encourage, or plot to excuse such acts, would place the international peace and security under grave danger".

This resolution has been followed up with many other resolutions to which Israel did not pay any heed at all. It continued to execute a destructive policy in Holy Jerusalem that aims at the displacement of its native inhabitants and of its glorious spiritual content, and by so doing, it hoped to eradicate all the links that pull the Muslims, the Christians and the Jews into Holy Jerusalem.

The continued Israeli occupation of the city of Holy Jerusalem has become a matter which cannot be by-passed in silence. The international community must not keep silence or be indifferent towards:

Firstly: Israel's changing of the religious, historical and civilization landmarks, since these measures do injure the feelings of Muslims all over the world and are a violation of the sanctity of this Holy City as well.

Secondly: The oppression and crimes perpetrated daily against the native inhabitants as well as their expulsion and replacement with others.

Thirdly: The violation of the legal status of the city which has been enacted by the entire international community.

Fourthly: The threat to international peace and security as a result of these practices.

The situation has now become one that calls for serious and objective consideration of the roots of this tension and to eliminate its causes by ending the Israeli forces' occupation of Holy Jerusalem, by its return to Arab Islamic sovereignty, and by the Palestinian people's regaining of their inalienable rights to return to their homeland, to self-determination and to the establishment of their independent state.

We are fully aware of the fact that all peoples who are committed to peace — peace based on justice and dignity — share with us the conviction of the need to find a just and comprehensive solution for the Middle East problem, whose core is the problem of Holy Jerusalem and Palestine.

These peoples do share with us the concern that the subjection of the area to a state of continued tension would inevitably lead to its explosion, a state of affairs that would constitute a serious threat to international peace and security.

Excellencies, Eminences and Honourable Gentlemen,

The peace that had been absent from the area as a result of these policies requires a much bolder attitude, as well as more positive positions in favour of the Arab and Islamic rights, from all and particularly from the governments of those states that had been behind the creation of Israel.

Experience has taught us that the timely action by intellectuals and scholars with their integrity, radiance and influence, has been — and continues to be — a basic factor in dispelling the ghost of war and in the triumph of just causes.

Excellencies, Eminences and Honourable Gentlemen,

Your voices will have an effective and far-reaching influence because they are the voices of men who are known for their honesty and their militant struggle for the establishment of the principles and moral values for the elevation of Man, whom God created as His representative in the world and to whom He had entrusted a message that is too heavy even for giant mountains to bear.

I thank you for your attention, and hope that the work of this symposium will be crowned with success in the cause of peace and justice.

May God guide us all along the right path.

Appendix IV

Address by H.E. Mr. Chazli Klibi, Secretary General, League of Arab States, at the Inaugural Session of the International Seminar on Jerusalem in London on 3rd December 1979.

Ladies and Gentlemen,

The speakers who preceded me have dealt with the various aspects of the Jerusalem issue in a way that leaves no need for adding or details, or for expanding upon what they have said. But what I would like to emphasize is that this conference on Jerusalem today is an intellectual, spiritual and political event at one and the same time. This multi-dimensional approach which makes the political stand supported by intellectual considerations and enhanced by strength derived from faith in spiritual values, is one that cannot be achieved except through work for Jerusalem, and it is an approach which cannot reach the level of creative interaction except through work for Jerusalem. At the mention of Jerusalem the chords of our hearts are touched; chords that could almost be supressed by our involvement in the affairs of our daily lives and by our acceptance of the standards imposed upon us without a moment of questioning on our part.

Perhaps this conference in memory of the late King Faisal Ibn Abdul-Aziz symbolises the moment required in the lives of individuals and in the life of societies for putting behaviour to the test. Through this test according to the highest standards — a test which is a prerequisite for redemption — we could avert the tragedy that befell us as a result of neglecting the spiritual values dictated by the monotheistic religion of Abraham and the blessed prophets who came after him. One of the characteristics of Jerusalem is that conscientious work for the sake of maintaining its authentic character purifies worship from the tinges of fanaticism, purifies politics from being a kind of pretention and falsehood, and gives our thought that purity which could only come through true commitment.

Gentlemen,

I do not intend to deal here with the history of Jerusalem or to describe to you the reality of the situation in the struggling city today, for you know that too well. What I would like to refer to today is the deep significance that this conference acquires, especially as it is being held in circumstances in which we need to remember Jerusalem and consider it a central issue in our lives.

Jerusalem is our strong yearning that transforms the tension in us into strength in order to revitalise our determination so that Jerusalem does not stay under the present conditions but is free, pure and glorious once more.

Therefore, our thinking of Jerusalem must be coupled with a plan of work for Jerusalem and its liberation, just as Jerusalem liberated us from the domination of materialism and kindled in our souls the flame of hope.

But Jerusalem, in addition to being the city of the three major religions and the place where the joint dimensions of these religions are revealed, is also the capital of Palestine and the conscience of the Arab nation.

Zionism has deliberately set out to destroy the historic character of Jerusalem and the existence of its Arab role, and to turn it into an extension of its own racism, claiming in the meantime that it is its capital. Israel behaves as if it means to go deep in wounding the feelings of the Arab nation in trying to destroy the special relationship that attracts the Arabs to

Jerusalem, in preparation for isolating Jerusalem from its destiny which is definitely linked to the peoples of the area.

Even the states that deal with Israel refuse to recognise Jerusalem as a capital for the Zionist entity. This shows that prejudice for Israel, whatever limits it reaches, does not reach the level of giving legality to the annexation of Jerusalem by Israel.

Jerusalem then, by its spiritual and human status, and by its Arab destiny remains a high torch to the eyes of those who, in moments of loss of memory, pretend to have forgotten the true facts about Zionism and its aims or turn their attention away from the central reality of the Palestinian problem.

Jerusalem then is, in the conscience of the world, that voice which Israel could not suppress, even amongst some of its own supporters. It is for this reason that Israel refuses to open the file of Jerusalem; it fears that this would lead to the opening of the whole file of the problem of Palestine from the start.

But Jerusalem, with the values it inspires and the conditions it suffers, is stronger than the mightiest armies and is able to awaken sympathy amongst the peoples of the world. It will always remain a word of justice held in high esteem.

Gentlemen,

Jerusalem and its inhabitants live in a tragedy renewed day by day under occupation. Perhaps when they know that the world remembers them and gives Jerusalem the attention it deserves, this knowledge will be a balsam that relieves their pains and renews their hope. Their steadfastness, whatever the sacrifices may be, gains political and spiritual dimensions that will be the basis for a reversal which will inevitably fulfil justice and put matters in their true Arab and human perspective. Thus the Palestinians will be able to transform the sacrifices into strength that permeates thought, deed and spirit.

This is the message of Holy Jerusalem: the source of spiritual light in the area, and the meeting place of the major religions, the destination of Arab hopes and universal prayers.

That is, through the Palestinian struggle, the historic message of Jerusalem: Renewal of determination until Jerusalem is Arab and free again.

Gentlemen,

I greet you and wish your conference success in awakening world public opinion to the true dimensions of the Jerusalem issue.

Appendix V

Address by Mr. Khalid al Hassan, Chairman, Foreign Relations Committee, P.L.O., at the Inaugural Session of the International Seminar on Jerusalem in London on 3rd December 1980.

> Bism Allah — by the name of God — the God of all of us, and by the name of the Prophets — the Prophets of all of us — because all of us belong to mankind and to humanity.

I would like to convey to you and to all those who care about a just and peaceful solution, not only for Jerusalem, but for the Palestinian people, the thanks of our people.

The PLO and myself had hesitations about coming here today, the main reason being that the Seminar is held in London, the place where the whole tragedy of Palestine was planned, directed and — with its support — it was implemented.

So, in accordance with the process of history, truth and justice is trying again to face the public opinion of Great Britain in order to realise how they created an uncivilised problem through which people were uprooted from their own home under the umbrella of "the land without people — for the people without land", as it was said more than once in the British Parliament. At last we feel that the public opinion of Great Britain will realise that they have done a great mistake in the past and through the truth, through facts that started to appear in this public opinion, they will have the duty to reform what they have achieved in order to release the history of Britain from that black point which has been achieved for purely colonial and selfish interests.

When I read the topics of this Seminar, I noticed that all of them, with the exception of the last, that is, "The Future of Jerusalem", were an academic exercise, discussing the history of Jerusalem from all points of view and all angles. We are not against that, because academic discussions must always deal scientifically and objectively with facts within the terms of an ideology and a civilization. If we believe that the individuals and people are the resultant of their history and their development for the future, we must start by understanding the history of mankind. The results of this Seminar must finally lead not only to discuss the history of Jerusalem, or to talk about its future or to think that Jerusalem is an isolated issue, but to realise that they can again take up their activity in building up civilization as they have done in the past.

The future of Jerusalem, as I said, is closely linked to the roots of the Palestinian problem, and, therefore, cannot be practicably isolated from it. Jerusalem is the core of the problem and forms part and parcel of any process aiming to achieve a just and peaceful settlement in the Middle East. Unfortunately, the Super Powers, who were the origin of our tragedy and who can still solve this problem if they wish to — are confusing the issue continuously by forgetting the essence and tackling the ramifications of the problem. Therefore, new terms and labels are continuously being invented to suit the selfish interests of the Powers.

First, in 1947, a Resolution was adopted by the United Nations General Assembly calling for the partition of Palestine and, in spite of the illegality of this Resolution and its contradiction with the Charter of the United Nations and the national right of nations, most of the Arabs have accepted it. But this was not the whole issue, because it is not the international or the national legality that we are dealing with; it is the legality of Power. And that is why when the Israelis planned their aggression in 1967, another Resolution was adopted and it was given the number 242, and all the Super Powers, and especially the Western, forgot what they decided in 1947 and in 1952, about the right of the Palestinian refugees to go back home. They forgot all that, and they said: let us apply this Resolution 242; which not only by-passed the Palestinian problem but ignored all the roots of the problem and dealt with the results of the aggression of 1967 as if the whole problem started from that date!

It was not only that. Recently, in 1979, a Camp David Agreement was signed. This agreement also forgot the Resolutions adopted by the United Nations General Assembly in 1947, in 1952, and all the other Resolutions concerning Jerusalem; and they forgot *even 242*. They by-passed the whole thing and they started with a new term of reference — the term of reference which contradicts all human values. There, in Camp David, they gave themselves the right to determine the future of the Palestinian people without the existence of this people, without the participation of this people, without the authorisation of this people. They confiscated the right of self-determination for the Palestinian people, and they are always asking us to be hopeful, tc be moderate and to co-operate with what they called the "self-rule" in the West Bank and Gaza.

Therefore, we could easily say that what is happening now, referring to our problem, although it is addressed by the Super Powers and the Super Power media — and, when I say the Super Powers, I do not only mean the United States but I mean Europe as a whole, and the other Super Powers — when they talk about our problem, they always use the term "peace" — but in reality they do not want "peace". They want "security and stability" to keep the oil flowing and to keep the industry running. They want something that we do not object to — that we are not against — not only as Palestinians but also as Arabs. This is not our nature, this is not our culture, and this is not our future thinking — but they say it that way in order to put the blame on the Arabs and the Palestinians.

There is great difference between *peace* and *security and stability*.

Peace is a way of thinking: it is that type of ideology and thinking, which includes deep in itself the process, the belief, and the future of peaceful relations that are based on justice and co-operation. This could only be realised by powers supporting this kind of thought.

Security and stability in the international parlance of our days is exactly like what dictators in local governments practice: "stability and security" by the police, the army, and the secret police. Security is a physical state, stability is a physical state that could be realised by power: but *it will not last*, because deep in itself it has the roots of revolt, revolt to realise justice, to realise peace through the ideology of peace.

Zionism, as it was described by the Zionist thinkers, is Grand Israel to be implemented — and here I am using their words — by "pumping in the Jews from outside and pumping out the Arabs from inside". This kind of philosophy has nothing to do with "peace". It is deeply related to war, aggression, discrimination and invasion. The Super Powers are only thinking of how to keep their interests, although through peace and co-operation and justice interests could be kept in a much better way — and in a more durable way — than that which is kept by the acts of force and colonialism.

Therefore, we Palestinians, who are a part of the Arab nation and the product not only of the Islamic culture but of the international cultures because of the location of our country and the history of our country in which all civilisations of the world mixed and developed: *we do believe* that there will be no peace in the Middle East and there will be no future for Jerusalem — a peaceful future for Jerusalem — without realising justice to the Palestinian people and without working through a peaceful and just settlement for the conflict in the Middle East.

Peace is always related to justice and justice is always related to truth: without that, no peace could be realised.

That is why, when we were told that "you are living now in the second half of the twentieth century, where you have to deal with politics in accordance with the terms of the 'balance of power' that exists these days", we said: "Those who are ready to sell half or three quarters of their homeland, are not even entitled to have the rest for themselves." And I am sure that this is not only a Palestinian phenomena, it is also a sort of a law that dominates all the nations of the world, including Britain. Indeed let us go thirty years ago to the Second World War and see what Britain did in order to lead freedom and democracy to victory against tyranny and Nazism. If *you* have the right to do that for your *own* people and for the international world, I think *we* also have the right to do it for *our* own people and the peace of the world.

Because we are Arabs, because we are Muslims and Christians who also believe in Judaism according to the instructions of our religions, because our history is clean from any kind of discrimination based on race or religion, and because we believe in humanity and the peaceful future of this world, we accepted the rest of all those who came from outside the Arab world, from Europe and Russia, whom you called Semites — although they are not — they are Aryans, and that is why they are called the 13th tribe in Judaism and they are not one of any of the twelve tribes. We said, alright, let us all live together, let us share with those people who have suffered all their history from the European civilizations, let us share with them our homeland and live all together in peace in a democratic state, all equal, as equal citizens in front of the law.

But they refused that because they want, as they say, "a

purely Jewish state". In reality they want a grand Israel that controls the Middle East and to be a partner of the international colonialism or, at least let us say it in the new terms: "international Super Power policy".

Then we were told: "go on you Palestinians, you are fighting a power that you cannot win against". Here again we say, it is only *states* that calculate too much when they want to enjoy a war; but when it comes to the *people*, it is the people's strength and the people's social values and the people's future that create revolutions, and revolutions prove to be always the fight of the weak against the strong, not like the wars between states; the fight and the aggression of the strong against the weak.

We believe in the *power of right* and we are against the *right of power*.

So we will continue struggling and struggling until we are fully recognised; and to display our good intentions for peace we say: let us have an independent mini-state on a part of Palestine provided this will not stop us from using our peaceful and democratic means to unite Palestine. Because by doing that we do not only restore justice in Palestine, we also help the Jews to survive from the filthy racism of Zionism and they will become Jews again, the followers of the Torah and the Bible, and they can live together as they lived for the many thousand years in the past as citizens without any kind of discrimination, without any kind of religious persecution, far from what they suffered in Russia and Europe. They can again be living in the land which originally belonged to the Arabs and, although 35 per cent of those who are dominating Israel are non-Arabs — they are Europeans — they are still accepted if they want to stay without Zionism.

You can see that in spite of our sufferings and in spite of our losses, which until now are more than 10 per cent of our population, we are willing to continue our struggle until we are recognised fully — people, rights, and leadership — and are able to practice our right of self-determination, to establish our independent state. Then the peaceful means will follow to re-unite Palestine, and *only then* the problem of Jerusalem will be solved for ever: when it becomes the City of Peace where followers of all religions can come freely, stay freely, and practice their prayers freely, in that city of God.

Appendix VI

Paper by Mr. Khalid al-Hassan, Chairman, Foreign Relations Committee, P.L.O., presented at the International Seminar on Jerusalem in London on 5th December 1979.

A feeling of irony and bitterness must overcome any well-informed person assisting in a discussion on the future of Jerusalem in London, the capital of a power which holds prime responsibility for the tragedy of the Palestinian people and for the dark fate that has befallen Jerusalem.

This was the price paid so that colonial policies such as those expressed by King George V, when he said to Colonel Miener Tsagen: "We would like to create a Jewish commonwealth in Palestine", are callously put into practice.

All the supporters of such a Jewish state — Zionists, British, French, German, in Palestine shared in the belief that such a state would be the only means of guaranteeing the economic and commercial interests of their respective countries. The leaders of the Zionist movement made tentative offers of services, first to Germany, then to Britain and the U.S., presenting themselves as guarantors of the interest of those powers in the Middle East.

From the Eighteenth Century and until the end of the First World War the world witnessed the struggle between France, Britain, Germany and Russia for the domination of the Middle East, in order to control all the routes of trade to the Far East and to become the dominating power in Europe. This was in no way related to any principles of civilisation, culture or religion.

The discovery of oil in the early years of the Twentieth Century in Iran and Northern Iraq and later in various countries of the Middle East, made it even more imperative for the colonial powers to attempt to dominate the area.

The following are historical examples of the interconnection between the idea of the Jewish state and European imperialist aims:

1. In 1799 Napoleon declared that he was ready to allow the Jews to return to Jerusalem and build the temple if they helped him financially in his war against Britain.
2. In 1837 the British Prime Minister, Lord Palmerston, asked his Ambassador in Constantinople to contact the Jews of Greater Syria (Palestine being part of it) and convince them as a religious minority to ask for British protection, thus providing Britain with the opportunity to enter the area as a protector of religious minorities in the same role as France, Austria and Czarist Russia.
3. Bismark proposed the creation of a Jewish state on both banks of the Euphrates to protect the trade route he was dreaming of building to India and in order to break up the British monopoly of the Suez Canal and the trade routes linking the Mediterranean to the Arab Gulf.

As for the Zionist movement, which Britain helped to create and support, Palestine was the last place it sought for the establishment of a Jewish state. First suggestions centred on Sinai, Syria, Libya, Uganda and Argentina, before the decision rested on Palestine. At the same time the majority of World Jewry was against Zionism.

The U.S. delayed giving its agreement to a British mandate in Palestine for two years until it secured from France and Britain equal economic rights in the area.

While Russia and Europe were busy in the last decade of the Ottoman Empire trying to dismember that Empire, they were simultaneously and paradoxically opposed to the independence of the Arabs from Ottoman rule. Consequently they supported Turkey in suppressing all the Arab movements of independence and unity: the most prominent example of this being the Anglo-French attitude towards the campaign of Ibrahim Pasha, hence their intervention which forced the Egyptian troops back from Syria and Palestine.

This was a brief survey of historical events resulting from the colonial policy carried out in the Middle East by European powers from the end of the Eighteenth Century to the end of the First World War. It entailed occupation, colonization, and dismemberment. All talk about European sympathy towards helping the Jews to establish a state for purely humanitarian reasons was nothing but an empty myth.

The age of European thought based on racism and religious fanaticism which flourished during the Eighteenth and Nineteenth Centuries, and which was accompanied by the European colonisation of various areas of Africa and Asia created a new political movement among some of the Jews of Europe centred upon the quest for a land to colonise. As this idea coincided with European ambition in the Middle East, it resulted in Britain embracing the Zionist movement represented by Weizman and Ben Gurion.

In his book, Charles Webster writes on page 124 that Britain's partnership with the Jews helped its strategic interests in Palestine, and consequently affected British plans in Europe and the Middle East after the War (First World War). He goes on to say that following Britain's promises to Egypt to grant it independence, it became imperative to have a British presence on the other bank of the Suez Canal.

After securing European and American support for the idea of the creation of a Jewish state, the Zionist movement realised that a part or even the whole of Palestine would not be enough for the establishment of a viable self-sufficient state, therefore it used the element of religion to realise the following:

1. The mobilisation of the Jews round a strong ideological doctrine.
2. The justification of the idea of "expansionism" to create a Greater Israel comprising a large enough number of Jews with a large area of territory whch would enable it to be independently self-sufficient, without having to continuously rely on foreign aid and protection, thus becoming a partner rather than a simple tool of European and American imperialism, and, eventually, a strong independent power able to control the Middle East.

Consequently:

(a) The constitution of Israel did not define the boundaries of the state.

(b) A resolution binding the Knesset to the strategy of a Greater Israel was passed and is still valid.

In addition, the state of Israel is based on the Zionist ideology which believes

(a) in a Greater Israel

(b) in Jewish immigration into Israel and the expulsion of the Arabs plus gradual expansion through wars.

Thus we can state categorically that as a result of the policy implemented by the Zionists in the past and in the present and which they are determined to implement in the future, that we cannot discuss the future of Jerusalem as a city in isolation from the Arab-Israeli or Palestinian-Zionist conflict in Palestine. This is an academic exercise which results in political numbness and to distraction from our objective.

Israel does not want Jerusalem for religious reasons — it wants Jerusalem and the West Bank and the Gaza Strip and other territories in Lebanon, Syria, Jordan and Egypt because it wants a Greater Israel.

But since we have agreed to participate in this Seminar on Jerusalem, we would like to say that any discussion on the future of Jerusalem will lead us inevitably to the conclusion that the whole of Jerusalem is an Arab city, and that it should remain under Arab sovereignty for established historical, political and cultural reasons:

1. *Religious Freedom:*

It is historically known that Jerusalem was a holy city before the advent of Judaism. In fact the only established connection between Judaism as a religion and Jerusalem came when the Kingdom of Israel was established through invasion. It merely lasted 78 years as a unified state and 200 years as a divided one. Judaism originated in Egypt and Sinai, not in Palestine or Jerusalem.

During the Jewish rule of Jerusalem no others were allowed into the city, whereas for the 3,000 previous years under Arab Canaanite rule, Jerusalem was free for all.

When Abraham came to Palestine from Iraq he was welcomed by the people and was offered a house and a tomb (which he insisted on paying for) because of his great religious prestige which was in no way connected with Judaism's claim on Palestine or Jerusalem.

When the Assyrians and the Babylonians invaded Palestine, the Jews were forbidden from entering Jerusalem and they were exiled to Babylon from whence they came.

With the Roman invasion of Palestine, the Jews were again banned from Jerusalem and their temples were destroyed.

When Christianity spread throughout the Roman Empire, the Christians forbade the Jews to live or pray in Jerusalem because of their attitude towards Christ.

With the liberation of Palestine from Roman rule during

the reign of Omar Ben Al-Khattab, the Christian religious leaders surrendered Jerusalem, and by virtue of an agreement between these leaders and the Caliph, the Jews remained barred from the city.

When the Crusaders took control of Jerusalem, they barred both Moslems and Jews from living there.

In fact the Arabs guaranteed the freedom of residence and praying in Jerusalem 3,000 years before Judaism and for 1,300 years after the fall of the Roman rule. They have never been known to forbid any one from practising their religious freedom in Jerusalem.

Byzantine-Roman rivalry which resulted in a division in the Church, led to an armed struggle between them over the holy places in Palestine. It was only through the good offices of the Moslem Arabs that religious freedom was restored and guaranteed for all Christian sects.

Thus we can see that it was only under Arab rule that all religions were fully guaranteed freedom of practice.

2. *Historical Sites:*

The various invaders of Palestine, starting with the Jews of Egypt and then the Assyrians, Babylonians, Hittites, Chaldians, Persians, Greeks, Romans and to a great extent the Crusaders destroyed the holy places belonging to others.

The Arabs were the only people since the days of the Caliph Omar who preserved the religious sites belonging to all the celestial religions. It is a well known fact that Omar refused to pray in the Holy Sepulchre lest his followers demand that it be converted into a mosque.

The Jews on the other hand not only destroyed all that did not belong to them in Jerusalem when they invaded Palestine before Christ, but they pursued the same policy in the Twentieth Century both in 1948 and after 1967.

They burnt Al Aqsa and carried on excavations beneath its foundations, in the search for a non-existent temple. They destroyed ancient historical buildings belonging to Islam. They worked on changing the architectural, geographical and cultural characteristics of the city: in itself a great historical crime against civilisation. These measures were over and over condemned by the United Nations and by many international cultural organisations.

This is yet another reason why Jerusalem should return to and remain under Arab sovereignty.

3. *Treatment of Human, Social and Religious Values and Respect for the Shrines:*

The Arabs, especially the Muslims amongst them who believe in the three divine religions, treated throughout history with respect all the values associated with those religions. This was not simply out of choice, but also because this was basic to their own religion. This, however, was not the case either with Christianity or Judaism. In the case of Christianity there was also the added factor of the sharp rivalries, often reaching violent levels, which were associated with the claims of various sects to the religious sites and shrines of Jerusalem and Bethlehem.

In any case Jerusalem and Bethlehem are rich with mosques and churches belonging to Christianity and Islam, while there is in this region not one single inch of land sacred to the Jews. Even the Wailing Wall which the

Jews claim as their own was declared a property of the Islamic 'Awqaf' or Trust by a British commission appointed in 1930 by the Mandate Government. The commission reached its findings after exhaustive research into the claim presented by the Jews. The Wailing Wall, all its stones and its pavements, was, according to the commission, Holy Muslim property.

In fact Levi Eshkol, the former Israeli Premier, admitted in August 1967 that the Wailing Wall was merely a historical site and not a sacred Jewish shrine.

—Abraham grew up in Iraq and he is the Patriarch of all Prophets and not the monopoly of Judaism.
—Moses was born and raised in Egypt and received his divine message in Sinai.
—Jesus was born in Palestine and lived in Nazareth, Galilee, Bethlehem and Jerusalem.
—Muhammed undertook the divine journey, 'Al-Isra', into Jerusalem whence he ascended to Heaven. The city itself was peacefully surrendered to the Muslims by the highest Christian authorities resident there and in accordance with a pact which Christian and Muslim Arabs have since observed with scrupulous care.

Hence it can be stated emphatically that the Aqsa, and the Dome of the Rock, the Church of the Resurrection, the Well of Al-Boraq, the Via Dolorosa, and many other sites and shrines are legacies of Muslims and Christians, and the Jews possess only the memory of a Temple built in the wake of a conquest and destroyed by another counter-conquest.

The Arab enters the Holy places of Islam, Christianity and Judaism (synagogues) with the utmost reverence and careful respect for all the rituals. As for the Jews, they have treated the Al-Aqsa with little more than contempt, desecrating its sanctity with all manner of profane behaviour such as the flaunting in its grounds of outrageous dress and promiscuous sexuality.

Omar Ibn Khattab refused to pray in the Church of the Resurrection to forestall any attempt by his followers to convert it into a mosque. But the Jews decreed over a year ago that it was permitted for them to pray in the ground of Al-Aqsa, hence contravening all accepted religious laws and values.

History has never recorded one incident during the reign of the Arabs entailing the theft of a religious or archeological relic from any of the holy places. However, the Jews have been guilty of numerous examples of such robbery including the plundering of the Cathedral of Saint Catherine in Sinai during the 1956 and later in the 1967 Wars. They have also plundered the Church of the Resurrection and attempted to set fire to the Aqsa Mosque. They stole the crown of the Virgin and destroyed many churches.

With such an appalling historical record, it ill becomes the Jews or those claiming an interest in the preservation of the Holy sites and the freedom of worship therein to demand or tolerate continuing Jewish control over these sites, especially as none of these belong to the Jews as such.

Hence Jerusalem must remain Arab and must revert to Arab sovereignty.

4. *Historical Rights:*

The first state in history created in Palestine was that of the

> Canaanites, created six thousand years go, i.e., three thousand years prior to the invasion of Palestine by Egyptian Jews.
>
> Palestine was subjected to continuous invasion throughout history as a result of its geographical position astride commercial and military routes. Yet its Arab inhabitants remained rooted to it and its Arab cultural identity was maintained while interacting with the historical developments that occured over its territory including the invasion by the Hebrews of ancient Egypt.
>
> These invasions were part of the unfolding of History with every invader in turn expelling the previous one. Each one of the latter never laid claim henceforth to the land that he had invaded and from which he had been expelled. The only peculiar exception is that of the Jews who claim a historical right they simply do not possess. Even that land which they occupied only made up part of Palestine. If the right of the Jews to Palestine should be upheld, then the same could be said about the Romans, the Greeks, the Persians, and the Egyptians, and the whole political map of the world must be drastically changed. But of course this cannot be the case, and no International Law can permit it. Indeed the Twentieth Century has, through such organs as the League of Nations and the United Nations, forbidden the acquisition of territory by force.

It might be useful in the circumstances to consider the name of Jerusalem as we deal with the subject of historical right. It is established scientifically that its first name was Ur Salim or City of Salim. And whether the word "Salim" referred to the King of the Canaanites, who first built Jerusalem or to the name of one of their gods, the name remains Canaanite in origin, hence Arab.

When the Egyptian Jews invaded part of Palestine and occupied Jerusalem the name of the city was Yibus relating to the Yibussy tribe which then ruled the city.

In the Old Testament the name Zion is that of the castle destroyed by David when he occupied Jerusalem, which he then named City of David. It was subsequently called several names according to the powers that controlled it. For example it was called Ibliya at the time when Umar Ib Al Khattab took possession of the City; henceforth it became known as Bayt Al Maqdess — i.e. the Home of Purity. The name remained in use by the Arabs and Muslims while the Western Christians called it Jerusalem and the Jews changed the word to "Urushalaym".

As for historical religious right, if we are to consider the promise given to Abraham cited in the Bible: "To your seed Abraham we have given . . . " it is obvious that the promise was granted to the genetic line, and not to any particular religious grouping. Hence the seed of Abraham comprised Arabs — Muslims, Christians and Jews — and excluded non-Arabs. In this connection Alfred Guillaume wrote in his book "The Zionists and the Bible" that the vague pledge giving the descendants of Abraham the Promised Land from the Nile to the Euphrates was a promise intended for all the Arabs descending from Abraham including Arab Jews, and was not restricted only to the Jewish inhabitants of the Land of Canaan.

It follows that the Palestinian position, which calls for the establishment of a democratic unified state in Palestine, in which Muslim, Christian and Jew may co-exist as citizens possessing equal rights and duties, corresponds with the above interpretation of the Promise handed down to Abraham, while the creation of a Jewish state to include only the Semitic Arab Jews and the non-Semitic Russian and European Jews contradicts the purpose of the text of the Biblical promise.

As for population sizes, that of the Jews since the Babylonian invasion did not exceed in Jerusalem the proportion of a very small minority and that despite the fact that no restrictions were placed on their presence, for at least 1,300 years. In 1947 the proportion of Jews in the Holy City was 7%. Property owned by them amounted to 0.6% of the total. As for their property in the new city of Jerusalem, it did not exceed 25%, and the majority ownership remained in the hands of Muslim and Christian Arabs. For this reason the mayors of Jerusalem, old and new, were always Arabs until the Jews occupied new Jerusalem in 1948 and a Jewish mayor was appointed for the first time in history. The mayor of old Jerusalem remains an Arab to this very day, despite its annexation into new Jerusalem.

Jerusalem and the Question of Internationalisation

All the information media of the U.S.A. and Europe expressed false sympathy for the Jews of Europe, the victims of anti-Semitism, pretending that these Jews were a race apart requiring assistance and seeking to "return" to an empty land called Palestine. In fact it is well established scientifically that the Jews of Europe were racially of European rather than Semitic stock. This propaganda campaign served to justify the creation of the Jewish state on Palestinian soil in the eyes of American and European public opinion.

Had this public opinion realised that Palestine was inhabited by Arabs and that the Jews of Europe were not Semites but belonged to the Aryan race — specifically descending from the tribe which settled round the Caspian Sea in Russia — then the governments of Britain and the United States would not have been able to bring about the tragedy that was cast upon the people of Palestine.

Nevertheless, and despite this effective propaganda smoke-screen, Britain, the United States and the United Nations could not dare go as far as incorporating Jerusalem into the Jewish State or declaring it capital of that state. Consequently, the idea of internationalisation whether under the authority of the British Mandate or the United Nations or of a neutral international commission emanated from the reality that while it was possible for the Western media to present Palestine as an empty land that should be handed over to the Jewish people who are without a land, the same media was incapable of convincing the Christians that Jews had primary claims to Jerusalem. Hence the suggestion of internationalisation which was rejected equally by Christians and Jews.

Ladies and Gentlemen

I have spoken to you about all aspects of rights to Jerusalem and the conclusion must be that Jerusalem is Arab and that religious freedoms were guaranteed only when Jerusalem was under Arab sovereignty. Also that peace for Jerusalem was historically never secure except when Jerusalem was Arab and free of foreign invasion.

I also spoke of the colonialist designs that led to the creation of the state of Israel and of the ambitions of that state in relation to Greater Israel.

Israel today occupies all of Palestine and Jerusalem and insists that Jerusalem belongs to it and is its capital. It is painful that the demand is being made today for an equitable or just or humanitarian solution to the problem of Jerusalem as a question apart from the wider conflict.

We are told that Israel is a reality. We say that it is no doubt a fact based on might and not one based on right. Israel has no *historical*, *religious* or *national* rights in Palestine or Jerusalem.

It is said that politics is the art of dealing with reality and attaining the impossible. Our reply is that some causes are more powerful than the politics of established facts. Principles of civilised behaviour, of historical, territorial, human and religious values are all more powerful than "established facts".

We have witnessed millions dying during the First World War in the cause of the right of self-determination and in opposition to German expansionist designs. And the same occurred at an even more costly price in the Second World War.

Churchill and Britain and the Allies did not succumb to the established fact and did not negotiate in spite of the vast military superiority of Germany, and despite the military defeats suffered by Europe and Britain at the beginning of the War. In fact they insisted that Nazi Germany should surrender unconditionally. Millions perished for the sake of democracy, freedom and national rights . . . and in defiance of the established facts that were inconsistent with these values.

Is not history a record of the struggle between freedom and slavery? Is not the liberty of a man a lofty civilised value for which man lays down his life and is not slavery a rejected value and the struggle against it worthy of the ultimate sacrifice?

They claim that they desire peace in the Middle East. And we say that there can be no peace within one society or amongst different societies without justice . . . and can we separate Justice from Truth. It is Truth that is always the basis of struggle and not established fact. History proves that facts established on tyranny and bondage and on usurpation of peoples' right will inevitably lead to a revolutionary uprising in the direction of Truth, Justice and Liberty.

It is also said that world military and economic peace — especially that of Europe — is directly linked with peace in the Middle East. Hence an explosion in that area of the world will spark off a Third World War or will lead to the destruction of the international economy and the spread of chaos and upheavals. For this end it is said that a solution is required for the conflict in the Middle East, while singling out the issue of Jerusalem and seeking a separate arrangment for that city.

The Solution in our eyes is as follows:

—One Jerusalem, capital of one democratic state embracing all of Palestine in which Muslims, Christians and Jews live as equal citizens enjoying the same rights and responsible for the same duties under the law. Thus will the freedom of religion and of worship be guaranteed in Jerusalem and elsewhere in Palestine.

This is our dream that we believe will be realised . . . and if it is to come true, peacefully, the following must take place:

1. The Palestinian people must be allowed to practice its right to self-determination and to the establishment of its independent state over its national territory with Jerusalem as its capital. The area of the Church of the Resurrection should be included in that state, as it should not be permitted that the enemies of the freedom of religious worship are left in control of that Church, of the Aqsa Mosque, the Dome of the Rock or any other Holy places.
2. The Palestinian state will ensure the continuation of its historical policy of guaranteeing the freedom of worship and religion to all, including the practice of Jews wailing at the Wall of Baraq.
3. The creation of this state will be accompanied by arrangements allowing for peaceful and democratic action leading to the unification of Palestine within one democratic state.

It is imperative upon the international community when seeking a solution to the problem of Jerusalem not to separate that problem from that of Palestine. It should also be stated that that community has no right, in view of its adherence to the principles of international legality represented by the resolution of the United Nations, to choose to apply those resolutions that correspond with the interests of the Big Powers and ignore the others.

The world today is confronted by three methods that could deal with the Palestine problem:

Firstly — it could apply the principle of natural legitimate rights as it affects the Palestinian people.

Secondly — it could apply the principles of international legitimacy.

Thirdly — it could accept the principle of might makes right and therefore annul the whole structure of the United Nations, including its Charter and its Resolutions, as well as annulling the principles of International Law.

If it chooses the third alternative it will also then sweep aside all consideration of civilization, and the noble aims associated with peoples' quest for freedom, democracy, sovereignty and self-determination.

Jerusalem is a part of the Question of Palestine, and the cause of the Palestinian people is the focus of the conflict in the Middle East.

Peace in the Middle East is the corner-stone of European and world peace.

The Camp David agreements have demonstrably failed in bringing about a just peace in the Middle East because these agreements ignored all of the above and remained conspicuously silent about Jerusalem.

These are realities which are understood today by the world as a whole, including Europe and America.

Hence the question that needs to be posed urgently:

—Can there be any discussion of the question of Jerusalem or Palestine without prior recognition of the people of Palestine amongst whom feature the people of Jerusalem?

And is it possible to recognise the people of Palestine without recognising the inalienable national rights of those people?

—And can all the above be possible without also recognising that the Palestine Liberation Organisation is the sole legitimate representative of the Palestinians?

If all the above is true — and there is no doubt that it is — is it acceptable that the United States and others should discuss the future of Palestine and its people in the absence of the representative of that people?

Hence you see, Ladies and Gentlemen, that the problem of Jerusalem is not an academic question to be dealt with by academic means; it is the essence of a political cause — that of the people of Palestine which the world recognises as being the central element of the conflict in the Middle East.

Appendix VII

Remarks by Session Chairmen

(i) H.E. Mr. Kamel Al-Sharif
First Session (3rd December, 1979)

(ii) Mr. Christopher Mayhew, M.P.
Second Session (4th December, 1979)

(iii) Dr. Musa Mazzawi
Third Session (4th December, 1979)

(iv) Lord Caradon
Fourth Session (5th December, 1979)

(i) H.E. MR. KAMIL AL-SHARIF, Minister of Islamic Affairs, the Hashemite Kingdom of Jordan, and Chairman of the First Session of the International Seminar on Jerusalem in London on 3rd December 1979:

Excellencies,
Ladies and Gentlemen,

Just a few minutes before I entered this hall I was asked by my brother Mr. Salem Azzam, Secretary General of the Islamic Council of Europe to say a word in this august meeting on behalf of Jordan. At the beginning I hesitated because I had nothing prepared for the moment and the issue is so serious that it cannot be dealt with in an off-hand talk. Nevertheless, I could not resist the desire to talk to you for a few minutes at least to convey the greetings and good wishes of His Majesty King Hussein of the Hashemite Kingdom of Jordan, the Jordan government and people, as well as to express our great confidence in this seminar which will discuss an issue of utmost importance to Islamic peoples including the Jordanians, namely, Jerusalem and the Palestine question.

I may not be exaggerating if I say that we in Jordan live this problem hour by hour since we are one integral body that was divided by occupation into two separate entities. Yet in spite of that, our feelings and our daily interests are the same; never an incident occurs in the occupied areas that does not have its consequences reflected among us in a few moments thereafter. The government organs and its institutions relentlessly follow up the peoples' affairs in the occupied territories, doing our best to alleviate the pains and pressures they undergo incessantly. All efforts, therefore, should be made by Islamic peoples and communities, as well as by all lovers of justice and humanity, to put an end to Zionist occupation and suppression of a peace-loving nation that seeks nothing except peace and dignity in its own land as other peoples of the civilised world do.

I have listened with utmost interest to the words delivered on behalf of His Majesty King Hasan of Morocco and His Highness Crown Prince Fahed Ben Abdul-Aziz, Deputy Prime Minister of Saudi Arabia. I was really impressed with the Islamic spirit displayed in those two addresses as they call for adherence to justice and encourage humanitarian brotherhood and participation in world peace, in fulfilment of the Quranic verse, "O Mankind! Lo! we have created you male and female, and have made you nations and tribes that ye may know one another. Lo! the noblest of you in the sight of Allah, is the best in conduct." (Surat Al-Hujurat; verse 13). No doubt, the points expressed by the two Muslim leaders represent our views as Muslims seeking friendship, co-operation, and universal fraternity among the various nations and religions.

In addition, the two leaders' adherence to the Arab and Islamic rights in Jerusalem and their resolution to continue the joint work to deliver it have increased our confidence in the future. In this context, too, they spell out the Islamic peoples' determination to remove the obstacles that stood in the way between them and their usurped lands and deprived them from access to the holy Islamic places.

We in Jordan live this case, as I have said, and follow its developments step by step. We realise the graveness of the Zionist measures sacrileging the holy places and seriously defacing the long standing aspects of the Islamic culture in the holy city. We are well aware of all the savage acts committed against the peaceful inhabitants, which the world public opinion ought to know. I have carried with me some of the documents and films that will demonstrate all these facts during the following sessions. I have brought also a book written by His Highness Crown Prince Hasan of Jordan about the Jerusalem case tackling, in particular, the legal aspects of the problem. I hope you will find them most useful as they give a good idea of the different dimensions of the question, so that you might come in the end to proper resolutions.

Finally, let me say that to have this seminar convened in London, the historical capital of Britain, purports more than a single significance especially when we call to mind the role the British government played in creating this problem from the outset. We do hope that this seminar and similar attempts will be the beginning of a continuous process in the way towards a desirable and just solution that eliminates aggression and returns to Jerusalem its everlasting role as the city of peace and fraternity for all mankind.

Many thanks to the Islamic Council of Europe, its Secretary-

General and all those who took part in this great event, wishing all success to this seminar in its noble endeavour. Thank you. *Wassalamu alaikum wa rahmatullahi wa barakatuh.*

(ii) **MR. CHRISTOPHER MAYHEW, M.P., Chairman of the Second Session of the International Seminar on Jerusalem in London on 4th December 1979:**

At this moment, the PLO's spokesman on foreign affairs, Mr. Kaddoumi, is paying a visit to London. I am informed that he is being cold-shouldered in the familiar manner by our Foreign Office ministers.

What possible grounds can there be for this boycott of the PLO by the British government?

It is said that the PLO has some links with the IRA, but no hard evidence is produced and this is strenuously denied by the PLO itself at the highest level. It is argued that the PLO is a terrorist organisation. This is inaccurate, and, even if it were true, it is not an argument which can properly be used by ministers who lay down the red carpet to Mr. Begin, Mr. Mugabe and Mr. Nkomo.

It is time the British government ceased slavishly following the example of the Americans and acknowledge that no peaceful settlement is possible in Palestine unless Palestinians themselves are involved in the negotiations through their own representatives.

Since when has it been a British custom to cold-shoulder those who are oppressed, and wine and dine their oppressors? I hope that all the British delegates here will use all means of pressure open to them to ensure that the British government's attitude towards the PLO is rapidly and fundamentally changed.

(iii) **DR. MUSA MAZZAWI, Chairman of the Third Session of the International Seminar on Jerusalem in London on 4th December 1979:**

We are going to discuss this afternoon (4th December 1979) the subject of "Jerusalem and International Organisations" and "Jerusalem and the Palestine Question in International Law". A very important and significant fact about the Palestine problem, and a sad fact, is that although the conflict between the Arabs and the Zionists has many aspects of law, and is very deeply involved in law, several attempts made by the Arab States earlier on to refer the dispute to the International Court of Justice at The Hague for a legal determination were rejected by the United Nations. I say "significant and sad" because the United Nations was established for this purpose of maintaining peace, and in its Charter the road to peace is the settlement of disputes by peaceful means, and the way in which disputes can be settled by peaceful means is to introduce an element of law to determine who is right and who is wrong. We do have a very distinguished body of jurists in The Hague, representing all shades of culture and tradition in the world, and they could have given us a decision as to the rights and wrongs of the dispute. But they were not allowed to do that. And I think the obvious reason for this was that one of the parties involved preferred to settle the dispute by means other than law. Hence, the mess which we have today.

This afternoon we have two speakers who will shed a great deal of light on the legal aspects of the Palestine conflict and the conflict involving Jerusalem. The first speaker, whom it is my privilege to introduce, is John Reddaway, who is known to almost everybody here and to many throughout this country and in various parts of the world as someone who has spoken the truth, and spoken it very forcefully and very courageously. John Reddaway has very wide experience of international organisations; he was with the United Nations Relief and Works Agency for Palestine from 1960 to 1968. I remember in 1967 that he publicly said things that were not in line with the official policy of the United Nations. I always admired his courage. He is certainly a man of convictions and strong views, and a man who is capable of expressing his thoughts eloquently. Since 1968 he has been Director of the Council for the Advancement of Arab-British Understanding, a body which was founded soon after the 1967 Middle East War for the purpose of promoting better relations between this country and the Arab world; and the path which this body has adopted for this purpose was to speak out for right and justice and to ensure that the Arab view-point, if they believed in it, was put forward. In that capacity John Reddaway has done a great deal. But it is not as a politician that he is going to be speaking now. He will speak as someone who was very much involved with the United Nations at a very important stage of its development and of its handling of the Palestine problem. His topic is "Jerusalem and International Organisations".

(*Later, introducing the next Speaker, Dr. Henry Cattan, Dr. Mazzawi said:*)
There has been some criticism of the point about *corpus separatum* for Jerusalem. I think perhaps the issue is not as simple as it might appear, and we all look forward very much to hearing the views of Dr. Cattan on this question. What *corpus separatum* means literally is "a body separate from all other bodies", and territorially not within the jurisdiction of either Jordan or Palestine or Israel, and having a special status. There is not in international law at the moment anything which we can compare with this. Jerusalem was intended by those who came to the decision about the partition of Palestine as something new in international law and international relations. We look forward very much to hearing what Dr. Cattan has to say on this subject.

There is another point that John Reddaway referred to, and which I would very briefly like to comment on. He said that the issue will be resolved by political action rather than by legal analysis. I hope he does not think that is because I am a lawyer that I come to the defence of law. I think we all appreciate that the development and establishment of law marked a stage in human progress generally everywhere, a stage of transfer from anarchy and backwardness to progress and civilisation, and I think law has a role in this issue. Look at every problem and at every conflict and you will always come to the conclusion that law has a role in this issue. Look at every problem and at every conflict and you will always come to the conclusion that law has something to do with determining who is right and who is wrong, and that it is the only sure basis for resolving disputes. I think the fact that there has been no reference to the International Court of Justice does not mean that there is no law on the subject: there is abundant law, and John Reddaway himself has referred to a great deal of it. There is a very strong case on one side of this conflict, and what is lacking is that political action on the part of people who should know better has not been forthcoming in support of the law.

I recall a few months ago that the American Secretary of Commerce wanted to visit Jerusalem and he was offered a guided tour by the so-called "Mayor of Jerusalem" (the only Mayor of Jerusalem that I know is here — here he is — Rouhi Al-Khatib). The imposter who claims that he is the Mayor of Jerusalem offered to give him a conducted tour. The American Secretary refused, he said: "No, because I would thereby be conceding the fact that you are sovereign in Jerusalem". Soon afterwards a dissident Arab leader visited Jerusalem and accepted an invitation there from someone who had no claim or right at all. It is a sourse of pain and shame to Arabs and Muslims that that man continues to plunder, and to behave in the manner that he has behaved so far.

May I now go on to the next Speaker. I want to say at the outset that when I was a young man — and it was not very long ago, otherwise Dr. Cattan might object — Dr. Cattan was my hero. He really was. Dr. Cattan has progressed from being a very distinguished lawyer to a very distinguished academic, and a very distinguished fighter for the cause of peace. His definitive work on "The Palestine Question in International Law" is now very well known, and he has another work on "Palestine, the Arabs and Israel". His topic this afternoon is "Jerusalem and Palestine in International Law".

(iv) **LORD CARADON, Chairman of the Fourth Session of the International Seminar on Jerusalem in London on 5th December 1979:**

I have always understood that it is prohibited that a Chairman should express any view of his own; I have strong views on the subjects we discuss, I do write and speak about them, but this must be one of the occasions when I must prevent myself from holding up the proceedings to which we look forward. I think you might permit me to say just a word or two, as someone who has listened to these proceedings in the two days that we have already met together. I am sure that it has been for everyone of us here a very remarkable experience to be able to give our minds wholeheartedly, for a day or two, to this central, unique subject of Jerusalem.

I went to Jerusalem when I was 21 years of age, more than 50 years ago, and I go back whenever I can — because once you have been to Jerusalem you are never the same again, and I have been anxiously following what has been said. I have learned a great deal. I have not always agreed, but I have been greatly impressed, and one or two things stand out in my mind if you will let me just say to you — to try to put them into three or four sentences.

First of all — we know now, do we not, it has taken a long time to teach the world, that the centre of the Middle East problem is the Palestinian problem.

I have felt for a long time — and many of us I am sure agree — that the centre of the Palestinian problem has been the problem of Jerusalem.

And then one thing I am sure that we are all absolutely agreed on is that there can never be peace in the Middle East if there is not peace in Jerusalem.

Then, again, we can be sure — can we not — that there will never be peace in Jerusalem if one part of the population is a subject people.

And then again, I am sure we could agree that there should never be any barriers, any denial of access to the holy sites of Jerusalem for everyone in the world.

And so I think that we can say that we join together — I am sure that we join together — in hoping to see the end of division by domination, and we all earnestly, hopefully, look forward to a unity and equality and freedom.

And so we proceed with the last day of our deliberations, and we join together, wherever we come from, whatever our preconceived ideas might be, we join together in hoping that we can contribute to the true peace of Jerusalem.

Appendix VIII

Text of the Communique

An International Seminar on Jerusalem, sponsored by the Ministry of Information, Saudi Arabia, and organised by the Islamic Council of Europe, was held in London from 3rd to 5th December, 1979 — 14 to 16 Muharram 1400.

Governments and organisations were represented at the Seminar by the following:

1 – H.E. Mohammed Ibrahim Masoud
Minister of State, Member of the Council of Ministers,
Saudi Arabia

2 – H.E. Dr. Abdul Aziz Khoja
Deputy Minister of Information,
Saudi Arabia

3 – H.E. Mohammed Boucetta
Foreign Minister,
Morocco

4 – H.E. Kamil El-Sharif
Minister of Awqaf and Islamic Affairs,
Jordan

5 – H.E. Habib Chatti
Secretary General, Organisation of the Islamic Conference
Jeddah, Saudi Arabia

6 – H.E. Chazli Klibi

Secretary General, League of Arab States

7 – Mr. Khalid Al-Hassan
Chairman of the Foreign Relations Committee of the PLO

8 – Mr. Salem Azzam
Secretary General, Islamic Council of Europe

9 – Mr. Muazzam Ali
Adviser to the President of Pakistan

At the conclusion of the Seminar the following statement was issued:

1 – *JERUSALEM*

Expressing concern about the Zionist threat to Muslim and Christian sacred sanctuaries in the holy city and the alteration of its demographic structure,

Emphasizing that Islam recognises both the Christians and the Jews as people of the Book and that historically it was only under Islam that shrines of all religions enjoyed full protection, respect and freedom of access and worship,

Asserting that the Zionist occupation of Jerusalem is illegal, and has neither historical nor racial basis,

Urge upon all those governments, organisations and members of the international community who believe in righteousness and justice to join hands for the return of Jerusalem under Arab sovereignty.

2 – *PALESTINE*

Asserting that the problem of Palestine is an international concern and that its continued Zionist occupation is a grave threat to world peace,

Noting with regret the callous indifference, particularly of major western powers and super-powers, towards the plight of about three million Palestinians living as refugees and as stateless persons for the past 31 years,

Doubting the sincerity of those leaders, powers and organisations who proclaim to believe in human rights, justice and fairplay but in practice aid, abet and support aggression when it suits their vested interests,

Call upon the international community, particularly the major western and super-powers to extend their full support, co-operation and active assistance to the just and fair cause of restoration of the usurped national rights of Palestinian people and their homeland.

3 – *ISRAELI SETTLEMENTS*

Denouncing the creation of Israeli settlements in the occupied territories,

Call upon Israel to desist from this illegal and provocative activity and dismantle the settlements already established.

4 – *ATTACKS ON SOUTH LEBANON*

Condemning the attacks by Israeli armed forces on South Lebanon and the civilian inhabitants of Palestine and Lebanon,

Urge all nations to persuade Israel to stop this aggression and the killings of innocent men, women and children and destruction of hospitals, houses and refugee camps.

5 – *PERSECUTION OF PALESTINIANS*

Noting the continued persecution of Palestinians in occupied territories, a recent example of which is the false and frivolous charges against the Mayor of Nablus,

Urge the governments and people of all nations to force and prevent Israel from persecution and violating the human rights in occupied territories.

6 – *CAMP DAVID ACCORD*

Fully aware of the dangerous implications of the Camp David Accord for the Arab people and the Muslim World,

Reject the Sadat-Begin Treaty which is designed to perpetuate the Zionist occupation of Jerusalem, Palestine and other Arab lands and to deprive the Palestinians of their inalienable national rights including the right of self-determination and establishment of an independent state.

7 – *UNDERSTANDING IN EUROPE*
Noting with satisfaction the signs of beginning of understanding of Jerusalem and the Palestine problem and the role of the PLO as sole legitimate representative of the people of Palestine by some countries of Europe,
Hope that with full and wider understanding, they will use all means at their disposal for a just and fair solution of the Jerusalem and Palestine problem.

8 – *PLO*
Recalling Britain's important role in the creation of Israel and the consequent injustices to the people of Palestine,
Call upon the British Government to help in finding a just solution of the problem and recognizing the PLO as the sole legitimate representative of the people of Palestine.

VOTE OF THANKS

1 – Thank His Royal Highness Prince Fahd Bin Abdul Aziz, Crown Prince and Deputy Prime Minister of Saudi Arabia, for his inaugural address which is a source of encouragement to us and underlines his commitment to the solution of the Palestine problem.
2 – Thank the Ministry of Information, Saudi Arabia, for sponsoring this Seminar which is an indication of the Saudi Government's and its people's stand on Jerusalem and the Palestine problem.
3 – Thank the Islamic Council of Europe for organising the Seminar and the speakers and delegates who made it a success.

4 – Thank the Secretary Generals of the Organisation of Islamic Conference and the League of Arab States, the Governments of Jordan and Morocco, and the PLO for their support and assistance to this Seminar.